Loss of Our Religious Identity

Loss of Our Religious Identity

How the term "Hindu" has hijacked our Vedic and Upanishadic Religion

Suresh Chandra Ghosh

Dev Publishers & Distributors
New Delhi

Published by:
DEV PUBLISHERS & DISTRIBUTORS
2nd Floor, Prakash Deep,
22, Delhi Medical Association Road,
Darya Ganj,
New Delhi-110002
Phone : 011-4357 2647, 98102 36140
e-mail: devbooks@hotmail.com
website: www.devbooks.co.in

ISBN 978–93–81406–08–3
First published 2013

Printed in India

Contents

Preface vii

Introduction xi

PART ONE 1

Our Religion and Religious Identity

1. The Four Vedas 3
2. The Genesis to the Brahmanas and the Upanishads 20
3. The Fifth Veda 33
4. The Persian and the Greek Invasion and Conquest of the North- West 40
5. The Sutras and the Sutrakaras 50
6. The Result of the Investigation of Our Sages into the Mysteries of the Universe 58
7. The Buddhism and the Jainism vis-à-vis the Brahmanism 66
8. The Decline of the Buddhism and the Brahmanism 80
9. A Retrospection on Our Religion in Ancient India 91

PART TWO **99**

Eclipse of Our Religion and Loss of Our Religious Identity

10. The Coming of the Islam and the Rule of the Islamic Rulers 101

11. Nature of the Islamic Rule in India 113

12. Islamic Education as an Indoctrination for the New Converts as well as for the Children of the Muslim Settlers in India 122

13. Persianisation of the Muslim India and Confirmation of the Loss of Our Religious Identity 132

PART THREE **147**

Survival of Our Religion

14. The Priestly Classes in the Muslim India and in the Bordering Non-Muslim Kingdoms 149

15. The Ascetics 175

16. Disciples of the Ascetics in the Sultanate Period kept up their Gurus'Work Alive in the Succeeding Centuries 181

PART FOUR **181**

Revival of Our Religion

17. Rebirth of Sanskrit 183

18. Back to the Vedas and the Upanishads 190

19. Ascetics and their Contribution to the Saga of Revivalism in the British India 206

20. Revivalism led to Militantism in Our National Movement and Politics 216

21. The Five Pillars of Our Religion 224

22. A Final Retrospection on our Religion 227

Bibliography 242

Index 247

Preface

India is a land of varied regions and places, people and religions, cultures and manners, social norms and practices. I belong to the group of people who are known as "Hindus." Why? Is it because I belong to the group of people who form the majority group among the people of the country, most of whom come from an area known as the Hindi belt and speak a language known as Hindi? The answer to my query is a firm "no". Obviously people and place come first before the language is born and so we can safely assert that our "Hindu" name has not been derived from the vast majority among us who speak Hindi.

Most European scholars I have come across and spoken to them on the subject believe that the term "Hindu" has been coined by the officials of the East India Company in the early nineteenth century. This is far from the truth. And on a further and deeper investigation into the subject I have found that the "Hindu" term has come into existence nearly two and a half thousand years ago when the civilisation and culture among the Aryan immigrants from the Central Europe was taking shape in the North-West part of the sub-continent which is now mostly in Pakistan since 1947.

The term has actually been coined by the Persians, the followers of Zoroaster whose religion recognizes the existence of both good and evil. The Persians came to the North-West India around 519 BC and settled down to rule this part of our sub-continent till 326 BC when they were replaced by the Greek under Alexander, the Great. The Persian conquerors bestowed the term on the conquered Indians living on the both sides of the river "Sindu" which they pronounced as "Hindu" as they had difficulty in the pronounciation of "S". They pronounced "S" as "H". With the replacement of the Persians by the Greek and the latter by the Mauryas in the succeeding centuries, the term which had earlier remained confined to the North-West, along with the Persian Satrap and Kharoshthi script, came to be gradually almost forgotten and revived only after the coming of the Muslim invaders and conquerors who ruled India for more than 650 years from 1206 to 1857 when they were finally and officially replaced by the British Crown.

The Muslim rulers introduced Persian language and literature, customs and manners, law and jurisprudence and along with these also revived the use of the term "Hindu" to refer to the conquered subjects known as Kaffers, infidels or unbelievers all over their extensive empire and called their conquered land from Kashmir to Kanya Kumarika and from Gujarat to Bengal as "Hindustan" or the land of the "Hindus". Both the East India Company and the Christian missionaries who came in the seventeenth century picked up these two terms from their contact with the Muslim rulers and used them in their home despatches, memoirs and travelogues. Thus both the terms were very much in use long before the time indicated by the European scholars about the coining of the term "Hindu"and "Hindustan".

The British only confirmed, around the time indicated

by the European scholars, that is, early nineteenth century, the religious connotation which had already been in use by the Muslim rulers who had always used the term to refer to the "Hindus" as Kaffers, idolaters or infidels. And the process of confirmation began in the early 1810s, when there was a debate in Parliament on the subject of sending missionaries to India for proselytisation on the eve of the passing of the Charter Act of 1813, to drive home the point by the old stalwarts of the East India Company, with their vast administrative experiences in India, like Warren Hastings, William Cowper and Lt. General J. Malcolm that the survival of the Company's territorial possessions in India depended on keeping alive the division of the Indians into two religious communities and groups, "Hindu" and "Islam", and any attempt to convert any member of these groups into Christianity would destroy this division and unite them in protest against the Company.

As a matter of fact, the appropriation of the term "Hindu" and "Hindustan" by the conquered subjects themselves began as early as the sixteenth century when both began to appear in occasional non-religious Sanskrit texts as well as in some hagiographic literature of the time. And by the time the East India Company settled down to rule we could not but think of ourselves as "Hindus" as against the past rulers, Muslims and this gave to our ancestors dominated by the Muslim rulers for more than six hundred years a kind of identity at the cost of our religion.

In the late nineteenth century in the hands of the militant nationalists like Bal Gangadhar Tilak, Lala Lajpat Rai and Bipin Chandra Pal this identity with its religious connotation became a fierce tool to fight the British for our national independence. The moderate leaders like Madan Mohan Malaviya did not also lag behind in adopting the term as an expression of our national identity and ideology in our struggles against the British for independence. And when independence came to us, it also came to us along with the British ideas and institutions as legacies of the British rule in India.Thus what began as a geographical identity given by the Persians invaders and conquerors to the people living on both sides of the river Sindu has ended as a religious identity for all of us and we have meekly surrendered ourselves to it, without raising any questions on its relevance to our religious scriptures and religion and are now known as "Hindus".

Our Aryan sages and ancestors had never looked themselves upon as "Hindus". And the "Hindu" term has never occurred in any of our religious scriptures consisting of Mantras or hymns composed and transmitted orally before and after 1500 BC which form the subject of the four Vedas, Rig, Sam, Yajur and Atharva as well as of the Brahmanas, Aranyakas and the Upanishads. The sages never described themselves as "Hindus" and were known as the Brahmanas who possessed the supreme knowledge of the Brahma or the Cosmos or the Universe obtained by Tapas or meditation through the composition of the hymns which form the subject matter of our religious scriptures. We are followers of the religion created by our sages who were known as the Brahmanas and in our description of us as "Hindus" whch invariably carries a religious connotation, we have lost our religious identity as the descendants of the Brahmana sages.

The book is the result of my investigation into the subject of our religion since 2000-2001 when as a Visiting Professor at the Friedrich-Schillar Universität, Jena,

Germany, I found myself in an indepth study of our religious scriptures while delivering lectures on the development of our system of education in ancient India. Our ancient system of education, often referred to by the officials of the East India Company in the early nineteenth century as "a classical and spiritual one", has emerged out of our sacred literatures of the four Vedas, Brahmanas, Aranyakas and the Upanishads and in the process I began to ask questions, using historical research methodology scientifically as a tool, on our religious identity as "Hindus". And after completing my lectures at FSU, Jena, subsequently published by Peter Lang at Frankfurt in 2002, as *"Civilisation, Education and School in Ancient and Medieval India"*, I resumed my investigation into the question of our religious idenity as "Hindus" and the present work is the result of this investigation.

Finally, I have addressed the work to a very wider non-specialist audience interested in the subject of our religion in India and abroad and have, therefore, discarded footnotes for a smooth reading. I have generally tried to avoid the use of the term "Hindu" except where its use is unavoidable. It is needless to add here that the responsibility for any error, either of fact or of interpretation, and for the opinion expressed, in the work, rests solely with me.

SURESH CHANDRA GHOSH

Introduction

We are known as "Hindus". Certainly not in the years between 1500 BC and 600 BC. These were the years when our sages were orally composing hymns through Tapas or meditation which were addressed to the understanding of the mysteries of the Brahman or the Cosmos. It was only in the years after 519 BC that the descendants of these sages and the rest of our Aryan ancestors living on the both sides of the river Sindu, came to acquire this description at the hands of the Persian occupiers and invaders of the North-West.

The use of the term was confined to the areas under Persian occupation and in our country it was not possibly known to the people outside these areas. The Persians ruled the North-West for more than two hundred years and many of the conquered subjects who participated in the Persian civil and military administration certainly knew that they were known as "Hindus" though it was extremely doubtful whether this term was in circulation among them. With the replacement of the Persians by the Greeks in the North-West in 326 BC and the latter's dislodgement by the armies of the Mauryas, it can be safely asserted that the term, "Hindu" fell into oblivion, though it lingered on after the break-up of the Maurya empire, in the invasion and occupation of the parts of the North-West by the group of foreigners like the Sakas, the Pahlavas and the Kushanas who spoke an Iranian language and occupied parts of the North-West India till the coming of the Guptas under Chandra Gupta 1 who ascended the throne of Pataliputra in AD 320 and subsequently built up the second great empire in the sub-continent after the Mauryas.

The use of the term was revived only after the coming of the Islamic invaders and the conquerors from AD 1206 onwards in the process of the Persianisation of the entire India under their rule from Kashmir to Kanyakumarika and Gujarat to Bengal. It was continued by the British who gradually replaced the Muslims as rulers of India between AD 1757 and 1857 and was accepted by our national leaders and religious pundits as the mark of an identity of a community struggling for freedom. After the British left the shores of India, the use of the term continues to remain with us along with the other legacies of the British ideas and instiutions.

Our Aryan ancestors began their sojurn in the country as Aryas. Our Aryan sages called their adopted land as Aryavarta and their religion emerging out of the hymns composed by their sages as Arya Dharma. Since most of the sages were descendants of the priestly class of the Bharata tribes, they also described Aryavarta as the land of the Bharatas and their religion as the Bharatiya Dharma or Brahmana Dharma as the priests who orally composed and transmitted the hymns addressed to the mysteries of the Cosmos, were known as Brahmanas or possessors of a mystical and supernatural power acquired from the Brahman or the Cosmos.

Yet we are known today as "Hindus" or worshippers of idols and images of gods and goddesses and our land as "Hindustan" and our religion as "Hinduism". Sometimes tradition is stronger than truth and fiction is more powerful than fact and under pressure ftom both, we have never questioned the genesis of this term, never bothered to find out its relevance to our religious scriptures, philosophy and practices spreading over a period of more than three thousand and five hundred years from now.

The beginning of the rule of a very young and energetic religion of Islam in India in the thirteenth century almost signalled the end of the old Bharatiya or the Arya Dharma, which had been earlier dominant in the country among our ancestors for nearly two thousand and seven hundred years as the theocratic Muslim state did not allow the existence of any other religion under its jurisdiction. However, our religion managed to survive among the dwindling priestly classes through guru-shisya parampara where the father was often the guru and the son shisya not only in Muslim India under great duress but also across the Vindhyas and the Himalayas in non-Muslim kingdoms and areas where they set up Vedic schools with royal support and patronage. Sanskrit, the language of our religious scriptures, groaned and withered in the Muslim India without support from the Muslim rulers except from Akbar who included it as one of the courses in the reformed Madrasah. And so the existence of our religious scriptures also gradually began to fade away from the minds of our contemporary ancestors.

A freer and fresher wind began to blow over our religion with the coming of the British as traders. In the late eighteenth century in Bengal a group of British officials known as Orientalists rediscovered Sanskrit and our religious scriptures and our Western educated ancestors were among the first to be galvanized into action and to reform our stagnant and moribund religion based on the teachings of the Vedas and the Upanishads. Rammohan

Roy was the first among them to read our newly discovered religious scriptures along with the Bible, the Quran and the Zoroastrian scriptures. After studying all these religious scriptures very carefully Rammohan Roy realized that we should better be known as the followers of the Vedas and of the Upanishads rather than as "Hindus" and set up the Brahma Samaj to propagate his ideas of religion. Swami Dayanand later also thought on the same lines and felt that as the descendants of the Aryans we should be known as Aryas and our religion as Arya Dharma. He set up the Arya Samaj to strongly propagate his views on our religion among us. Ramakrishna echoed the concluding ideas of the Rigveda which saw only one god in the different forms of gods and goddesses as in the case of the god, Agni who appears here and there in different shapes and forms. All the gods and the goddesses, though different in forms and shapes, are one and are the manifestaions of the Brahman. Ramakrishna saw Brahman in the Goddess Kali and his disciple, Vivekananda saw it not only in one image but also in the images of all the gods and the goddesses. He further discovered Brahman in the souls of the poor and the down-trodden. And Aurobindo realized his Brahman by blending the Vedas and the Upanishads through "the Integral Yoga" in a "Life Divine."

Thus began a revival of our old religion often under the garb of the ideologies of the reformers but the attempt of these schools of religious reformers to restore our lost religious identity was only partially successful. They were not certainly in the majority group who think otherwise and against the backdrop of the national movement and the rise of militant nationalism, the term, "Hindu", became a mark of our national identity as the real inheritors of our country against the past conquerors and found its fulfillment in such political organizations as the "Hindu Mahasabha" set up by the Pundit Madan Mohan Malaviya in 1909, or the "Vishwa Hindu Parishad" in 1964, which traced its emergence to the Rashtriya Swayamsevak Sangha, founded by K.V. Hedgewar, a very influential member of the "Hindu Mahasabha" in 1925 in the pre-independece days.

Malaviya was an orthodox Brahmin and, in all probability, as a learned person he was fairly acquainted with our sacred religious scriptures. Yet, as a member of our very influential priestly class he had never questioned the use of the term, "Hindu" to describe us and our religion. Our religious scholars and pundits had, perhaps, little time to seriously discuss the question when an intense agitation for the freedom of the country had been going on and the term "Hindu" had become a mark of our national identity and ideology. But after independence we have scarcely had, perhaps any time or interest, to indulge in such theocratic exercise, given the host of problems faced by a newly emergent nation as well as our much proclaimed secularism inherited from the British which has not, perhaps, allowed any of our universities in the country, to seriously study and research in our ancient religion.

Our religious identity as the descendants of the Aryan sages of the Bharata tribes who became Brahman by acquiring a mystic power from the Brahma, through Tapas or meditation and who composed various hymns addressed to the mysteries of the Brahma or the Universe or the Cosmos, which form the basis of our religious scriptures, before and after 1500 BC, thus gets lost in our description as "Hindus". A geographical identity given by the first Persian invaders who were mosly the followers of Zoroastrianism, nearly two thousand and a half years ago from now, to the people living on both sides of the river, Sindu, has now become our religious and cultural identity.

To put in a nutshell, our Brahmana, Arya or Bharatiya Dharma or to be more precise, our Vedic and Upanishadic Dharma, lies buried in the description of our religion as "Hindu Dharma" or "Hinduism" and our land as "Hindustan". We have lost our religious identity bestowed on us by our old sages and are now known under an imported one, "Hindus", embossed on us first by the Persians in the sixth century BC, revived by the Muslim rulers from the thirteenth century AD, continued by the British and absorbed by us after independence!

SURESH CHANDRA GHOSH

Part One

Our Religion and Religious Identity

1

The Four Vedas

Our religion incorrectly and traditionally known as "Hinduism" is not the work of a single prophet or a single saint but that of many sages spreading over many centuries which took place more than a thousand and a half years before Christ appeared on the earth at Bethlehem and nearly more than some two thousand years before Muhammad was born in Mecca in AD 570. And unlike Christianity and Islam our religion initially started not as sermons on the well-being and salvation of the human beings but as an investigation into the mysteries of the Cosmos or the Universe by the priestly class of the Bharata tribes of the Aryans immigrants to the sub-continent.

The Coming of the Aryans

The Aryans came to India in the early part of the second millennium BC from the great Steppe land stretching from Poland to Central Asia, when they were on the move in different directions, westwards, southwards and eastwards, either from pressure of population, desiccation of pasture lands or from both causes, conquering local lands and populations and inter-marrying with them to form a ruling class. In India they settled down in the North-West after vanquishing an old civilisation which flourished on both sides of the river Indus and which is known to us, thanks to the archaeological excavations carried out by Sir John Marshall between 1924 and 1931 at Mohenjodaro in Sind and Harappa in the Punjab, as the Indus Valley Civilisation.

The Aryan invasion of India was not a single concerted action, but one covering centuries and involving many tribes, perhaps not all of the same race and language. There were frequent internal conflicts among these tribes as well as prolonged struggles with the non-Aryans or the survivors of the Indus Valley Civilisation and kindred people of the Punjab and the North-West described as the Dasas or Dasyus, a dark skinned, flat-nosed race who spoke a language unintelligible to the Aryans and possessed forts and herds of cattle coveted by the new-comers. In the campaign against the Dasas, the Bharatas among the Aryan tribes were ably supported by their rivals, the Purus, one of whose kings bore the significant name of Trasadasyu or Terror to the Dasyus.

The geographical area eventually occupied by the Aryans is clearly indicated by the mention of certain identifiable rivers which implies the possession by them of a considerable portion of the country stretching from eastern Afghanistan to the upper valley of the river Ganges. The major part of this area came to be known as Sapta Sindu or the Land of the Seven Rivers. However, the whole of the extensive tract of land could not have been occupied entirely by the Aryan tribes but also by the clans of the Dasas who must have occupied some part of this territory as their supersession and later absorption was a very slow and gradual process. The

Aryans adapted their original language to the tongues of the conquered people and as they gradually settled down in their new habitations, they transplanted their patrilineal organizations, their horses and chariots and their worship of the Cosmos or the Universe.

Attempt to understand the Mysteries of the Universe through the Composition of the Mantras or the Hymns

The priestly class of the Bharata tribes of the Aryans who had mainly settled down in the region in the East of the Punjab and in the Doab between the Sutlej and the Yamuna called their adopted land as the Brahmavarta and described themselves as the Brahmanas or possessors of the Brahman or the supreme knowledge of the Brahma or the Universe, acquired by Tapas or meditation through composition of the Mantras or the hymns. These hymns are the outcome of the pursuit of the highest truth and of its direct realisation by the seeker through ascetic austerities and concentrated contemplation and meditation called Tapas, yogas or meditation, which marks out or makes a Rishi or a seer.

The hymns composed orally in their new home were, as said earlier, addressed to the understanding of the different aspects of the Cosmos or the Universe and were carefully handed down by word of mouth and early in the first millennium BC were collected and arranged. They were still not committed to writing, but by now they were looked upon as so sacred that even minor alterations in the texts were not permitted, and the priestly schools which preserved them, devised the most remarkable and effective system of checks and counter checks to ensure their purity. Even when the art of writing was widely known in India, the hymns were rarely written, but thanks to the brilliant feats of memory of many generations of the Brahmana and the extreme sanctity which the hymns were thought to possess, these have survived to the present day in a form which, from internal evidence, appears not to have been seriously tampered with for nearly three thousand and five hundred years. The great collection of hymns is the Rigveda, the most sacred of our numerous sacred scriptures and the mother of all the three Vedas and the Brahmanas which followed it over the subsequent centuries.

The Rigveda

The Rigveda which alone contains 1028 hymns has been dated back to the years between 1500 BC and 1000 BC. However, since the composition of the Rigveda could not have been made without the availability of a number of hymns, it can be safely presumed that many of the hymns in the Rigveda were long in the making and must be dated centuries before 1500 BC. The European scholars like Arthur A. Macdonell and M. Winternitz who have worked on the Rigveda readily agree on this point. As Winternitz has observed in his work on the history of Indian literature : "Centuries must have elapsed between the composition of earliest hymns and the Samhita of the Rigveda." Max Muller describes the Rigveda in his *Origin and Development of Religion* as the oldest religious text in the world.

The hymns in the Rigveda present the worship of 33 gods and goddesses divided into three groups of 11 each and assigned to the three planes of the Cosmos or the Universe—dyurloka or the celestial, antariksha or the intermediate and bhurloka or the terrestrial. And each of these assigned gods and goddesses was identified with a force of the nature or natural phenomenon by the sages in order to understand the mysteries of the Cosmos or the Universe. The celestial gods include Varuna and Mitra (both sons of Aditi, the goddess of eternity), Indra (the god associated with storm and thunder), Yama (the lord of the dead), Surya(the illuminator), Savitri (the enlivener), Pushan (the nourisher), Vishnu Urukrama (the wide-striding Sun), the Asvins (the morning and evening stars, later the gods of healing) and Usha (the lovely goddess of the dawn). In the intermediate the chief gods, besides Indra, are Maruts (storm gods), Vayu and Vata (wind gods), and lacking Indra's popular and genial character was Rudra or the howling god of storm and lighting who lived in the mountains and was invoked to ward off his arrows of plague and disaster. The terrestrial gods include Soma, Sarasvati and Agni. Soma was originally a plant, from which a potent drink was produced, which was drunk only at sacrifices and which caused the most invigorating effects. Sarasvati was a river deity once flowed in the river Sindu below the confluence of the river Sutlej and now an insignificant stream almost lost in the desert of Rajasthan and later came to be identified with the goddess of learning. Agni was the fire god who received special homage for no sacrifice could be performed without offerings to him.

In the beginning Varuna is said to preside over the Universe and to guard the moral laws and quite in keeping with his status, he is said to have been worshipped in a spirit different from the worship of other gods. However, Indra, the war god associated with storm and thunder soon came to replace Varuna as the chief among gods. With the passage of time and contact with the new people eastwards and southwards, some less prominent gods later became more prominent than before. Siva or Rudra, Vishnu or Vasudeva now became the favoured gods among the ascetics who had begun to dislike the domination of the Brahmanas in the Aryan religion. Needless to say that these ascetics who existed since the days of the Rigveda later became the torch-bearers of the Upanishadic message of love and devotion to the deities as the manifold manifestations of the universal soul, as well as of detachment from the earthly things, which began to sweep the eastern part of the country from the sixth century BC onwards.

Ten Mandalas or Sections

As said before, our sages addressed their hymns orally composed through Tapas or meditation to worship these deities to find an answer to the mysteries of the Cosmos or the Universe. In the Rigveda these hymns were grouped under ten mandalas or sections. They are as follows:

> Six mandalas from 2 to 7 are attributed to the six Rishis or seers and form their family books and serve as the nucleus of the whole Rigveda. These six Rishis are: Gritsamada, Visvamitra, Vamadeva, Atri, Bharadvaja, and Vasishtha. Mandalas 1, 8 and 10 are later, especially parts of 10, while 9 mandala was compiled by extracting the hymns to the god Soma from the other parts of the Rigveda. In this way, the whole compilation came to include 1, 028 hymns and 10, 580 verses in 70, 000 lines (including 5, 000 which are merely repetitive) of 153, 826 words.

Oneness of the Gods and the Goddesses

The hymns in the Rigveda reveal from the very beginning an attempt at understanding which moves towards the oneness of the gods. Thus, there are hymns which describe Agni as the god dwelling in the waters of heaven in the form of lighting, and on earth in many forms such as the one hidden in the fire-sticks with which the sacrificial fire was kindled and which were personified as his parents. Agni was thus here, there and everywhere. Was there only one Agni, or were there many Agnis? How could Agni be one and many at the same time? Such questions as were asked of Agni in the Rigveda reveal the earliest signs of the tendency towards monotheism or monism, which later bore fruit in the Upanishads. Indeed there are many hymns in the Rigveda which foreshadow the idea of universal unity and oneness of gods although known by many names such as the following ones: "They call him Indra, Mitra, Varuna and Agni; he is the heavenly bird Garutmat." "To what is One, the poets give many a name. They call it Agni, Yama, Matrisvan." Such monotheistic conception appears more prominently towards the end of the Rigvedic period in the hynms addressed to Hiranyagarbha or the gold-germ and to Visvakarman or the all-creating: "Who is our father, our Creator, Maker, /Who every place doth know and every creature, /By whom alone to gods their names were given, /To him all other creatures go to ask him"

Yajnas or Sacrifices

In the Rigvedic pantheon, the male gods dominated though there were also important goddesses as we have already seen. And none of them could be worshipped without any yajnas or sacrifices which formed the central part of the Aryan religion. Sacrifices involved offerings by the worshippers of milk, ghee, grain, flesh and juice of the Soma plant. Sacrifices were complex rites, involving much preparation, the slaughter of numerous animals, and the participation of the several well trained priests. In the days of the Rigveda such sacrifices were generally organized and financed by the chiefs and the wealthier tribesmen to gratify the gods in order to obtain boons from them. The gods descended to the sacrificial venue, ate and drank with the worshippers, and duly rewarded them with success in war, progeny and long life and almost in everything asked for. The worshippers came to possess a magical power, a sort of supernatural electricity identified with the Brahman or the Universe by uttering the sacred Mantras or the hymns. The possessor of the Brahman came to be known as the Brahmana, the tribal priest and mystician. The supernatural power of the Brahmana lay in the words of the hymns he uttered in the alphabets "OM" which contains the essence of the Vedas and is pregnant with the utmost power and mystery.

By the end of the Rigvedic period, it was widely believed from the mystical identification of the god, the victim and the sacrificer that the Universe itself arose from a primeval sacrifice involving the god, Prajapati, the Lord of Beings, later called Brahma, the masculine from the neuter Brahman. In the "Hymn of the Primeval Man", Prajapati was thought of as a primal man or purusha who existed before the foundation of the Universe and who was sacrificed, presumably to himself, by the gods, who apparently were his children. The Universe came into existence out of the body of the divine victim. With the sacrifice of the primeval man, a new attitude to sacrifice developed. It became a supernal mystery. By means of it, the priests mystically repeated the primeval sacrifice and the world was born anew. All cosmic process would cease and chaos would return without such sacrifices. Thus the order of nature was ultimately dependent not on the gods but on the Brahmanas who by the ritual of the sacrifice maintained and compelled them. And so the Brahmanas were more powerful than any earthly kings or gods, who could, by the slightest variation of the ritual, turn the sacrifice against his patron and destroy him.

When the Aryans entered India, there was already a class division in the tribal structure as in the use of the terms, Kshatriya or the nobility, and the Vis or the ordinary tribesmen. As the Aryans settled down among the darker aboriginals, they laid greater stress than before on the purity of blood, and class divisions hardened to exclude those Dasas who had found a place on the fringes of Aryan society, and those Aryans who had intermarried with thc Dasas and adopted their ways. While both these groups sank in social scale, the priests whose sacrificial lore was becoming more and more complex and who therefore required greater skill and training, were arrogating higher privileges to themselves. By the end of the Rigvedic period the Aryan society was divided into four great classes, and this four-fold division was given a religious sanction in the "Hymn of the Primeval Man", where the four classes are said to have emanated from the dismembered Primeval Man, who was sacrificed by the gods at the beginning of the world—the Brahmana grew out of his mouth, the Kshatriya or the warrior out of his arms, the Vaishya or the trader out of his thighs and the Shudra or the server out of his feet. As said before, the Brahmanas or the priests who belonged mainly to the Bharata tribes, and had settled down mainly in the East of the Punjab and in the region betwccn the Sutlej and the Yamuna were the most powerful group in the Aryan society. They were the possessors of "Brahman", a supernatural electrical power, which they had derived from their composition and uttering of the Mantras or the hymns addressed to gods and sung at the sacrifices performed by the tribal chiefs or kings to ensure the prosperity and success of their tribes in war and peace.

The Rigvedic Religion changed in Response to Changes in the Aryan Society in the Succeeding Centuries

Quite in keeping with the progressive changes in the Aryan society, in the succeeding three centuries, the Rigvedic religion showed considerable developments of ceremonial and priesthood out of their beginnings in the Rigveda. These developments centered on the fixed order of sacrifices. However, the order of the hymns in the Rigveda had nothing to do with the order of the sacrifices while it included many hymns which had no use for any sacrifices. The need was felt for the composition of new hymns which could be exclusively used for purposes of ritual application and in course of time, say by 600 BC, three more Vedas, Sama, Yajur and Atharva, came to be compiled.

How ritualistic the religion of the Aryans had become since the days of the Rigveda could be seen in an increase in the number of the personnel of the priesthood participating in sacrifices. The Rigveda mentions only 8 priests including Hotri, Udgatri, Adhvaryu and Brahmana, each with an assistant, besides the institutor of the sacrifice. Now the number of assistants under each of the four categories of priesthood had increased from one to three so that the priesthood had a personnel of 16 members to participate in sacrifices. The Hotri priests specialized in the recitation of hymns; the Udgatri priests specialized in the chanting of hymns, which required a special training; the Adhvaryu priests specialized in the actual performance of sacrifice involving a number of operations and material details and the Brahmana priests had to acquire such a proficiency and knowledge in the matter that they could easily detect and correct errors in the performance of the different parts and operations of sacrifice and pass judgements on all doubtful points and disputes, thereby laying the beginning of the systems of Nyaya and Mimansa.

The Samaveda, the Yajurveda and the Atharvaveda

The Samaveda is the compilation of all the hymns recited on the ocassion of the Soma Yajna. While the Udgatri priests had contributed 78, out of 1549, verses, the bulk of the verses had been taken out of the 8 and 9 Mandalas of the Rigveda. These verses have been classified into two parts: the Archika of 585 single stanzas or riks and the Uttararchika comprising of 400 chants, mostly of three stanzas each. The text of the Samaveda is tailored to the learning of melodies and the student who wanted to be trained as the Udgatri priest had first to learn the melodies with the aid of the Archika where is given only text of the first stanza of each song as an aid to the recollection of the tune. While a stanza can be sung to various melodies and one melody can be applied to different stanzas out of which are formed the Stotras to be sung at the sacrifices to the tunes which the Archika teaches. While the Samaveda can give only the texts as they are spoken, their melodies are taught by oral and instrumental rendering. Music is known to the Rigveda as well as the instruments producing music by means of percussion, wind and string such as drum, lute and lyre or harp with its seven notes recognized and distinguished, together with the flute of reed called Nadi.

Yajurveda

While the Samaveda is the song-book of the Udgatri, the Yajurveda is the prayer-book of the Adhvaryu priests. Prayers were accompanied by the sacrificial acts about which differences of opinion were more likely to arise leading to the formation of numerous schools, the number of which was 100 in the time of Patanjali (*c.* 200 BC), as stated in his Introduction to his Mahabhashya.

The Yajurveda consists of two divisions, the Black or Krishna and the White or Shukla. The White Yajurveda contains only the Mantras or the hymns, the prayers and the sacrificial formulae which the priest has to utter while the Black Yajurveda contains the Mantras in verse and also a portion in prose, presenting the sacrificial rites that go with the Mantras along with discussion thereon, anticipating the later Brahmana literature.

The Yajurveda has thus made a material contribution to the prose literature which later culminated in the literary masterpieces of the Upanishads. The Yajurveda fixes the religious life of the Aryans in the course of ceremonies it prescribes such as those for the New and the Full Moon, the Father or Pinda-Pitri-Yajna, Fire or Agnihotra to be performed both morning and evening, seasons or Chaturmasyas to be performed every four months, Rajasua for kings only. Asvamedha for a king of kings and Agnichayana or building of the Fire-altar lasting a year and possessing a mystical significance.

Atharvaveda

While the Samaveda and the Yajurveda came into existence to meet the highly complex religious requirements on sacrifices, the Atharvaveda largely meets the needs and the requirements of the growing Aryan society including the kings and the chieftains. It is also more original than the Sama and the Yajur Vedas in the sense that the majority of its hymns have not been adapted from the Rigveda. Only 1,200 stanzas out of 6,000 have been derived largely from 1, 8 and 9 Mandalas of the Rigveda. It refers to appropriate herbs as remedies against diseases like fever, leprosy, jaundice, dropsy scrofula, cough, opthalmia, baldness, impotence and surgical ailments like fractures and wounds, bite of snakes and other injurious insects and against poison in general, mania and other complaints.

Thus, the Atharvaveda is the earliest medical treatise in the country and perhaps also the earliest in the world which prescribes nature's herbs and plants as cure for the treatment of the discases and thereby also soothes body, mind and soul. Our indigenous medical science which emerges from the Atharvaveda is most appropriately termed Ayurveda or the secrets of longevity or life. Its ninth book anticipates astronomy by its mention of lunar mansions and deals with domestic rites at birth, marriage and death, thereby anticipating the later Grihasutras. As a matter of fact, the Atharvaveda is more original than the Sama and the Yajur Vedas not merely in the sense that the majority of its hymns have not been adopted from the Rigveda but also in the sense that it is the first authentic account of the political and philosophical life of the contemporary Aryan society.

Aids to the Understanding of the Four Vedas

Six subsidiary studies or auxiliary sciences–Siksha, Kalpa, Vyakarana, Nirukta, Chhanda, and Jyotisha---were subsequently developed as aids to the understanding of the four Vedas.

It is the lips of the guru that are uttering the hymns—in other words, the guru is giving the Veda or knowledge to his pupil by uttering it. This is Siksha which is from the root Siksh, to give. Secondly, the hymns are to be uttered correctly bringing out their meaning clearly. The first that comes is Chhanda while giving Veda to a pupil by his guru and then Vyakarana or grammar and Nirukta or etymology to convey its meaning correctly. And all these subjects, Siksha, Vyakarana and Nirukta had to be studied as aids to the comprehension of the meaning of the Vedic texts upon which so much stress was laid. A mere crammer of Vedic texts was compared to an ass carrying a load of sandal wood without sensing its sweet and fragrant smell but only feeling its weight. Again, the hymns correctly learnt are to be uttered by the Adhvaryu priests who are fully in the actual performance of the sacrifices. The operational aspect of the sacrifices means measuring the ground, building the altar and the platform, ascertaining proper seasons and moments for them. It is also necessary to cultivate a knowledge of the parts of the bodily frame of the animals to be immolated at the sacrifices. The Adhvaryu priests had to learn Kalpa and Jyotisha in discharging the responsibilities imposed on them by the Yajurveda. As far as Jyotisha is concerned, it finds expression in the recognition of an immutable cosmic order or laws of nature as Dhata, Satya and Dharma. While Dhata refers to accomplished fact like the tree growing from a seed, the Sun rising in the east, Agni consuming objects thrown to it, Satya refers to the law by which a tree grows out of a seed, the Sun rises in the east, and Agni gives heat. Dharma is that which holds in the midst of change.

These subsidiary studies or auxiliary sciences—Siksha, Kalpa, Vyakarana, Nirukta, Chhanda and Jyotisha—were developed in the Vedic schools as aids to the study of the Vedas and are known as Vedangas or the limbs of the Vedas. In course of time, say, by the time of the Sutrakaras (400 BC) they gave birth to a number of independent disciplines and allied sciences like Philosophy and Yoga, Grammar and Philology, Anatomy and Physiology, Astrology and Astronomy, Music and Songs, Arithmetic, Algebra and Geometry while still serving the needs and requirements of our religion.

Transmission of the Vedic Knowledge

The knowledge of the Vedas was transmitted from one generation to another orally, thanks to the brilliant feats of the memory of the Brahmanas, through guru-shisya-parampara. In the age of the four Vedas, the other three classes of the Aryan society, the Kshatriyas or the Warriors, the Vaishyas or the Traders and the Shudras or the Untouchables as well as the women had access to the study of the Vedas at a Brahmanical or Vedic school. While the Brahmanas spent a longer time at a Vedic school and mastered the whole or the four Vedas, the other three castes were possibly instructed in the same way as the women who were given a knowledge of one of the four Vedas to participate in the religious life of the Aryans. The Kshatriyas further learnt the art of warfare and administration, the Vaishyas trade and commerce and the Shudras agriculture and animal husbandry. And as we have just said, it was only the priestly class or the

Brahmanas who stayed at the Vedic schools till they obtained complete mastery of the four Vedas. They learnt not only the hymns of the Rigveda, the ritualistic details of sacrifices of the Samaveda and the Yajurveda as well as the hymns of the Atharvaveda throwing light on diseases and their cures, domestic rites at birth, marriage and death as well as on spells for warding off evils and for securing good to the Aryan society.

The Upanayana Ceremony

They all had to perform the Upanayana or the sacred thread ceremony while entering the Vedic schools at the age of 12 after an enquiry into their Vamsha or family of birth, individual merits and capability to serve their teachers called Gurus, Acharyas or preceptors. The students after admission through the Upanayana ceremony were known as Dvija or twice-born; at the second birth they had as parents their teachers who pierced their ears with needles of truth and knowledge without causing them any physical pain or injury. While at the residence of the guru for not less than 12 years studying the Vedas, they had to observe Brahmacharya which meant leading a hard and Spartan life. The system of Brahmacharya also covered the women who were admitted to the Vedic schools after the performance of the Upanayana ceremony and were given prescribed courses of study to enable them to assist their husbands in the sacrificial offerings.

The Brahmacharya

The Atharvaveda gives us an insight into the rigorous physical and mental discipline of a shisya observing Brahmacharya while studying Vedas at the residence of his guru. He had to let his hairs grow and wear the Kusha girdle and the deer skin as his dress, had to collect fire-wood, tend the house-hold fire and beg alms from the neighbourhood. His spiritual discipline included offering fuel to the Agni and worshipping him twice daily, controlling senses, practicing austerities and living a dedicated life as well as satisfying, either by service or gifts, to his guru who was variously extolled as Yama, Varuna, Sun and Moon as the givers of light and happiness. While underging through his rigorous course of discipline, the Brahmachari would pray for his success in his study of the Vedas without any interruptions as well as for his faith, insight, progeny, wealth, longevity and immortality.

A Day in the Vedic School

The Vedas were always described as Sruti which should appeal to the ear and not to the eye. And the texts of the Vedas were imparted to the learners by recitation. Every day the students started recitation of the Vedic texts before the birds started chirping, announcing the break of the day. The air in and around the Vedic schools became resounded with the recitation of the hymns and it was the sight of such a familiar phenomenon that inspired the composition of a hymn in the Rigveda which compared the monotonous recitation at a Vedic school to the croaking of frogs exhilarated by the advent of rains after summer.

The study of the Vedas was forbidden under the shade of the trees and within the sight of green barley and hearing of the cattle. And the Vedic schools observed holidays during the session only on the occasions of cloudy or windy weather.

2

The Genesis to the Brahmanas and the Upanishads

By the time of the composition of the Atharvaveda, the Aryans had already spread from the North-West to the East across the Ganges and to the South across the Vindhyas and their organizations had transformed themselves from tribal into monarchical. Small kingdoms beginning with the Kuru-Panchala in the North-West and Kashi, Kosala, Videha and Magadha in the East with permanent capitals had appeared on the scene, and a rudimentary administrative machinery to rule them had come into existence. In the process the power of their tribal organizations gave way to the rising autocracy of the kings limited only by the power of the priests, the weight of tradition and the force of the public opinion. The popular assemblies, like the Sabha and the Samiti, were replaced by the relatives, courtiers, and palace officials of the king, collectively known as Ratnins or the jewel-bearers. The latter were considered so important that special sacrifices were performed at the king's Rajasua or royal consecration to ensure their loyalty to him. After Rajasua, the king could perform Vajapeya or drink of strength to revitalize an aging health and Asvamedha to raise his status from a mere Raja to that of a Maharaja, Samrat or king of kings receiving allegiance of all kings subordinate to him. The Aryans had by now all the ingredients of an ancient civilisation. They cultivated a large range of crops, including rice, and they understood something of irrigation and manuring. While the Rigveda speaks only of gold and copper or bronze, there is now reference to tin, lead, silver and also of iron. In place of the few occupation in the Rigveda, specialized trades and crafts including jewellers, goldsmiths, metal-workers, basket-makers, rope makers, weavers, dyers, carpenters and potters had appeared. They had a variety of domestic servants and a host of professional entertainers like acrobats, fortune tellers, flute players and dancers which the Atharvaveda describes as Deva-Jana- Vidya.

However, class distinctions were becoming rigid and change of caste was becoming difficult, if not impossible. The higher classes were still free to inter-marry with the lower orders, though marriages with Shudras were not much approved. The ranks of Shudras were constantly swelled by the admission of new aboriginal tribes into the Aryan society. The Shudras were not infrequently grouped with the Vaishyas, and the two together were set against the priests and the Kshatriyas who enjoyed privileges denied to the former. It was at this period that the seeds of untouchability began to be sown when the touch of a carpenter, usually a Shudra, is said to impart ceremonial impurity and the Shudras in general were not allowed to touch the milk needed for oblations to the Agni or the fire-god. The power and prestige of the Brahmanas who claimed themselves to be gods on earth and the protectors of the realm had increased immensely. They had developed a unique system of memory-training for transmission of the Vedic texts to a choosen few, usually their own progeny and possibly zealously guarded their unique privilege and so frowned upon writing which was certainly known in some form or other in the days of the Buddha.

This transformation took a couple of centuries since the composition of the Atharvaveda by 600 BC. With the changed circumstance in the life of the Aryans, the Vedic religion now began to concentrate more and more on yajnas or sacrificial ceremonies, the details of which were more and more elaborated and called for suitable texts by which they could be regulated, fixed and conserved.

The Brahmanas

A new type of religious literature came into existence to meet the demands of the Brahmanas where ritualism runs riot. These religious texts are known as the Brahmanas which deal with the worship of the Brahma, the soul of the Universe, through devotion and prayer. They are textbooks for rituals or treatises in the science of sacrifice and are composed in prose to explain the relations between the Vedic texts and their corresponding ceremonials as well as their symbolic meaning with reference to each other. An Aranyaka or forest portion is annexed to each of these Brahmanas for study in the sylvan solitude of the forests by those sages who had become its denizens and were not required to perform sacrifices. It is also possible that the Aranyaka portion was added to the Brahmanas to cover the Vratyas who, though Aryans, led a nomadic life. The Brahmanas group themselves round the three Vedas which thus determine their subject matter. Thus, while the Brahmanas of the Rigveda are concerned with the task of collecting the hymns suited to a particular occasion as its Shastra or canon by the Hotri priests, the Brahmanas of the Sama and the Yajur Vedas occupy themselves with the duties of the Udgatri and the Adhvaryu priests.

Thus, an age of creation is now succeeded by an age of conservatism and orthodoxy partly in answer to the changing conditions in the socio-economic and political conditions of the time and partly in answer to the changed position of the Brahmanas whose power and position as protectors of the realm had increased considerably following it. Poets, Rishis or seers of the Rigvedic days are now replaced by the priests and the theologians.

The Reaction to the Brahmanas

Soon a reaction against the sacrificial ritualism practised by the priests and the theologians of the Brahmanas began and expressed itself in the birth of the Upanishads which revived the atmosphere of abstraction and pure thought of the days of the Rigveda. This reaction came mainly from the Kshatriya kings and princes. The Kshatriyas were the warrior castes of the Aryan society and as such they were constantly called upon to protect and administer their kingdoms against the attack of their neighbours and enemies. The Kshatriya kings and chieftains were constantly engaged in warfares with their neighbours either for defence or for expansion of their power and territorial possessions. They had frequent rendezvous with death and disasters, sufferings and miseries of human lives and finally ups and downs in their own fortunes. When the priestly classes were engaged in an investigation into the mysteries of the Cosmos or the Universe, the Kshatriya rulers and administrators were asking a different set of questions and these were about the mysteries of life and death and the most enlightened among them like Sanatkumar, Janaka and Ajatasatru, found the answers and kept these as their secret possessions and administered them only to the deserving seekers such as Narada of this knowledge through secret sessions. The priestly classes initially kept themselves away from this knowledge possessed by the Kshatriya kings. However, when they found that they were gradually losing their monopoly in religion, they soon came forward to claim it as its authors and added it to the end of the four Vedas and called this knowledge Vedanta or the end of the Vedas. This they did it through Yajnavalkya's Brihadaranyka Upanishad where there has been a reconcilation of the worship of the Vedic gods and goddesses as the different manifestations of the Brahman.

The Upanishads

The term, Upanishad, literally means "a sacred session" which means sitting at the feet of a teacher who imparts secret or esoteric doctrines in discourses to a select band of pupils or disciples towards the end of their studentship. For in a Vedic school run by a teacher, the latter can not teach the subject of a Upanishad as it can only be taught by one who knows the Brahman. In the words of the Upanishads, subjects taught in a Vedic school are Apara Vidya as they could not throw any light on the Brahman or the knowledge of the Supreme Being. As the Katha Upanishad forcefully points out, "Not by the Veda is the Atman attained, nor by intellect, nor by much knowledge of books."

Para Vidya or the Knowledge of the Brahman

The Vedic schools could not teach Para Vidya or the knowledge of the Brahman, known as Vedanta which was the final and the highest stage of the Vedic wisdom. However, the Bramacharya at the Vedic schools was preparatory to the realization of the knowledge of the Brahman. With the passing of the Aranyakas in the Upanishads the conception of the scope of the Brahmacharya is widened to include not merely the student period but the entire course of life regulated by the disciplines of its four successive stages as the way that leads to the Brahman. The students as Brahmacharis passed the first stage at the Vedic schools. The second stage as Grihasthas or householders began when they entered family life. The third stage of Vanaprastha started when in well-advanced middle age they left their homes for the forest to become hermits and in the final stage as Sannyasins they became homeless wanderers with all earthly ties broken.

However, a student returning home from a Vedic school and entering family life could still achieve Brahmavarcha or knowledge of the Brahman by Svadhyaya or self study, first by going to a place outside the town or village, north or north-east, from where only the roofs of the houses could be seen and secondly by reciting the Vedas at that place from sunrise till sunset when he returned home and offered a gift. The importance of such Svadhyaya has been pointed out by Satapatha Brahmana which regards it as a form of sacrifice to the Brahman by which an imperishable world is gained—one becomes calm in mind, independent of others, the best physician for himself with his restraint of senses, uniformity of mental attitude, growth of intelligence and fame as well as power of protecting the people.

The Indispensabiliity of a Guru

Both the Katha Upanishad and the Mundaka Upanishad emphasise the indispensability of a guru for a student who did not go for self-study. A teacher is needed, explains the Chandogya Upanishad, to disperse the mist of empirically acquired knowledge at a Vedic school from the eyes of a student. However, the Maitrayana Upanishad forbids communication of this most secret doctrine to anyone who is not his son or pupil. Thus, Svetaketu learnt this esoteric doctrine from his own father, a Rishi or a seer, after his return from a Vedic school where he had spent 12 years in studying the Vedas. So did Bhrigu from his Brahmana father, Varuna. There are indeed many such cases where the student had obtained the knowledge of the Brahman from their fathers.

Search for a Guru

However, those who did not possess Rishis as their fathers, they had to search for gurus to obtain this secret knowledge and this could involve them in travelling from one part of the country to another. In the Chandogya Upanishad we have the classic example of Narada who after learning all the subjects in a Vedic school found himself "not learned in the Atman" or the Atma-vid and approached the Kshatriya king Sanatkumar, the Guru of Sri Krishna, who had known Atman with a request to teach him this knowledge: "Yet have I heard from such as are like you that he who knows the Atman vanquishes sorrow. I am in sorrow—lead me then over, I pray, to the farther shore that lies beyond sorrow."

Transmission of the Knowledge of the Brahman through Discourses

As we have said earlier that this knowledge is imparted to a shisya by a guru through discourses, dialogues, questions and answers very similar to the method later used by Socrates in ancient Greece as well as by Jesus Christ in the form of parables or short stories with a moral in the Middle-East. In these discourses the need for contemplation and introspection on the part of the disciple was never overlooked. Thus, Svetaketu's father who was teaching his son how the functions of the mind and its faculties were dependent upon the body, how psychological conditions were bound up with the physiological, put him through a course of actual fasting so that he could achieve a direct perception of the truth by his own experiments and experiences. The father first made him fast for 15 days, cutting of all foods except drinks of water to show that Prana or life depended on water. After this fast, the father asked him to recite the Vedas and the son found to his surprise that the knowledge of the Vedas had vanished from his mind and it began to dawn on his mind as he started taking food. By this experiment Svetaketu realized the truth that Manas or mind depended on Anna or food and that it could not function in a famished body. Similarly, the Yak or the faculty of speech depended upon Tejas or heat of the body.His father thus made the concluding observation: " Just as by covering it with a piece of straw or Trina, one make a single small spark or Khadyot left in it to blaze up, so is it with you."

Upanishads imparted a New Meaning of the Brahman

From the days of the Rigveda to the dawn of the Upanishads

the term Brahmana underwent a transformation in its meaning as the Aryan sages began to gather more knowledge not only about the mysteries of the Cosmos but also of the birth and death. In the Rigveda the term means the magical power of the sacred word of the hymns but in the Upanishad it means the entity or consciousness that pervades all forms and phenomena and from which the whole Universe, including the gods themselves, have emerged. The knowledge that the Upanishads impart lies not in the mere recognition of the existence of the Brahman, but in continual consciousness for it.

The sages of the Upanishads used imagery of every possible kind to express the idea of Brahman. Sometimes Brahman is described as a tiny manikin in the heart or the breadth or the mysterious fluid which flows in the veins but often is thought of as quite incorporeal and immeasurable as in the Chandoyga Upanishad where the father of Svetaketu, the sage Uddalaka Aruni, thus taught his son:

"Fetch me a fruit of the banyan tree."
"Here is one, Sir."
"Break it."
"I have broken it, Sir."
"What do you see?"
"Very tiny seeds, Sir."
"Break one."
"1 have broken it, Sir."
"Now, what do you see?"
"Nothing, Sir."
"My son, " the father said, "what you do not perceive is the essence, and in this essence the mighty banyan tree exists. Believe me, my son, in that essence is the

Self of all that is. That is the truth, that is the Self, and you are that Self, Svetaketu."

As a matter of fact, the identity of the souls of the individual and of the Brahman or the Universe is reiterated through out the Upanishadic literature with varying emphasis and interpretation on the nature of the identity and character of the Brahman or the universal soul.

There are said to be 108 Upanishads. The earlier ones are composed in prose and consist of a series of short expositions of some aspect of the new doctrines, often in the form of questions and answers. The later Upanishads, like the Katha and the Svetasvatara, are in verse and their contents are more closely related.

The Doctrine of Samsara or Transmigration and of Karma or Deeds

The Aryans from the beginning were most affected by "death" as the central fact of their life. In the Rigveda the fate of the dead was finally decided when they died—they went either to "the World of Fathers" or to the "House of Clay" where they remained infinitely though a late hymn in it suggested cryptically that they might pass to the waters or remain in plants before being reborn in a human body. In the Brihadaranyaka Upanishad often ascribed to the authorship of the sage Yajnavalkya who adorned the court of the king Janaka, is given the first form of the doctrine of transmigration after the Aryans had pressed down the river Ganges and had absorbed new ideas about life after death. According to it, the souls of those who have lived the lives of sacrifice, charity and austerity first go to "the World of Fathers," then, after a period of bliss, go to the moon and from moon they go to the air and desecend to earth in the rain. On earth they "become food, . . . and are offered again in the altar fire which is man to be born again in the fire of woman." And those who have failed to live their lives righteously are reincarnated as worms, birds or insects.

However, this doctrine of Samsara or transmigration, and Karma or deeds which seems to rest on a primitive belief that conception occurs through the eating by one of the parents of a fruit or vegetable containing the latent soul of the offspring, was not universally held at the time of the composition of the Upanishad which first propounded it but by the sixth and fifth centuries BC, it has gained wide currency and universal acceptance among the Aryans.

In whatever way the doctrine of transmigration was developed, it involved a belief in the repeated passage of the soul from life to life, either for all eternity or for an inestimably long period of time. And this is applicable to all forms of life. Death is always terrible, and the prospect of having to die innumerable times is certainly not a very happy one. Again, life is often an acute suffering, physically and mentally and nobody who is born again and again can escape the sorrows and the sufferings of life. Our sages set out to find a way to escape from these sufferings involved in the cycle of birth and death and they found it in the Upanishads.

The Brahman never dies or changes

They realized that it was the Atman or the self who died and not the Brahman or the Cosmos which was not subject to change, decay and dissolution. Selfishness results from the pursuit of objective knowledge which connects the mind with the worldly matter. When the sage Yajnavalkya was about to take up the life of an ascetic, he thus instructed his favourite wife, Maitreyi, on immortality, the Brahman or the universal soul:

> "A husband is not dear for love of the husband—a husband is dear for love of the Self. Similarly, wife, sons, wealth, cattle, priests and warriors, worlds, gods, the Vedas, everything–none of them are dear in their own right, but all are dear for love of the Self. Truly you can see and hear and perceive and know the Self, Maitreyi. And when you have seen, heard, perceived and known the Self, you will know all things. When there seems to be duality of Self and non-Self, one sees, smells, tastes, perceives, hears, touches and knows something other. But when all is the Self, there is no consciousness of anything other than Self. Thus, Maitreyi I have instructed you—this is immortality."

For the Brahman resides in the human soul, and indeed the Brahman is the human soul, is the Atman, the Self. When a man or a woman realizes this fact fully, the soul of that person becomes one with the Brahman, and the person transcends joy and sorrow, birth and death. Thus, the merger of the Self or Atman with the Absolute or Brahman is immortality and when this is achieved, one is free from bondage and attachment and ultimately is free also from the cycle of birth and death.

How to achieve the Brahman

And how is this to be achieved? It is through knowledge or Veda, from root Vid, to know which is the culmination of the knowledge on Sravana, Manana and Nididhyasana. Sravana means listening to the words or the texts as they are uttered by the guru or the teacher, Manana means deliberation, reflection on the the topic taught by the guru and Nididhyasana means Yoga or meditation through which the truth is to be realized. Our sages achieved liberation through this method, so did the Mahavira and the Jaina sages as well as the Buddha and his followers. And so also did the Buddha's guru, Alara Kalama, a Vedic ascetic, who taught the Buddha the doctrine of Nirvana. It is said that Alara Kalama was so used to meditation that "he would not, sitting on the roadside, be conscious of a caravan of 500 carts rattling past him."

3

The Fifth Veda

We have already cited the case of Narada to illustrate the point that the Vedic schools could not teach the Brahman and one needed a guru to learn it as he did from the Kshatriya king Sanat Kumar. Narada gave a list of subjects he had earlier studied at the Vedic school to Sanat Kumar before making his request. They were: "the Rig Veda, Yajur Veda, Sama Veda, the Atharva Veda as fourth, the epic and mythological poems as fifth Veda." As far as we know there is no "fifth Veda" but description of the epic and the mythological poems as "fifth Veda" by Narada suggests their religious importance and we can presume that in all probability the two great epic poems, the Ramayana and the Mahabharata, were taught at the Vedic schools and that Narada learnt them as "fifth Veda" in one such school.

Narada belonged to an age when the Vedas and other allied religious scriptures were put into Sutras and the Age of the Sutras which began with the composition of Asthadhyayi by Panini around 400 BC, came to an end with Patanjali's Yogasutras around 200 BC. We can reasonably argue that before the Age of the Sutrakaras, the composition of both the epics, the Ramayana and the Mahabharata, had begun and were known in some elementary form or other by the time of Narada, though both of them later took many centuries till they were finally completed in the Age of the Guptas by the sixth century AD.

The Ramayana and the Mahabharata

These two epics blossomed out of many martial ballads sung on the occasion of great sacrifices like the Rajasua and the Asvamedha. Among the sacfrificers who performed Rajasua and Asvamedha were many kings of the Kuru or Kosala realms. Some of the most famous lays and tales found in the Vedic texts celebrated the benevolence and prowess of Kuru kings like Parikshit and Janamejaya and of Ikshvaku and Kosalan monarchs like Harishchandra and Para Atnara. Both Mahabharata and Ramayana though worked out by a succession of priestly editors give their origins as martial legends.

Their religious importance lay at first in the royal sacrificial ritual, part of which involved in telling stories of the heroes of the past. This put the martial ballads into the hands of the priesthood, who, in transmitting, often interpolated many long passages on theology, morals and statecraft.

The Mahabharata

Traditionally, the author of the Mahabharata, consisting of more than 90, 000 verses was the sage Vyasa, son of Parasara, who taught it to his pupil, Vaisampayana. The latter recited it in public for the first time at a great sacrifice held by king Janamejaya, the great grandson of Arjuna, one of the heroes of the story. Stripped of its episodes and interpolations the poem tells of the great civil war in the kingdom of Kurus, near modern Delhi, and the victory of the Pandus, helped by Krishna and the Panchalas over the Kurus proper, the sons of the blind king, Dhritarashtra Vaichitravirya.

The name of the king Dhritarashtra Vaichitravirya, father of the Kurus has been mentioned in the Kathaka recension of the Yajurveda and the ruin of the Kurus is hinted at in the Chandogya Upanishad and one of the Srauta Sutras. In the Chandogya Upanishad Krishna has been identified as the son of Vasudeva and Devaki, and in the Taittiriya Aranyaka, he is identified with the god, Vishnu or Narayana. In the Satapatha Brahmana Arjuna has been identified with Indra though in the epic he is the son of Kunti, wife of Pandu, by Indra.

It will not be out of the way to mention here that the Gupta Age saw the completion of the Mahabharata containing some 100, 000 verses which has been mentioned for the first time in an inscription of the time. The Mahabharata is not merely a song of victory but a collection of old legends of high-souled kings and pious sages, of dutiful queens and beautiful maids like Sakuntala and Savitri, Nala and Sibi, Amba and Vidula.

The Bhagavad Gita

Among the religious poems which form part of the Mahabharata, the most famous is Krishna's address to Arjuna who was reluctant to fight his dear and near ones, which form the subject matter of the Bhagavad Gita or the Song of the Lord, later the bed-rock of Aryan theism. As the Upanishads represent the Vedanta or the end of the Vedas, the Bhagavad Gita represents the essence of the teachings of the Upanishads such as the one when Krishna tells Arjuna that the soul never dies, is everlasting, dwells in all things, firm, unmoving, eternal. In other words, the Atman is the Brahman.

The essence of the teachings of the Bhagavad Gita may be summed up in the maxim: "Do your work without concerning yourself with the result." This seems to be inconsistent with the idea imparted by the doctrine of the Law of the Deeds according to which the fate of a person is decided by one's own deeds or actions after birth. However, there is no inconsistency at all. By advising one not to expect the result of the work done, the Bhagavad Gita is actually teaching the Upanishadic doctrine of detachment as revealed in the last two Asramas, Vanaprastha and Sanayas in a contemporary person's life.

In an organized society each individual has his special role to play and in every circumstance there are actions which are intrinsically right as are laid down by the sacred law of the Aryan society. The right course must be chosen according to the circumstances, without any considerations of personal interest or sentiment. Thus, man serves god, and in so far as he lives up to his ideal he draws near to god. As a matter of fact, the stern ethics of the Gita are clearly intended as a defence of the order of the Aryan society against the attack of the reformers and the unbelievers. The virtue of the Brahman is wisdom, of the Kshatriya, valour; of the Vaishya, industry; of the Shudra, service. By fulfilling his class function to the best of his ability, with love and devotion to god and without personal ambition, a man will find salvation, whatever his class. As Krishna in Sloka 26, Chapter 9, of the Bhagavad Gita says: "Whosoever offers to Me, with love or devotion, a leaf, a flower, a fruit or water, that offering of love of the pure and self-controlled man is willingly and readily accepted by Me."

The Ramayana

The author of the Ramayana, a little more than a quarter of the size of the other epic, was Valmiki, a contemporary of its hero, Rama, the eldest son of Dasaratha, a prince of the Ikshvaku family of Ayodhya, the capital of the old kingdom of Kosala. Rama married Sita, the daughter of Janaka, the celebrated king of Videha, in North Bihar but had to leave his home and go into exile for a period of 14 years. Rama, with the help of his half brother Lakshmana, Sugriva, Hanuman and other monkey chiefs of Kishkindhya in the Bellary region of South India, recovered Sita, from Ravana, the Rakshasa king of Lanka who had kidnapped her after slaying the latter, and then repaired to Ayodhya. However, he had to banish his faithful consort Sita to please his subjects to the hermitage of Valmiki where she gave birth to the twins, Lava and Kusha who subsequently returned to their ancestral home and succeeded to their heritage.

The names of Rama and Sita though met with in the Vedic literature often as appellations of human beings are in no way connected in the Vedic texts with the illustrious lines of the Ikshvakus or the Videhas and the name of Ravana is absolutely unknown to Brahmanical and non-Brahmanical literature till we come to the epics themselves or to works like the Kautiliya Arthasastra. Whatever may be the kernel of historical truth underneath the Ramayana, there is no doubt that the Ikshavaku princes from Kosala kingdom played a leading part in the colonization of the southernmost part of South India as names of the Ikshvaku kings figure prominently in the early inscriptions of Southern India.

Which was composed first—Mahabharata or Ramayana?

Both the epic poems were known before the Sutra Age and by sixth century AD, their fame spread to far off places in the South Asia like Combodia. Both of them contain a good deal of pseudo-epic or didactic material which came to be included at a comparatively later date. The question that may be asked now is: Which one of the two saw the beginning of its compositon first, Mahabharata or Ramayana?

Since both the epics were more or less contemporaries, worked over through years by a succession of priestly orders, it was always possible for them to interpolate materials from each other and these can not be used as arguments for advancing the date of the composition of one over the other. For example, the Mahabharata contains as an episode the story of the Rama in a form which suggests the editor of the final version of the Mahabharata knew the Ramayana. Similarly, the Ramayana mentions Janamejaya and "Vishnu who upraised a mountain with his hands, " that is, Krishna. However, the tale of the Pandus is known to the Jataka Gathas or the collection of folk-tales and other Buddhist stories and is hinted at by the Greek writers of the fourth century BC in the confused legends about the Indian Herakles and Pandia. It is also known to Panini who composed his Asthadhyayi by 400 BC and Asvalayana, the author of the Griha Sutras as well as the grammarians, Katyayana and Patanjali. Patanjali who came towards the end of the Sutra Age and composed his commentary on Panini's grammar seems to be acquainted with the Kishkindhya episode of the Ramayana, which has never been mentioned by any of his predecessors.

Secondly, the style of the Ramayana is less rugged than

that of the Mahabharata which contains occasional grammatical and prosodical errors and has a close relationship to that of classical Sanskrit poetry in post-Panini age.

Finally, the scene of the Mahabharata is the holy Brahmanical heartland of the Kuru-Panchalas where the Aryans settled first when they came to India and that of the Ramayana is Kosala in the eastern part of the Ganges valley where the Aryans expanded later.

All these point to the fact that the main narrative portions of the Mahabharata, admittedly at first only about a quarter of its present size, are appreciably much earlier than those of the Ramayana.

4

The Persian and the Greek Invasion and Conquest of the North-West

All these religious scriptures from the Rigveda down to the Upanishads as well as the two great epics, the Ramayana and the Mahabharata which were regarded as the "fifth Veda" in the contemporary Vedic schools were orally composd, transmitted and preserved by the priestly classes of the Bharata tribes.They had developed a unique system of memory-training for retention as well as for transmission of the Vedic texts to a chosen few more than a thousand years before the Persians under Darius 1 came and occupied the countries washed by the river Sindu and its five tributaries.

In the sixth century BC when the star of the Magadhan kingdom was rising under Bimbisara (542-490 BC) and his son, Ajatasatru (490-458 BC) in the eastern part of the country where the Buddha was roaming with his band of disciples preaching Nirvana, the Persians were knocking at the gates of the North-West which included Gandhara with the city of Taxila then famed not only as a great center of trade and art but also as a great seat of Vedic learning where students from places as far off as Varanasi and Pataliputra used to come for higher study and learning.

In an inscription of around 519 BC Darius I, the third of the Achaemenid emperors after Cyrus the Great (558-530 BC) who built up the greatest empire the world had then ever seen, claimed possession of Gandhara and in a slightly later one he also claimed *Hindush* or the North-West. According to the Greek historian, Herodotus, *Hindush* or the North-West became the twentieth and the most populous and rich satrapy of the Persian or the Achaemenid empire under Darius I and his successors. We do not know the exact extent of the Persian province of *Hindush* but it is certain that it included much of the pre-partitioned Punjab and Sind which is now in Pakistan and its boundaries reached as far as the deserts of Rajasthan.

For nearly two hundred years the Persians ruled the North-West through their satraps or provincial governors till they were replaced by the Greeks under Alexander who invaded our country in 326 BC. During all these years the North-West part of our country was known to them as *Hindush*, the western extension of the Himalayas bordering their satrapy as *Hindukush* and the Sindu river which flowed from the *Hindukush* mountains down through the Punjab and the Sind with five tributaries to the Arabian sea as *Hindu*.

Why did the Persians call their North-West satrapy of the Punjab and Sind as *Hindush*, the western extension of the Himalayas as *Hindukush*, and the river Sindu as *Hindu*? The answer is simple: the Persians found it difficult to pronounce the alphabet *"S"* and replaced it with *"H"* and so *Sind* became *Hind* and Sindu became *Hindu* and the whole of their North-West satrapy and beyond came to be known as *Hindush*.

In the history of time and space two hundred years

even in the absence of any technological innovation and development were not certainly a small period to measure changes that happened under the rule of the Persians in the North-West part of our country and in all probability the Persians might have ruled their satrapy with the help of local Aryans. Their armies might have offered good opportunities for earning livelihood to the lower castes of the Aryan society as it happened much later under the Muslim and the British rulers in our country. For example, as Herodotus reported that over a hundred years before Alexander's invasion, a detachment of Indians fought in the Persian army with the Greeks at Plataea. And again when in 330 BC. Alexander defeated Darius III, the last of the Achaemenids and set out to subdue the whole of the former Persian empire, he found in the decisive battle of the Gaugamela a small contingent of soldiers from the west of the river Indus with fifteen elephants fighting with Darius.

It is obvious that these two terms, *Hindu* and the *Hindush,* used by the Persians could not under any circumstances have occurred in our religious scriptures composed much earlier and since the Persians stayed there for nearly 200 years and had interaction with the original residents in administering the country, it is possible that the latter knew that they were called *Hindus* and their country as *Hindush* but this knowledge had never misled the priestly classes or their followers in describing themselves and their creations as *Hindu* and the countries inhabited by them as *Hindush.* They remained Brahmanas or the possessors of the supreme power, their land as the Brahmanavarta or the Bharatvarsha and their followers or the people from the other three castes as the followers of the Brahmanical or the Vedic religion.

Impact of the Persian and the Greek Occupation of the North-West on Our Religion

Yet the occupation of the land of the Bharata tribes and their successors, the Kurus and the Panchalas, which was the scene of the religious activities of the Aryans for centuries, by the Persians and the Greeks for more than 250 years had significant consequences for the Aryan society and the religion. The Persian occupation of the North-West till they were replaced by the Greeks, lasted alone more than two hundred years. In the absence of any authentic account based on historical evidences (in those years such evidences were indeed not only very meagre but also difficult to come across) on the Persian occupation of the North-West, it will be silly to dismiss this episode as a bubble in a sea of time. We know that the Muslims ruled India for more than six hundred and fifty years in the middle ages and the British less than two hundred years in the modern times. We also know of the tremendous changes that took place in our country and society in both these periods though the pace of changes was much faster under the British administration because of the advancement of knowledge in science and technology than under the Muslim rule.

So there were definite changes in the Aryan society in the North-West under the occupation of the Persians and later of the Greek though the pace of such changes was much slower than the one witnessed in the later periods under the Muslims and the British. And as in the case of the changes in the medieval and modern India, it was the society which was first affected under the Persian rule.

The Persian conquerors like their Muslim and British

counterparts in medieval and modern India respectively were not accompanied by their females. Certainly in those days hardly an army set out to conquer a neighbouring territory had ever been accompanied by the women members of its families. As far as the Persians and later the Greek were concerned only a very few among their married higher-ups intially brought their wives to settle down in the country. The rest which was the majority among the Persians and later among the Greek picked up their women from the members of the Aryan society, as did the Muslim and the British officials in the subsequent centuries. And we all know that while the Muslims married them after converting them into their religion, the British formed an illegal *liaison* with them thereby giving birth to a community which we know as Anglo-Indians or Eurasians. As in the cases of the Muslims and the British, the women mostly came from the lower castes like the Vaishyas and the Shudras who often felt oppressed by the higher castes–the Brahmins and the Kshatriyas. The women from the Dasas or the Dasyus, the descendants of the people of the Indus Valley Civilisation, vanquished by the invading Aryans over the several centuries before they finally settled down in the country formed the bulk of the majority of the wives acquired by them.

With the Persian conquerors around and their women becoming their wives, our sages later known as the Sutrakaras stepped in to protect the sanctity of the Aryan society and took a number of retrograde measures to uphold it. First, in the days of the four Vedas, the women at the time of the Persian occupation, were admitted to the Vedic schools after the performance of the Upanayana ceremony and were given prescribed courses of study in the Vedas to enable them to assist their husbands in the sacrificial offerings. Now as the Persian and later the Greek occupiers began to make an inroad into the Aryan society by marrying their women, the sages like Manu and Yajnavalkya stepped in to protect the Aryan society by debarring them from attending the Vedic schools and advised the parents of the girls in their Dharmasutras for their early marriage as soon as they reached puberty. This means that unlike the Age of the four Vedas which produced many women sages called Rishikas and Brahmanavadinis like Romasa, Lopamudra, Apala, Kadru, Visvavara, Ghosha, Juhu, Jarita, Urvasi, Yami, Indrani, Savitri, Devajani, Nodha and Gaupayana, the years following Manu and Yajnabalkya would not be able to boast of any such learned and accomplished ladies. The sages in the Age of the four Vedas advocated knowledge of the Vedas to the women of their society to the extent it was required not only for the purpose of assisting their husbands in the performance of their religious duties and obligations but also for the purpose of discharging their own domestic responsibilities as good and dutiful house-wives. The sage Heemadri says that "Kumaris, unmarried girls, should be taught Vidya and Dharmaniti. An educated Kumari brings good to the families of both her father and husband. So, she should be married to a learned husband or Manishi as she is a Vidushi." However, after the Persian occupation following the advice of Manu and Yajnavalkya, most parents preferred to marry their daughters off as soon as they reached puberty or even earlier before it, and this fact explains not only the disappearence of scholarly ladies from the Aryan society but also the beginning of an increasing illiteracy among them. And from this point of view, one can say that the Aryan women almost became equal in status to that of the Shudras in respect of learning in the succeeding centuries.

Secondly, simultaneously with the act of putting a stop to the continuation of further studies by the Aryan women at the Vedic schools, the sages also banned the entry of the Shudras to the Vedic schools .In the days of the four Vedas the Vedic schools were open to all classes including the Shudras who were along with the other castes were admitted to study the Rigveda. The Yajurveda clearly enjoins the imparting of the Vedic knowledge to all classes, Brahmanas and Rajanyas, Shudras, Anaryas and Charanyas, not to speak of women. In the same catholic spirit the Vajasaneyi Samhita or the Atharvaveda states that "all classes have an equal right to study the Veda." The reason why the Shudras were particularly singled out for this kind of treatment was not because they were not regarded as bonafide Aryans but because of their proximity to the Persian and later the Greek occupiers. The latter not only found their wives mostly from among the Shudra women but also provided occupation to many of the Shudra men as helpers and soldiers in their civil and military administration.

Thirdly, the sages also made the society more rigid by banning hitherto prevalent inter-marriage, inter-dining and change of occupation or commensality among the four castes. In the days of the four Vedas we have not only instances to show that the Rishis or seers were not merely the monopoly of the priestly classes but also we have evidences to know about the marriages of Brahmanas with Rajanya women, of the Aryas with the Shudras, and of the instances of the families who were not wedded to a particular profession. We do not also have any evidences to suggest that there was a ban on the taking of food cooked by the Shudras or that impurity was communicated by the touch or contact with the inferior castes. However, it was at this time of the Persian and later the Greek occupation of the North-West that along with the ban of inter-marriage, inter-dining or change of profession, the seeds of untouchability began to be sown in when the touch of a carpenter, usually a Shudra, is said to have imparted ceremonial impurity and the Shudras in general were not allowed to touch the milk needed for oblations to the Agni or fire-god.

And finally, a decline in advanced surgical knowledge in Ayurveda began when the sages like Manu and Yajnavalkya imposed a taboo on touching a corpse and provided ceremonial purifications for the violators.

The Aryan sages looked upon the Persians who were then mostly the followers of Zoroastrianism and later the Greek as foreigners or outsiders and considered these retrograde steps necessary to preserve the purity and the sanctity of the Aryan race and culture against their occupation and administration of the North-West.

Yet, many of these foreigners, often described by the Aryan sages as "Mlecchas" and "Yavanas" became gradually Indianised by accepting our religion and culture to such an extent that they soon found a place in the Dharmasutras of Manu as "degenerate Kshatriyas" or warriors and became known as "Hindus" or "Indus" to their friends and relatives at home in Persia and Greece respectively, not because of the religion and culture they adopted but because of their settlements in the valley of the river Sindu which the Persian occupiers pronounced as "Hindu" and the Greek as "Indus".

The interaction of the members of the Aryan society

with the Persian and later the Greek rulers in the civil and the military administration led to many far-reaching consequences, the most important of which was the development and use of the Kharoshthi script among them as against the Brahmi and the Nagri scripts of the language. The Kharoshthi scripts indeed posed a challenge to the survival of the Prakrita language and it was left to Panini to refine it with his grammar known as *Asthadhyayi,* which later came to be known as Sanskrita or refined.

One of the most important impact of the prolonged Persian and later Greek occupation of the North-West was that the Kuru-Panchala country gradually lost its prominence as the centre of Aryan culture and religion which now came to be enjoyed by the Eastern and the Southern kingdoms such as Kashi, Kosala, Videha and Magadha. Yet there is no denying the fact that the Vedic learning in the North-West, which now became exposed to the Persian and later the Greek influences, went through a period of metamorphosis and apart from the Vedas, it now began to offer new programmes and courses in the Vedic schools at Taxila in the province of Gandhara, which attracted students from far-off places where the Buddhist learning was more dominant than the Vedic.

However, the most immediate and perhaps the most direct impact as reflected in our earlier discussion was the fact that the Aryan priestly classes who had developed a unique system of memory training for retention and transmission of the Vedic texts now began to consolidate their past religious works orally transmitted through the guru-shisya-parampara into special Sutras to save the Vedic religion from oblivion under an alien occupation by making it easily and readily accessible to all.

Subsequently the simplified and the compiled works of our religious scriptures into various Sutras were also found to be extremely convenient to ward off the challenges to Brahmanism of a tremendous growth of asceticism which was then blowing over the Eastern India under Mahavira and Buddha and which, however, took nearly more than two hundred years to reach the North-West areas under Asoka's patronage. Needless to say, some of these Sutras which have miraculously survived the long period of Islamic rule in medieval India till they are rediscovered by the British Orientalists in the late eighteenth and the early nineteenth centuries, form the backbone of our present religion.

5

The Sutras and the Sutrakaras

The sages began their work nearly hundred years after the Persian occupation of the North-West around 400 BC. The work of compilation and codification of our religious scriptures into Sutras began with Panini who came from the area known as Peshawar and is now in the State of Pakistan. Panini wrote the Sanskrit grammar, the *Asthadhyayi* or eight chapters, which effectively stabilized the Prakrita language of the Vedas, which was threatened by the language of the Persian occupiers. The Prakrita language could now develop further but only within the frame work of Panini's *Asthadhyayi*. Panini, in all probability, based his grammar on the language as it was then spoken in the North-West. And with Panini, the language of the Vedas had virtually reached its classical form and thence forward it developed little except in its vocabulary. It was from the time of Panini onwards that the language of the Vedas began to be called Sanskrita or refined, perfected as opposed to the Prakritas which though unrefined developed naturally as popular dialects. It is interesting to note here that the sages completed their last work of putting our religious scriptures into various Sutras also with the one that had a bearing on their language and Panini's grammar. This is *Mahabhasya* or the great commentary by Patanjali, also the author of the Yogasutras, who flourished around 200 BC and his work aimed at explaining Panini's terse grammar which was often found difficult to be comprehended by not too learned a person.

In between Panini and Patanjali flourished quite a number of sages whose work on the Sutras have survived the ravages of time and now form the most substantial basis of our knowledge in our religion. Their work survived through the oral transmission of knowledge to the Brahmacharins in the Vedic schools which now took definte form and shape at their hands. A child's Vidyarambha began at the age of 5 with offering worship to the deities, Hari, Lakshmi and Sarasvati or the goddess of learning as well as to the Vidya cultivated by his family and was admitted to the Vedic schools after perfoming the Upanayana ceremony at the age of 8 if he was a Brahmana, 11 if he was a Kshatriya and 12 if he was a Vaishya. The students as Brahmacharins were taught the "Whole Veda" with the allied Angas and the Rahasyas or the esoteric sciences and had to observe some special Vratas for a certain period of time before starting a course. And, as said before, only the Brahmana students stayed at the Vedic schools to complete the full course lasting for a period sometimes for more than 12 years to retain their monopoly on our religion and religious scriptures.

The school session started on a full moon day in the month of July-August, now called Guru-Poornima day and it lasted till the month of December-January when the students returned home and stayed there recapitulating the lessons learnt till they came back and joined the schools again in the month of July-August. The sages Baudhayana, Apastamba and Gautama, now also provided for the gradation of teachers as Acharya and Upadhyaya as well as for the payment of fees to them in lieu of services. They also made provision for teaching by non-Brahmin teachers under duress and at difficult times when the Brahmana teachers were not available for the sake of continuity and finally they also provided for payment of parting gifts, in the words of Manu, "a field, a cow, a horse, a parasol and shoes, a seat, grain, even vegetables" by students depending on their abilities to their teachers after completion of their studies which, often lasted beyond 12 years. The Brahmacharins now shaved their heads and beards, discarded their old robes, took a perfumed bath and came to be known as Snatak and wore new garments, two ear-rings and a perforated pellet of sandalwood, overlaid with gold to bring them gain and superiority in battles and assemblies at its aperture. At a function called Samabartana the teachers advised them on leading a fruitful life of a house-holder or the respected life of a teacher as the case may be.

The sages who compiled the Sutras out of our existing orally transmitted religious scriptures which were then threatened under the occupation of the Mlecchas or the Persians were known as the Sutrakaras. Their Sutras represent the quintessence of all the knowledge acquired and assimilated through study and meditation spreading over the past several centuries. The Sutrakaras generally claimed no originality or inspiration for themselves except perhaps credit for making the religious scriptures of the past centuries more easily accessible to all. They adopted a business like style and condensed the vast mass of literary material of the past within the smallest possible compass. As Patanjali, one of the Sutrakaras, who came around 200 years before the beginning of the Christian era, observes in his *Mahabhashya,* "an author rejoiceth in the economizing of half a short vowel as much as in the birth of a son."

Among the various forms of Sutras were the Srauta-sutras which are said to be the continuation of the Brahmanas on their ritual side, the Grihasutras which deal with the various domestic ceremonies of birth, marriage and death, the Dharmasutras which deal with the various customs and manners of Aryan social life and are our earliest legal treatises and finally the Sulvasutras which deal with the various practices of the time such as measurement required for the construction of a Vedi or altar for sacrificial ceremony. The last one may be regarded as our earliest mathematical treatise incorporating an advanced knowledge of geometry and algebraical propositions.

Further Development of Religious and Allied Subjects

Yet the Sutra Age which is said to have begun around 400 BC when Persians were ruling the North-West and ended around 200 BC when Buddhism was having its sunny days under the great Maurya Emperor, Asoka, is known for developing many religious texts and disciplines further. Thus, in law there were further studies on the Dharmasutras of Vasishtha and Baudhayana though only the chief surviving representatives of the Age are the Dharmasutras of Manu and Yajnavalkya. Many of the Vedangas also became independent disciplines in the works of the Sutrakaras. Kalpa or ritual reached large dimensions in the Sutras of Baudhayanaiyas and Apastambaiyas, Vyakarana or grammar developed as an independent science in Panini's *Ashtadhyayi* or eight chapters which laid down the rules applicable to the language of the Vedas, which now came to be known as Sanskrita or refined and finally in both Gargi Samhita and Vasishta Samhita which were composed later, astronomy developed as an independent discipline showing no connection with the Vedas except that the authorship is attributed to Rishis or descendants of their families.

Similarly, in Philosophy, as in Law and Angas, there was a tremendous growth and development in the hands of the Sutrakaras. The result was a multiplicity of schools of thought, of which six systems have till today held their own as the most typical and representative of them all. These six systems of philosophy have come to be distinguished as orthodox systems from the heterodox philosophical systems of the Buddhists, Jainas and Charvakas, as they are somehow reconcilable with the philosophy of the Vedas and the Upanishads. They are: (1) the Samkhyha of Kapila, (2) Yoga of Patanjali, (3) Nyaya of Gautama, (4) V aiseshika of Kanada, (5) Karma or Purva Mimansa of Jaimini, and (6) Sariraka or Uttara Mimansa or Vedanta of Badarayana.

The foundations of these six systems of philosophy rest on a common system of discipline, known as Varnasramadhrama or the regulations belonging to different castes and asramas or stages in the life of the Aryans first developed in Yajnavalkya's Brihadaranyka Upanishad. These comprise the various samskaras or sacraments prescribed for different stages in life: Upanayana, Brahmacharya, and Samavartana for its first stage; various sacrifices prescribed for the householder's life in the second; the rules for the gradual detachment from the world in the third stage of the forest dwelling hermit and finally various forms of meditation prescribed for the wandering mendicant in the last stage of emancipation or liberation from the cycle of birth and death. Thus, in the Aryan society, the study of philosophy aimed at the attainment of the supreme knowledge or truth, that is called mukti or emancipation, through different stages of life or experience, each representing a specific degree of conquest achieved over the body, mind and the material world.

Birth of New Disciplines

These are the disciplines which have cut off their umbilical cords from the Vedic scriptures or the Vedic schools where the latter were orally transmitted by the priestly class to their students or Brahmacharins who stayed at their residences. Yet there were many new subjects or disciplines the Sutrakaras wrote about to meet the needs and requirements of an emerging Aryan society. One such subject is the study of statecraft or treatise on governance and the most outstanding work of the Age is Kautilya's Arthasastra. Kautilya whose original name was Chanakya, was the Brahmana scholar who helped Chandragupta Maurya to usurp the last of the Nandas and capture the Magadhan throne at Pataliputra between *c.* 324 and 317 BC. Kautilya's Arthashastra which compares well with Machiavelli's *The Prince* in modern times deals with the education and training of the monarch and provides the necessary guidelines for him to successfully administer a kingdom. Kautilya himself served Chandragupta Maurya who founded the illustrious Maurya dynasty at Pataliputra as his Purohita or Brahman adviser and it is possible that many of his experiences were embedded in his work.

Thus, the Sutrakaras not only collected the past

knowledge of the scriptures, compiled and edited it but also developed the disciplines allied to our scriptures such as the six Vedangas and put each one of them on an independent track as well as opened new frontiers of knowledge and learning to meet the needs and the requirements of the time

The Vedic Schools at Taxila

Many among the Sutrakaras like Panini and Kautilya were students of the Vedic schools at Taxila we have earlier spoken about. Taxila was named after Taksha, son of the king Bharata and was situated in Gandhara to the east of the river Sindu and on the highway connecting Central and Western Asia to the interior of India by way of the river Ganges. Exposed as it were to a variety of influences including those from Persia and later from Greece, vast and varied subjects such as Vedatrayi, Vedanta, Vyakarana, Ayurveda, eighteen Sippas or Arts, Astronomy, Agriculture, Commerce, Law, and Military Science were studied at the Vedic schools at Taxila. From 326 BC, as Taxila came under the Greek influence, Greek Language, Greek Military Science and Greek Arts were also included in the courses offered at Taxila. From the evidences in the Jatakas, it may be said that except in religious scriptures, lessons were imparted from written works and most of the lessons taught were followed by practical applications. While the practical application in some subjects like medicine where search for medicinal plants and surgery was to be conducted under the careful eye of a teacher, in other subjects the practical course was left to be completed by the students themselves after they had left Taxila. The duration of studentship at the Vedic schools at Taxila was seven years and students came from all classes except the Shudras from different parts of India, especially from Kashi, Rajagriha and Mithila of the Eastern India which was then fast coming under the spell of Buddhism and gradually losing its importance in the Vedic religious studies.

6

Result of the Investigation into the Mysteries of the Universe

We have said earlier that our religion has emerged out of the investigations started by our sages into the mysteries of the Universe or the Cosmos. Since the Sutrakaras directed that all further original works were to be within the framework of their Sutras , it is almost clear that there could not be any further discovery of original knowledge and learning into the mysteries of the Universe after the Age of the Sutrakaras.

Discovery of the Seven Planets

Yet by the time the Sutrakaras started their works, our sages had been able to unveil a number of mysteries about the Universe, which are still valid. Thus our sages had come to know about the existence of the seven planets through observation with the naked eye and later added two more to the list, Rahu and Ketu, the ascending and the descending nodes of the planet, Moon. The seven planets are Surya or Sun, Chandra or Moon, Budha or Mercury, Sukra or Venus, Mangala or Mars, Brihaspati or Jupiter, and Sani or Saturn. They also knew the existence of the twenty-seven nakshatras or stars which formed the constellations of these seven planets. They knew further through Greek influence that the zodiac was divided into twelve parts—Mesha or Aries, Vrishabha or Taurus, Mithuna or Gemini, Kataka or Cancer, Simha or Leo, Kanya or Virgo, Tula or Libra, Dhanus or Sagittarius, Mina or Pisces, Vrishchik or Scorpion, Makara or Capricorn, Kumbha or Aquarius. With their achievement in Mathematics, our sages, however, outdistanced the Greeks in their knowledge of astronomy which they considered sufficient by the time of the Sutra Age for the purpose of setting the dates and the times at which periodical sacrifices were to be performed. And they never used their knowledge of astronomy for prognosticating the future which they used to do by the Art of Divination, a course taught in the many of the Vedic schools, particularly in those at Taxila.

Discovery of the Tithi or Lunar Day, Month and Year

For purposes of calculating the date and time of a sacrifice, the Aryan priestly class relied mainly on the Moon. It was the tithi or lunar day which formed the basic unit of such calculations. Approximately thirty tithis formed a lunar month of 29 and a half days. A tithi or a lunar day might begin anytime of the solar day; the tithi current at sunrise was taken into consideration for the whole day which was given its number for the pakshas, Sukla and Krishna, which divided a lunar month into two halves of fifteen tithis each. A year consisted of 12 lunar months which was again divided into six seasons of two months each—Grishma or Summer, Varsha or Rains, Sarad or Autumn, Hemanta or Mild Winter, and Sitha or Extreme Winter.

Five Elements of the Universe: Pakudha Katyayana and Uluka Kanada's Theory of Atom

Secondly, the Aryan priestly classes by the time of the Sutra

Age realized that the Universe was classified by five elements—earth, air, fire, water, and akasha or ether. These five elements were thought of as medium of five sense impressions—earth of smell, air of feeling, fire of vision, water of taste, and ether of sound. The Brahmanical and the Buddhist schools of thought believed that all the elements other than ether were atomic and therefore eternal. Pakudha Katyayana, an older contemporary of the Buddha, used to teach on this subject long before the Greek philosopher, Democritus, who first thought of atom in Europe and the world came to know about it from him. Pakudha Katyayana's teachings on atom were further developed by theVaiseshika School of Uluka Kanada, who was more interested in physics than in theology as his Sutras indicate. According to this School, the atom or anu which was quite invisible to the naked human eye was a mere point in space, completely without any magnitude. A single atom had no qualities but only potentialities, which came into play when they combined with others. And before coming to form any material objects, atoms made primary combinations of diads and triads. Thus, the Vaiseshika School of Philosophy was the School of Atomism par excellence.

Ayurvedic Science: Rhinoplasty and Chaulmugra Oil

In many other similar areas related to the study of the Vedangas in the Vedic schools search for further knowledge had led to its substantial advancement as in the field of surgery where the art of rhinoplasty reached such an excellence in the hands of the Ayurvedic surgeons by the time of the Sutra Age that nearly two thousand years later the surgeons of the East India Company in the eighteenth century were not ashamed to learn it from their modern successors. The Ayurvedic Pharmacopoeia became quite large and comprised animal, vegetable and mineral products and by the end of the Sutra Age many Ayurvedic drugs such as the oil of the Chaulmugra tree traditionally used in curing leprosy in ancient India and which still serves as the basis of its modern treatment, were known to the outside world in Europe through Persian, Greek and Arabic contacts.

Aryan Minds of the Sages faltered in the Conception of the Shape and the Structure of the Universe

Yet in the conception of the shape and the structure of the Universe, the Aryan minds faltered. The Aryan sages believed that the Universe was shaped like an egg and called it Brahmanda and further thought that it was divided into 21 zones or regions, of which earth was seventh from top. Above the earth were six heavens of increasing beatitude and below it the seven stages of Patala or the nether world which was abode of the nagas or the serpents and other mythical beings. And below the Patala lay the Naraka which was again divided into seven zones of increasing misery and inhabited by the souls in torment. The Universe hung in empty space and was isolated from other Universes

Our Aryan sages postulated earth as a flat disc of enormous size with mount Meru in its centre round which the Sun, the Moon, and the Stars revolved. Around Meru were four dvipa or continents separated from it by oceans, and named according to the great trees which stood on their shores opposite Meru. The southern continent, on which human beings dwelt, had a Jambu as a distinctive tree and was therefore called Jambudvipa. The southern zone of this continent separated from the rest by the Himalayas was "the Land of the Sons of Bharata, " or the Bharatavarsha. Jambudvipa was separated from the next continent, Plakshadvipa, by an ocean of salt. Plakshadvipa in turn formed a concentric circle round Jambudvipa, forming seven circular continents, each divided from its neighbour by an ocean of different composition of treacle, wine, ghee, milk, curds and fresh water respectively.

This fantastic geographical scheme of the Universe and the earth held by the Aryan priestly classes in the Sutra Age aroused, much later in the nineteenth century, the scorn and the contempt of Macaulay for Oriental learning while advocating the case for the introduction of English education in the British India in his Minute of 2 February 1835. It was really amazing to believe how the Aryan sages could hold such a view of the Universe and the earth when many of the people over whom they held sway believed otherwise. Certainly the kings who led their armies thousands of miles on their campaigns, the merchants who carried their wares from one end of India to the other end and beyond it, the sailors who sailed the ocean from Socotra to Canton or from Sopara to Alexandria and the scholars who travelled from one place to another, say, from Kashi to Taxila in search of furher knowledge as well as the pilgrims who visited the Buddhist sacred places and stupas spread all over India, had a far greater and wider practical knowledge of geography than our Aryan theologians.

The Sutra Age is more of an Age of Retrogression rather than of an Age of Innovation

The reason why the Aryan priestly classes held such a

fantastic view of the Universe and of the earth is because of the fact that this was the view that had been handed down to the Sutrakaras by the past sages over the centuries. And the Sutrakaras who compiled and edited this past knowledge into simple and easily accessible Sutras for an enlarged audience declared it to be a final one and prohibited any further addition and alteration to it through any further search or quest for knowledge about any subject concerning any aspect of our religion. In other words, the Sutrakaras who collected their remarkable knowledge from the past religious scriptures and put it in the framework of their Sutras wanted to leave it as an ultimate authority to the posterity for any judgement in any sphere of life. While they thus did a great service to us by preserving knowledge and culture from oblivion, they equally did us great harm by discouraging any further search for knowledge in areas where doubts about the truth existed.

Thus, the astronomers who knew through Greek influence the conception of a flat earth to be an incorrect one, had nevertheless to accept it and adjust it to their correct knowledge of a spherical earth by making Meru the earth's axis and the continents zones on the earth's surface. Similarly, there was little development in the Sanskrit language later since any such development was to be within the framework of Panini's grammar, *Ashtadhayayi* which the latter composed at the beginning of the Age of the Sutrakaras around 400 BC. How strictly was forbidden any original thinking could be seen as late as the eighth century AD when the great religious reformer, Sankaracharya, had to spend a lot of time and energy, to prove that his Philosophy of Advaitaism or Monism was quite in conformity with the teachings of the Upanishads. This partly explains why in the succeeding centuries there have been little or no attempts at the composition of an original or a masterly work either in philosophy or in religion and almost all the existing religious and philosophical works that we have today are either commentaries, explanations and elaborations on the works of our past sages within the framework of the works of the Sutrakaras who completed their works around 200 BC.

The Sutras were put into Writing to preserve them from Oblivion in the face of the Persian Occupation

The Sutrakaras started their works almost a hundred years after the occupation by the Persians of the land called Bramhavarta or Aryavarta by the Aryan priestly classes and during this early period the transmission of our religious scriptures through guru-shisya-parampara must have been affected by the presence of the Yavanas in their midst. The majority of the Persian conquerors who merged with the local people through inter-marriage and change of religion and were accepted by the Aryan society as "degenerate Kshatriyas," to quote Manu. Yet the Aryan priestly classes must have been concerned about the smooth oral flow of the transmission of our religious scriptures in the land of their birth now occupied by rulers who did not originally belong to their society and had no knowledge of the creation of their Brahmanical religion. There was indeed a great urge to save our orally transmitted religion from oblivion particularly in the face of the use of the Kharoshthi script and language by the Persians, which posed a great challenge to the orally transmitted, Sanskrita and what easier way could have been available to them to do so, than by putting their compilation into writing which was then known to the Buddhists and was fast emerging as the medium of transaction with the rise of the monarchial kingdoms in the East. The Sutrakaras mainly put many of their edited and simplified Sutras that emerged out of the original orally transmitted knowledge of the past sages into writing. They left the original hymns intact and this way the Sutrakaras were also able to honour the wishes of our sages who forbade the posterity never to put their orally transmitted hymns into written words to preserve their original purity.

7

Buddhism and Jainism, vis-à-vis Brahmanism

Yet there was a further, and perhaps the most remote and important, factor other than the Persian and the Greek occupation of the heart-land of the Vedic religion, which made it almost imperative for the Sutrakaras to simplify our past religious scriptures into Sutras and made them easily accessible to all members of the Aryan society. The need was also badly felt to ward off the future challenges as visualized by our sages of the two heretic religions which had emerged as protests against the extravagant sacrificial ritualism of our Brahmanical religion. They remained mostly confined by the time of the Sutrakaras to the eastern part of India till the days of the great Maurya emperor, Asoka. These two religions were the Buddhism and the Jainism.

It was, however, Buddhism rather than Jainism that later threw a formidable challenge to the dominant Brahmanism. In Jainism the layman was a definite member of the Jaina Order, encouraged to undertake periodical retreats, and to live as far as possible the life of a monk for specified periods. The saints and the prophets of Jainism were not altogether different from those of Brahmanism and the Jainas did not altogether dispense with the worship of the old deities or the services of the Brahmanas at their homes on occasions like birth, death, and marriage.

As long as Buddhism was concerned with the settlement of mere theological and speculative issues, there was no confrontation with Brahmanism. However, a struggle for self-preservation and self-assertion for Brahmanism began when Buddhism addressed itself to the practical points of religion, worship and life and soon developed itself into an easily accessible system of religion among the Aryans. The doors of Buddhism were thrown open to all members of the Aryan society and anyone seeking relief from the sorrows and the sufferings of the world could join it by renouncing the world. On the other hand Brahmanism was the monopoly of the priestly class who mastered its very complex and difficult scriptures composed and transmitted orally. The extravagant and elaborate ritualism of Brahmanism had already angered and alienated many members of the Aryan society and many of them including some members of the priestly classes itself now turned to Buddhism as a shelter for succor and relief from the daily problems of survival. In this circumstance, Brahmanism was forced to forge a suitable weapon of defence to combat against the rising onslaught of Buddhism by making Brahmanism easily accessible to all members of the Aryan society through compilation, codification and simplification of the existing religious scriptures into a set of easily understandable Sutras under different heads and categories, which we have already referred to and discussed in the preceding chapter.

Asceticism

Both Buddhism and Jainism represent asceticism which

is an inherent aspect of our religion since the days of the Rigveda. The Upanishadic teachings prescribe asceticism as the last of the four stages of life leading to the liberation of the soul from the cycle of birth and death and it is in the days of the Upanishads when every body was talking about the Upanishadic doctrine of the Brahman as the Atman that asceticsm in the country rose to its climax in Buddhism and Jainism.

Krishna-Bhagavatas and Siva-Bhagavatas

However, these two ascetic movements which apparently ran counter to our Vedic religion were preceded by others such as Vasudevakas or Krishna-Bhagavatas and Siva-Bhagavatas which preached the attainment of the liberation of the soul through love, devotion and identification of the soul with the divinity. However, both the Siva and Krishna-Bhagavatas while preserving their distinct identity never made a complete break from Brahmanism and attempts at a synthesis were made in the epics and later literature whereby the gods of the Bhavagatas were recognized as emancipation of the supreme divinity of Brahmanism. This leads to enunciation of the doctrine of Trimurti which in its mature form belongs to a much later age.

The Genesis of Asceticism

The years which saw the occupation and the administration of the vast territory in the North-West by the Persians and the Greeks and the compilation of the Sutras by our sages were also the years which witnessed a large number of ascetic movements and most of them occurred in the Eastern part of the country. This resulted from the expansionist policy pursued by the kings of Kosala and Magadha at the expense of their neighbours. Chieftains were overthrown, their courts dispersed and their lands and tribesmen absorbed in their kingdoms. The break-up of the old tribal units led to the disappearance of the feeling of a group solidarity among the people who now stood face to face with the world, with no refuge in their kinsmen. They became alone, lonely and isolated and many of them now turned to asceticism as a means of their salvation from the worldly life as preached by the Upanishads. This goal of the ascetics substantially differed from that of their brethren in the Vedic years when the sole object of the ascetics in undergoing rigorous penance and hardships was the acquisition and possession of magical and mystical power, already possessed by the priestly classes or the Brahmanas by virtue of their birth and training as sacrificial priests.

Spiritual Leadership in Eastern India passed from the Hands of the Priestly Theologians to the Ascetics

In the Eastern part of the country, with the growth of free speculation as presaged in the Upanishads, humanitarian and theistic movements began to gather momentum and the spiritual leadership passed from the hands of the priestly theologians and sacrificiers to ascetics and wanderers called Sramanas or Parivrajakas. They believed in the doctrine of transmigration and the law of the deeds but rejected the authority of the Vedas and the Vedic priests. They denounced the blood sacrifices that constituted so large a part of the Brahmanic ritual and even the existence of god and consequently the efficacy of divine grace. They laid the utmost stress on non-injury to living beings and the cessation of craving for the material things of the world and declared that the only way of getting out of the meshes of Samsara and Karma was through detachment and renunciation of the world.

Mahavira and the Buddha

Among the wandering ascetics were Vardhamana Mahavira and Gautama Buddha, the scions of Kshatriya clans, like the lord of the Bhagavatas, who created history as founders of new religions, Jainism and Buddhism. Mahavira came from the Jnatrika clan of Kundapura or Kundagrama near Vaishali in North Bihar and Gautama Buddha from the Sakya clan of Kapilavastu near Rummindei in the Nepal Tarai.

Buddhism

As we have said before, it was Buddhism rather than Jainism that provided a formidable challenge to the Vedic religion dominated by the Brahmanical ritualism. The doors of the religion founded by the Buddha were open to all castes and creeds and it offered no struggle for survival and existence to a person who chose to follow the paths of the Buddha as the Buddhist monks lived on the charity of the laity or the Upasakas and the Upasikas who supported them as a religious duty. However in the beginning of the Age of the Sutrakaras who started the process of simplifying the Vedic religion by converting the orally transmitted religious scriptures into a number of Sutras under different categories, this challenge was not so formidable as it later turned out to be nearly more than two hundred years after the Nirvana of the Sakyamuni when Asoka succeeded his father Bindusara as the Magadhan emperor in 269 BC.

Heydays of the Buddhism

Asoka began as a traditional inheritor of a king's devotion to devas or gods and the Brahmanas but the sight of misery and bloodshed following his conquest of Kalinga smote his conscience and awakened in his breast sincere feelings of repentance and sorrow. He became a lay-worshipper or Upasaka of the Buddha, went out to Bodh-Gaya and established intimate relations with the Buddhist Samgha or Order. Asoka imbibed the true spirit of Buddhism and by precepts and deeds he made Buddhism a living force regulating the lives of his subjects in his empire. As a matter of fact, he spent 24 years of his 36 years' reign in providing active support to the spread of Buddhism in and outside India, particularly to his Tamil, Ceylonese and Hellenestic neighbours though it was only in Ceylon that his mission which converted the Ceylonese ruler and his subjects into Buddhism was fully successful. When the emperor, his family members and his officials were firm believers in Buddhism, the people at large could not but choose otherwise–and the Buddhist viharas now came to dot the different parts of the Magadhan empire stretching from Afghanistan to Andhra and Karnataka and from Gujarat to Bengal. One such vihara which came into existence in the days of Asoka was at the village of Nalanda near Rajagriha, the old Magadhan capital, where Sariputta, a favourite disciple of the Buddha was born. Thus, whatever may be the position of Buddhism immediately after the Nirvana of the Buddha, it became a distinct religion centuries later; strong and prominent enough to attract Nagasena, a Brahmin scholar well-versed in the four Vedas to profess Buddhism.

However, the religious scriptures of Buddhism which were based on the teachings of the Buddha and classified as Vinaya or Conduct, Sutta or Sermon and Abhidhamma or Metaphysics grew by a long process of development of accreditation spreading over several centuries. And the process started with the meeting of the followers of the Buddha who were asked by the latter to diligently work out their salvation, shortly after his Nirvana, at Rajagriha, the capital of Magadha, where Upali recited the Vinaya rules as he recalled having heard them from the lips of the Buddha and another disciple, Ananda, recited the Sutta or the Buddha's sermons on matters of doctrine and ethics. A century later, the second council which met at Vaishali, condemned disputes on Vinaya and revised the scriptures. The third council met at Pataliputra, 236 years after the Nirvana of the Buddha, under the patronage of Asoka and made a final compilation of the scriptures and the fourth was held under Kanishka at Purushapura or Peshawar and prepared elaborate commentaries, Upadeshashatras and Vibhasashastras, on the sacred texts, in the first century AD.

Buddhism and Brahmanism in the Post-Asokan Years

Despite the break-up of the Mauryan empire following the death of Asoka, Buddhisim continued to flourish side by side with the Vedic religion and even attracted the attention of a host of foreign invaders and conquerors of the North-West India beginning with the Bactrian Greeks who poured in once more in the second century BC into the Kabul Valley, the Punjab and even the Gangetic region and threw all these provinces into confusion.

The Sakas

However, the Greeks in Bactria were soon replaced by the Scythians and they moved on from Bactria to attack first the Parthian rulers of Iran and then the Greeks in India and as a result by the middle of the first century BC only a few petty Greek chiefs still ruled in the North-West while the power of the Scythians, known as the Sakas in India and who spoke an Iranian language, reached as far as Mathura, though for a brief period, a line of kings with Iranian names, usually known as Pahlavas which included such important name as Gondophernes to whose kingdom St. Thomas first brought the knowledge of Christanity in the country, gained suzerainty of the North-West India.

The Kushanas

The Pahlavas werc, in turn, conquered by the Yue-chis of Turkish origin, who spoke an Iranian language like the Sakas and the various autonomous tribes of the Yue-chis were consolidated by Kujula Kadphises of the tribe of Kushanas and at sometime in the first century AD, Kujula and his son Vima Kadphises between them gained control of the North-West India.

Kanishka

Vima Kadphises was succeeded after a short interregnum by Kanishka who controlled all the western half of Northern India at least as far as Benares and whose dominions in Central Asia were very extensive. Numerous remains testify to the importance and popularity of Buddhism during the reign of Kanishka and it was at this time that Buddhism spread not only to the Central Asia but also to the Far East as both the Kushana and the Chinese empires were then in close contact with each other. His reign saw not only the flourishing of the Gandhara School of Art but also of the Vedic schools at Taxila which attracted students from places as far as Benares. A patron of Asvaghosa, author of the Buddhacharita at his court at Peshawar, and founder of an era, known as the Saka era (AD 78) though Kanishka was not, strictly speaking a Saka, he was next only to Asoka in popularising Buddhism in and outside India.

Kanishka's Successors

Kanishka's successors continued to rule in the North-West India but their empire was soon reduced by the middle of the third century AD when Shapur 1 of the new Sassanian dynasty of Persia defeated one of Kanishka's successors, Vasudeva and from now on the North-West came much under the Iranian influence.

Patronisers of the Aryan Religion

In the North-West Deccan the Satavahanas who were driven by the Sakas of the clan of Ksaharata returned to their seat of power under Gautamiputra Satakarnin around AD 130 but another Saka dynasty known as Western Satraps remained in control of Kathiawar and Malwa till about AD 388 when they were defeated by Chandragupta ll (*c.* AD 376-415) and by the third century AD all India east of the Punjab and Malwa was in the hands of small Indian kings and tribal chiefs, many of whom were originally Persian and Greek invaders and now had become thoroughly Indianized patronising either Buddhism or Saivism, Vaishnavism or Jainism. Many of the Greeks supported the orthodox creeds of Brahmanism as the Besnagar column which was erected by the Greek ambassador Heliodorus in honour of the early Vaishnavite deity Vasudeva shows. The Sutrakara Manu described in the Age of the Sutras such earlier Greek rulers as the "degenerate Kshatriyas" and thus gives them a place in the contemporary Indian society. Still many more became the followers of Buddhism and one of them Milinda or Meander, the king of Sialkot in the Punjab is still remembered for his long discussions with Nagasena as recorded in a Pali text Milindapanha or the Questions of Milinda.

The Imperial Guptas

The successors of Kanishka continued to rule in the North-West India but their jurisdiction was soon much reduced about the middle of the third century AD and in AD 320, a new Chandragupta arose, whose successors in great measure restored the splendour of the Mauryas. The Guptas–Chandragupta 11, his father Samudragupta and his grandfather as well as his successors—were followers of the Brahmanical faith and revived some of the Vedic rites that had been in abeyance for a long period. However, Brahmanism in the days of the Guptas became more gentle and more humane than 700 years ago in the days of the Mauryas. In place of the old sacrificial Brahmanism, the religion that had appeared now, did not seem to be greatly different in form from that of recent centuries. Bhakti, that is intense devotion to god conceived of as personal, a saviour worthy of trust and ready to be gracious, is an important element of Vaishnavism and Saivasim as expounded in the Gita and the Svetasvatara Upanishad: "He who with unwavering practice of devotion does god service has crossed beyond the strands" and is fit for salvation. The growing importance of Bhakti or loving faith and devotion in god and the love of fellow-beings found expression in benevolent activities and toleration of the opinion of others. The wide prevalence of a feeling of toleration is well illustrated by epigraphic and literary references to the employment by the Vaishnava kings of the Saivite and the Buddhist officials as well as by the affection felt by the Jainas for the Brahmanas and by the latter for the Tirthankaras and the Buddha.

Fa-hien

As a matter of fact, the existence of a mutual toleration and a reciprocal affection, between the two major religions, the Vedic and the Buddhist, reached its peak under the reign of Chandragupta II which saw a perfection of Indian civilisation and culture never to be seen again in the history of India. And this was attested by none other than a Buddhist scholar from China, Fa-hien whose travels through the different parts of India in search of the Vinaya texts for the Buddhist viharas in China roughly coincided with the last fifteen years of the reign of Chandragupta II or the first decade and a half of the fifth century AD. En route from Udyana or modern Swat on the North- West to Tamralipti on the East, Fa-hien saw an abundance of the Buddhist viharas or monasteries, inhabited by monks who were either followers of Hinayana or Mahayana form of Buddhism and was pleased to find that "the Law of the Buddha was very flourishing" in the doab between the Ganges and the Yamuna as well as in the Buddhist heart-land of Magadha. In these monasteries, he found some eighteen schools of Buddhist thought, each following the views and decisions of its own master. This multiplicity of thought in the Buddhism which continued to grow with each subsequent century may well be compared with the multiciplity of thoughts and ideas leading to the liberation of souls set up by varied sects under their respective gurus over the past centuries within the Vedic religion itself.

Religious Harmony between the Followers of the Buddhism and the Brahmanism

Thus, for years since the appearance of the Buddhism on the Indian scene, it peacefully co-existed and prospered along with the Vedic religion even when the contemporary monarchs were not its partrons as we have seen in the days of the Guptas. The same care and affection was also shown by the successors of the Guptas, the Maukharis claiming descent from Asvapati of epic fame, when the dynasty rose to prominence, north of the river Ganges and its capital, the city of Kanyakubja or Kanauj, became the cultural center of the North India until the coming of the Muslim invaders and conquerors. In AD 606 the greatest among this dynasty, Harsha-vardhana or Harsha ascended the throne and was destined to revive the imperial memories of the Gupta epoch and obtain recognition as the lord paramount of the Northern India from Kathiawar to Bengal, even from his bitterest enemies. Only in the Deccan , Harsha could make no progress and was checked by the Chalukya king, Pulakeshin II. Harsha was a follower of Saivism, but in his last days he fell increasingly under the influence of the Buddhism and invariably included the Buddhist monks among those consisting of courtiers, officials and the Brahmin priests who accompanied him on his journeys while ceaselessly travelling from one province to another, both in his own domains—and in those of his feudatories.

Nalanda

It was towards the end of his reign between AD 629 and 645 that the Buddhist vihara at the village of Nalanda which had now grown into a huge complex of learning from a very humble beginning in the days of Asoka through a continuous series of endowments in the form of lands and buildings from a succession of sovereigns over the centuries was visited by the Chinese Buddhist scholar, Hiuen Tsang.

Hiuen Tsang

Hiuen Tsang enjoyed the patronage of Harsha and despite his chief interest in the Buddhist life and thought left a very valuable account of India which, unlike the account of Megasthenes, has survived intact. Hiuen Tsang enrolled himself as a student at the Nalanda for five years to study Yogashastra followed by a study of Naya, Hetu-vidya and Sabdavidya under its head, Silabhadra, a Brahman prince, unique in learning and character, who had renounced the world and become a Bhikkhu.

Unlike Fa-hien, Hiuen Tsang traversed widely from Kashmir to Kanchipuram and Negapatam, and from Surat to Tampralipti and found both the Brahmanism or the Vedic religion and the Buddhism were prospering under Harsha. He described India as the "the country of the Brahmanas" and observed that Sanskrit, the language of the Vedas and spoken by the Brahmanas had now become the language of all the cultured classes including the famous Buddhist teachers. He also described the growth of numerous ascetic orders or sects, each distinguished by its own special garb within the fold of the Brahmanical cult. And as far as the Buddhism was concerned, he found that it was represented by a good number of schools, each of which claimed and counted many monasteries, specializing in the study of its doctrines and practices. He estimated the number of active monasteries at 5000 and the number of the monkish population at 2, 12, 130.

I-Tsing

Another Chinese Buddhist scholar, I-Tsing who came to Nalanda nearly forty years after the departure of Hiuen-Tsang also spoke about the flourishing state of the Brahmanism and the Buddhism. By that time Nalanda had grown further and had been visited in the interval by nearly fifty-six scholars from China, Japan and Korea, some of whom came by sea via Tampralipti and others by land via Khotan, Tibet and Nepal. I-Tsing studied at Nalanda for a long period of ten years from AD 675 to 685 and collected some 400 Sanskrit texts of 500, 000 slokas from the library situated at Dharmaganga or the mart of religion. The library comprised three huge buildings Ratnasagara, Ratnadadhi and Ratnaranjaka—of which the first one was a nine storeyed one, specializing in the collection of rare sacred works like Prajnaparamitasutra and Tantric works like Samajaguha.

8

Decline of the Buddhism and the Brahmanism

It would seem from the accounts of Hiuen Tsang and I-Tsing that all was well with the two major religions in the other parts of the contemporary India. As a matter of fact, both the Buddhism and the Brahmanism had began to suffer a setback since the beginning of the Huna invasions of India in the middle of the fifth century AD. The repeated incursions of the Hunas and their temporary rule for nearly thirty years in the Western India did create havoc with the Buddhist monasteries there as the Hunas were known persecutors of the Buddhism. They adopted Saivism as their faith but this did not deter them from ravaging the excellent centres of the Vedic learning in Taxila in Peshawar which they retained along with Kashmir and other parts of the North-West India after they had been driven out from the plains of the Ganges.

And when Hiuen Tsang came to India towards the end of Harsha's reign, he did not speak much about Taxila where the Buddhist influences had firmly established themselves since the days of the Kushana king Kanishka and spoke about many Buddhist monasteries in the North India which were either in ruins, dilapidated or destroyed.

Hiuen Tsang's estimate of the total number of the monkish population of India including Ceylon at 2, 12, 130 was not certainly an indicator of the flourishing state of the Buddhism and pales into insignificance before the number of the militia men maintained by Dhana Nanda of Magadha nearly seven hundred years ago which stood at 2, 20, 000. Unlike Fa-hien who came in the early fifth century AD before the invasions of the Hunas, Hiuen Tsang faced enormous dangers and difficulties while travelling down the river Ganges–he was twice robbed by the bandits in Harsha's domains and on one occasion he was nearly sacrificed to the Goddess Durga by the river pirates in the very heart of Harsha's empire!

The deterioration in law and order in Harsha's time was an index to the degeneration that had set in, following the break-up of the empire of the Guptas, in the Aryan society. The stability of the Aryan society in the Ganges valley deteriorated further when a severe struggle for supremacy ensued after Harsha's death in 647 AD. The bone of contention was the possession of Kanyakubja or Kanauj and the city became, to the upspringing dynasties of the Northern India in the seventh, eighth and ninth centuries AD, "what Babylon was to the martial races of Western Asia, what Rome was to the Teutonic barbarians and Byzantium to the medieval world of Eastern and Southern Europe."

In such a situation no religion could either flourish or prosper and it badly affected the people who now became more defensive than before and the relationship among the various groups of the society began to be governed more strictly by the rules of endogamy, commensality and craft-exclusiveness. In such a society creative thinking, and original ideas were likely to be buried under an obstinate desire to preserve, expound and comment on the outstanding works of the past since canonized by the Sutrakaras. And reason and logic, truth and knowledge were likely to be sacrificed at the altar of popular beliefs and myths as endorsed by theologians of the day.

Thus, in the seventh century AD, Brahmagupta who attempted to measure the circumference of the earth as 5, 000 yojanas and knew well the reason behind eclipses of the Sun and the Moon, endorsed the popular belief in his *Brahmasiddhanta* that they were caused by the Rahu and the Ketu attacking and swallowing the luminaries! He even went further in denouncing both Aryabhatta and Varahamihira for their beliefs that eclipses were caused by the shadow of the earth. However, in mathematics which was not as canonized as astronomy, the same Brahmagupta, followed by Mahavira in the ninth century AD, was able to make several discoveries which in Europe were not known until the advent of the Renaissance. Both understood the import of the positive and the negative quantities, evolved sound systems of extracting square and cube roots, and could solve quadratic and certain types of indeterminate equations. In the fourth century AD, long before Brahmagupta and Mahavira, the anonymous author of a surviving mathematical text, "Bakshali Manuscript, " first devised the simplified system of writing numerals and in AD 499, Aryabhatta in his terse treatise, "Aryabhattiya, " suggested the existence of zero which Europe came to know through the Arabs who had settled down in the Western India in the beginning of the eight century AD. Aryabhatta's discovery has since revolutionsed the world of mathematics and is the basis of our own modern digital technology which now governs our lives on the planet.

The Vedic religion provided the necessary strength for the smooth continuance in many of the activities of the people in the society. When the religion began to decline following a decline in the peace and stability of the country, the performance of the people in other areas were also affected. The age saw an abandonment of the commercial activities of the Aryans, which in turn affected trade and commerce and agriculture which was earlier highly held by the upper castes now came to be the sole occupations of the Vaisyas and the Sudras. And Ayurveda also saw little progress in surgery since the prohibition of the dissection of the corpses by the Sutrakara Manu.The worst affected were, however, the arts and crafts which now failed to attract the best brains of the Aryan society partly because of the rigidity of the caste system and partly because of the low esteem in which these professions began to be held now. Consequently, there were not many flashes of genius as in the past age except occasionally at places where they were held in high esteem as shown by the construction of the Kailasanatha Temple at Ellora (AD 756-773)and that of the Trimurti at Elephanta a century or two later.

The Vedic Religion in the South

Indeed, the only silver lining in an age of decline is the South India which not only saw the revival of the Vedic religion under Sankara but also in the setting up of the new centres of learning in Sanskrit and Astronomy at Dhara and Devagiri respectively while in the far south the Pallava kings extended their traditional patronage to educational institutions at Kanchi and Bahur. In the ninth century AD, Bahur which was situated near modern Pondicherry was famous for the study of the Vedas,

Vedangas, Mimansa, Naya, Puranas and Dharmashastras. From the ninth century onwards the development of such centres which combined both religion and learning had been a novel phenomenon in our religion and these first developed mostly and primarily in the South. The reason why this did not develop earlier because ancient India did not believe in the external and mechanical methods of organization and therefore did not develop any religious or ecclesiastical institutions like the Buddhist viharas or the Christian churches to serve the purposes of the religion. In our religion the interests of our religious life and spiritual growth were not handed over to any institutions and their regimented life of routine, but were left to be dealt with between the guru and his disciple in their personal relationships from which the whole world was excluded. This explains why most of our temples that survived the wrath of the foreign invaders could hardly be dated before the ninth century. Nevertheless in the wake of the emphasis laid by Jainism and Buddhism upon organized brotherhoods in rockcut caves and halls, viharas and monasteries, the Brahmanical religion followed suit with similar institutions like the mathas and the regular learning institutions as the religio-Ieaming centres from the tenth century onwards following the revival of the Vedic religion by Sankaracharya who himself set up organized monasteries at Shringeri in Mysore, Dwaraka in Kathiawar, Puri in Orissa and Badrinath on the snowy heights of the Himalayas.

The extent of such religio-learning centres concentrating on mathas or temple-colleges was widespread as could be gathered from the various inscriptions describing the deeds of endowments in the southern kingdoms of the Rashtrakutas, Pallavas, Cholas, Hoysalas and Pandyas. Such religio-learning centres not merely looked after the religious and the spiritual needs but also the physical requirements of the community as could be seen from the different categories of the staff maintained by them. The staff of all these institutions usually included (a) three teachers for teaching the three Vedas, (b) five for teaching Logic, literature and the Angas, (c) one accountant who could be a Kayastha, (d) one physician, (e) six Brahmana servants for the mathas and the feeding houses, (f) village guards called Vira-Bhadras, (g) village craftsmen called Vira-Mushtis to work as goldsmith, coppersmith, mason, bamboo-worker, blacksmith, potter, architect, carpenter, barber and artisan. In the feeding houses, were fed at all hours men of all castes from Brahmana to Chandala—a remarkable instance of Saiva catholicity. Besides, the establishment of temple-colleges and colleges with hospitals and practical arts, arrangement was often made by some specific endowment to take care of the food and the clothing of the Vedic students, teachers and ascetics.

The study of the religion which went together with the study of other allied subjects was not, however, solely confined to these religio-learning centres but often spread outside in select areas to the settlements of pious and scholarly Brahmanas invited from the North who devoted themselves fully to an advanced study of religious scriptures and allied subjects. These learned settlements created through royal and public benefactions were centres of light and life, showing how theory and practice should go together, how precept should be supported by example, ethics by conduct, how learning was to be lived, and how truth of religion was to be realized in daily activities.

And thus, the South India kept the lamp of the Vedic religion and of learning burning while it was almost flickering in the North India suffering under great stress created by the frequent internecine warfares among the ruling potentates for the possession of Kanauj.

Buddhism in the Post-Harsha Years

However, in the post-Harsha years, it was Buddhism rather than Vedic religion which suffered most despite the creation of two new Buddhist viharas by the Pala kings of Bengal at Uddandapura and at Vikramshila in Bihar.

In the first place, the Buddhist viharas which were open to all classes, castes and creeds had become, over the centuries, a haven for all kinds of people of the Aryan society who found in them an escape from the various problems of life. The Buddhist brotherhood lived on the charity of the sympathetic laity or the Upasakas and the Upasikas who supported the brotherhood as a religious duty. And so there was no struggle for existence within the Order and in many places, the Buddhist viharas failed to live upto the expectations which had brought them into existence.

Secondly, the Buddhist viharas, composed as they were of a heterogeneous mixture of residents coming from different classes of the Aryan society with their own ideas and beliefs, and also exposed as they were particularly in the North-West to the ideas of Zoroastrianism, and the multifarious influences of the Greeks, the Sakas and the Kushanas, gradually began to make room for the development of theism with its division into two distinct sects, the Mahayana or the Great Vehicle and the Hinayana or the Lesser Vechicle. The Bodhisattva doctrine which formed the hallmark of the Mahayana form of the Buddhism peopled the heavens with mighty forces of goodness, and presented Buddhism with a new mythology and brought Buddhism near to the Vedic religion. The Buddha came to be worshipped as a Vedic god with flowers, incense, waving lamps and with deep devotion from the first century onwards as the carvings on the stupas of Bharhut and Sanchi indicate. With the deification of the Buddha and his gradual admission into the Vishnuite pantheon as an incarnation of the Narayana-Vishnu, there was little to distinguish the Buddhist laity from their Brahmanical neighbours. The Great Vehicle which promised to carry many souls to salvation became rapidly popular in many parts of India as it fitted the moods of the time and the needs of many simple people better than the Lesser Vehicle which, however, held its ground firmly in Ceylon from where it was taken to Burma, Siam and other parts of the South-East Asia where it became the national religion.

Thirdly, there was a further development in the Great Vehicle which brought Buddhism much nearer to the religious practices of the people of the Eastern India. From the end of the Gupta period onwards religion in ancient India became more and more permeated with primitive ideas of sympathetic magic and sexual mysticism. With the coming of the feminine divinities in the pantheon of the Great Vehicle, the Buddhas and the Bodhisattvas who were earlier thought of as males, now became like the gods of the Vedic religion, endowed with wives, who were the active aspect, called "Sakti", the "force" or the "potency" of their husbands. The productive activity of the divine was thought of in terms of sexual union, an idea as old as the Rigveda, and led to the development of a third vehicle, the Vehicle of the

Thunderbolt or Vajrayana in the eight century in the Eastern India where the Mahayana form of Buddhism was very strong and popular and it grew very rapidly in Bengal and Bihar. It was this form of Buddhism, modified by primitive local cults and practices, which was finally established in Tibet, in the eleventh century , as a result of the missions sent out from the Vajrayana monastery of Vikramsila, in Bihar, when the Palas were ruling the Eastern India. This development in Buddhism almost wiped away any substantial differences that till now existed between it and the Vedic religion in the Eastern India, the heart-land of the Buddhism in the sub-continent.

Finally, in the ninth century when the growth of Tantrism had made the Vajrayana Buddhism and certain forms of Saivism and Saktism purely nominal, a revived and reformed Brahmanism or the Vedic religion began to travel northwards from Kerala when the great theologian Sankara (AD 788-820) travelled the length and breadth of India disputing with the Buddhists. An ardent Vedantist and the most powerful exponent of the doctrine of Advaita or pure monism which he elucidated in his commentaries on the Upanishads, the Bhagavad-gita and the Brahmasutras of Badarayana, he died at a comparatively very early age at Kedarnath but left behind him an organized body of Vedic monks to carry on his work of spreading the message of our devotional religion which now made a vigorous appeal to the ordinary men and women who would have otherwise preferred Buddhism as the later not only made no distinctions among the four castes for admission into the Buddhist Order but also solved the problems of daily survival with the existence of a sympathetic neighbourhood. As no new messiah now turned up to revitalize Buddhism and to prevent it from being swallowed up by a revived Vedic religion from the South, Buddhism remained in the post-Harsha centuries in a degenerate condition removed far away from the form in which the Buddha wanted to see it flourish in the sub-continent.

For example, Buddha did not believe in the authority of the Vedas but now the Vedas came to be studied along with his teachings in almost all the important Buddhist viharas in the country. Secondly, the Buddha advocated regional dialects as the preferred medium of his teachings but now the preferred medium was not the regional dialect but Sanskrit, the language of the Vedas, as mentioned by Hiuen Tsang and I-Tsing who visited the Buddhist viharas in the Harsha and the post-Harsha years. Thirdly, the Buddha did not believe in the existence of a Supreme Soul or god but now the Buddha himself came to be worshipped as a Vedic deity. This happened because over the past centuries those who joined the Buddhist monastries came from the followers of the Vedic religion. The Buddha himself was born in a Kshatriya family which followed the Vedic religion, was a disciple of the two Brahmana ascetics, Alara Kalama and Uddaka, who could not quench his thirst for the knowledge about the human suffering. If the Buddha had got the sage Yajnavalkya or the king Janaka as his Guru, the history of the religion of the world would have been perhaps different. The Buddha's Nirvana which basically means extinction of all desires or attachment leading to the freedom of the human souls from the sorrows and the sufferings of the world could very well be compared with the last two asramas or stages of our religion, that is, the Vanaprastha and the Sannyasa as prescribed in the Upanishads and practiced by those who renounced the world after going through the first two asramas or stages of life as Brahmacharis and Grihasthas. Thus, after traversing more than a dozen centuries and experiencing many ups and downs in its career, the Buddha's religion which emerged as a revolt against the Vedic ritualism was now rife in the post -Harsha years to take an about turn and return to its mother religion which is the religion of the Vedas and the Upanishads created by our sages centuries before the Buddha was born in a Kshatriya family in 566 BC.

9

A Retrospection on Our Religion in Ancient India

We are now in a position to have a critical look at the developments in our religion, since the days of the Rigveda till the coming of the Muslims, which had changed in intensity and degree in response to the changing conditions in the society and the polity and adjusted itself with the needs and the requirements of the time.

We are known as "Hindus" in our own country and abroad as worshippers of mythological gods and goddesses at homes and outside at the temples and the mathas. We may begin our analysis with the question how far this description of ourselves as "Hindus" is justified with reference to the religious developments in ancient India briefly discussed in the preceding chapters.

It will be an act of sheer folly if we start looking for the use of the term "Hindu" in the religious scriptures orally composed and transmitted by our sages nearly one thousand years before the coming of the Persians who occupied and ruled the North-West for more than two centuries from 519 BC onwards. As we have already said before, the Persians described their conquered subjects living on the both sides of the river Sindu in the North-

West as "Hindu" as they could not pronounce the initial "S" of Sindu and pronounced it as "H". And it is obvious that initially the term had nothing to do with the religion followed by the latter. However, as religion was a part and parcel of the life of these people it came to be used as a mark of their identity which the Persian rulers used to distinguish themselves from their conquered subjects.

We have alredy seen that in the pre-Persian days when the members of the priestly classes of the Bharata tribes who created our religion, by orally composing and transmitting through guru-shisya-parampara, the four Vedas, Brahmanas, Aranyakas and the Upanishads, none of them could have the slightest chance either to use the term "Hindu" in their orally composed scriptures or describe themselves to each other as a "Hindu." Indeed it would not only be ludicrous to think that they did so but also historically a travesty of truth by putting the cart before the horse.

However, the Sutrakaras who started their works mostly as a reaction to the Persian occupation of the North-West did have a chance to use this term in their compositions and to say that they were known as "Hindus" by the Mleccha rulers. But this never happened. There has never been an occasion at any place of their compilations to make a reference to the term, "Hindu". And as far as they were personally concemed, they used the societal norms of castes and professions, supported later by the hymns of the Gita, in describing themselves to each other. Thus, the priestly classes or the composers of the hymns were known as the Brahmanas or the possessors of the supreme knowledge of the Brahman or the Cosmos or the Universe, which in the pre-Upanishadic days used to mean possessors of the mystical or supernatural powers through Tapas or meditation. And the other three classes of the Aryan society who were the followers of this religion were not also known as "Hindu". They were known like the priestly classes either by the castes they belonged to or by the professions they followed such as the Kshatriyas or the rulers and the warriors, the Vaishyas or the traders and the merchants and the Shudras or the servers of the upper three castes as the carpenters, artisans and craftsmen and doers of various other odd manual jobs. And in all cases the people at large were known generally by the kingdoms they belonged to.

Similarly, a follower of the Buddha or of the Mahavira was never known as a "Hindu" though the former were almost contemporary to the invasion and occupation of the North-West India by the hordes of Cyrus(*c.* 519-326 BC), who bestowed this term on us. We have already seen that a Buddhist monk was known as a Sramana or a very senior Sramana as a Bhikkhu. And it will not be illogical to argue that most probably the Buddha and his followers were not aware of this term as they lived far away from the scene of the Persian occupation of the North-West which lay thousands of kilometers away from the capital of the Mauryan empire of Chandragupta and could not be easily accessed in view of a very difficult communication in those days either by roads or by rivers. In none of the Buddhist scriptures based on the Buddha's teachings or in those of the Mahavira one could ever come across the term "Hindu" and its use was mostly confined to the Persian occupiers of the North-West India.

The Persian occupation of the North-West saw not only the birth of two major rebels in our religion, Buddhism and Jainism in the Eastern part of the country far away from the scene of the Persian occupation of the North-West but also the composition of some of the most important Upanishads which govern our lives even today through the enunciation of the doctrine of transmigration or the cycle of birth and death. The compositions of the Upanishads began much earlier, and immediately before the coming of the Persians, these were rivalling the dominance of the Vedic ritualism with a host of believers gathering round the ascetics as gurus for deliverance from the cycle of birth and death. These Upanishads were first supposed to be the treasured knowledge of the Kshatriya kings only like Janaka, Ajatashatru and the Sanat kumar, the Guru of Krishna, who taught Narada the knowledge of the Atman. It was from them that the sage Yajnavalkya who adorned the court of the king Janaka learnt the knowledge of the Brahman and the Atman. In none of the 108 Upanishads that we have been able to recover till date is there any reference to the term, "Hindu".

Again almost contemporary with the birth of the Upanishads was the birth of the two great epics, Ramayana and the Mahabharata which were taught at the Vedic schools before the Sutrakaras started their work around 400 BC. The Bhagavad Gita which forms a part of the Mahabharata represents the essence of these Upanishads and is now the bed-rock of our religion. Both the two great epics continued to be interpolated by a succession of sages through the Mauryan years down to those of the Guptas when such interpolations came to an end and their compositions were said to have been formally completed. It will be a miracle for one to find the term "Hindu" in any pages of these two great epics either to describe us ethnically or ecclesiastically.

So, the question that we may ask now is what does the term "Hindu" signify in our religion if the sages who have composed our religious scriptures orally centuries before Jesus was born and, in written words from fifth century onwards, have never used it in their compositions and have never described themselves as "Hindu" and their religion also as "Hindu Dharma"? This question, however, does not imply that the Aryans living in the North-West under Persian occupation as well as later under their successors, the Sakas and the Kushanas who spoke an Iranian language, as late as AD 388 were not acquainted with the term "Hindu". Indeed they were, as many of the conquered Aryan subjects had direct interaction with their rulers and participated in the latter's civil and military administration in and outside India; and they knew very well that they were known as "Hindus" to the Persian conquerors and later their successors, the Sakas and the Kushanas as people who not only worshipped Agni or fire liked them but also worshipped an innumerable number of other gods and goddesses as the manifestations of the Brahman or the Cosmos first suggested by the Brihadaranyaka Upanishad. It could be said that the "Hindu" term was very much in circulation, merely as a geographical identity, among the Persian occupiers and the settlers in the Northern and the Western India till AD 388 and perhaps beyond that date among those with Persian connexions who remained in control of the North-West India.

The South of the Vindhyas

We have already seen how the rule of the foreign invaders who gradually became Indianised and how the internecine warfares among the Aryan rulers in the post-Harsha years shifted the interests of our religion mainly to the regions beyond the Vindhyas. In the south of the Vindhyas the term "Hindu" was comparatively little known and it mostly remained confined to the Aryan people in the Northern and the Western India as a geographical identity having contact and dealings with the Persian occupiers and their successors like the Sakas and the Kushanas who spoke an Iranian language.

Our Religious Identity as the Followers of the Vedas and the Upanishads remained Intact

It is now obvious that the term "Hindu" coined by the Persian occupiers of the North-West towards the end of the sixth century BC has nothing to do with our religion based on religious scriptures such as the Vedas, the Brahmanas, Aranyakas, Upanishads as well as the two great epics orally composed and transmited by our sages centuries before the Persian invasion and occupation took place in the North-West. Again, the term "Hindu" was also conspicuous by its absence in those religious scriptures known as the Sutras composed, between 400 and 200 BC, by the Sutrakaras like Manu and Yajnavalkya as a reaction partly to the Persian intrusion into our Aryan society and partly to the challenge of Buddhism to the Vedic religion, which emerged in the Eastern India. And also the various elaborations and the commentaries on our Vedas and Upanishads by noted religious scholars and philosophers that adorn the pages of our religious history in the post-Sutras years till the dawn of the middle ages carry nowhere a single reference to the term "Hindu".

In ancient India the term "Hindu" was never used by our ancestors to describe their religious identity. They were known to each other, as we have already said before, not only by their castes but also by the religion and profession they followed as well as by the kingdoms and the tribal groups they belonged to. They were not certainly known as the Bharatiyas though united by the religion created by the priestly classes of the Bharata tribes. The concept of nationality was not there though the name Bharatvarsha or Aryavarta was given to the land of their settlement by the priestly classes of the Bharata tribes of the Aryans. As a matter of fact, the name Bharatvarsha or for that matter, the name Aryavarta remained a mere geographical expression of the areas and the lands snatched away from the original inhabitants who later merged with the Aryan society either as Dasas or Dasyus and fled to the East by the river Ganges and the Yamuna.

Yet, the identity of the people lay in the pursuit of the religion which may be called the Bharatiya Dharma or the Arya Dharma and it was never impaired or lost. As a matter of fact, in ancient India in the pre-Muslim days our religious identity lay in our religious scriptures, that is, the Vedas, the Brahmanas, the Aranyakas and the Upanishads. The priestly classes who composed these scriptures and possessed a knowledge of the Brahman were known as the Brahmanas, first, as possessors of some supernatural power and later, as the possessors of the knowledge of the Brahmana or the universal soul. And often our religion was called the Brahmana Dharma or religion and our ancestors were known simply as Brahmans , as described by the Chinese scholars like Fa-hien, Hiuen-Tsang or I-Tsing who visited India in the fifth, sixth and the seventh centuries respectively. If the followers of the Dharma created by the Buddha were known as the Buddhists and those of the Dharma preached by Mahavira, the Jina, known as the Jainas, it would have been appropriate for us to describe the followers of the Vedas, the Brahmanas the Aranyaks and the Upanishads either as Vedic or Upanishadic.

From sixth century BC Vedanta or the Upanishads largely replaced the Brahmanical ritualism of the Vedic Dharma with love and devotion and from that date onwards various religious cults preaching love and devotion for the identification of the Brahman with the Atman leading to the liberation of the human soul appeared on the religious scene with a large number of followers. The most important among them were Saivaism and Vaishnavism and their followers were known, as they are still known today, either as Saivas or Vaishnavas. The Vedic religious umbrella also fully covered the rest of those who did not follow any particular sects or religious groups other than Saivaism or Vaisanavism but worshipped various gods and the goddesses as the manifestations of the Brahman or the universal soul.

Part Two

Eclipse of Our Religion and Loss of Our Religious Identity

10

The Coming of the Islam and the Rule of the Islamic Rulers

We lost our religious identity and our religion suffered an eclipse when the Muslim invaders came through the North-West, gradually conquered the whole of the sub-continent and settled down at Delhi and Agra as rulers. The Muslims were followers of the Prophet Muhammed who was born in AD 570 in the city of Mecca in Arabia .It was he who founded a new religion called Islam which preached the unity of God among the Arabs and roused the desert people to unbounded energy and enthusiasm. He fought 35 wars against heathenism to spread the message of the Allah in and around the capital of his kingdom, Mecca. Under his succcssors, the Caliphs of Baghdad, the arms of Islam advanced from AD 632 onwards in all directions and the banner of Islam floated over many countries from Iran to Spain and Saudi Arabia to India.

The Arabs

The Arabs were the first to come to India in the early cighth century, taking advantage of the struggle for power among the Indian dyanasties in the North over the possession of Kanauj, the imperial capital which had become synchronized with power and culture after the fall of the imperial Pataliputra under the Guptas. In AD 712 the Arabs under Muhammad-bin Kasim overran Sind by defeating the Brahmana King Dahir, son of Chach, the founder of the ruling dynasty of Sind and captured the rich seaports of Western India. However, the further progress of the Arabs was resisted by the Chalukyas in the South, the Pratiharas in the East, and the Karkotas in the North. Kasim's work was greatly facilitated by the treachery of certain Buddhist monks and renegade chiefs who deserted Dahir and joined the invader.

Ghazni

A new scene opened with the foundation of the kingdom of Ghazni in Afghanistan by Alptigin in AD 962. Alptigin's son and successor, Sabuktigin carried fire and sword into the territory of the king Jaipal of the Shahiya dynasty of Waihand, which extended from Lamghan to Kangra. In AD 997 Sabuktigin died and his successor, Mahmud, inflicted a crushing defeat on Jaipal near Peshawar in AD 1000. Jaipal burnt himself on a funeral pyre and was succeeded by his son, Anandapala. In AD 1008 Mahmud routed the troops of Anandapala under prince Brahmanapala at the battle of Waihand and penetrated further into the territory beyond the Punjab, capturing Thaneswar in AD 1014, burning the temple of Mathura, sacking Kanauj in AD 1018 and thereby almost extinguishing the once powerful empire of the Pratiharas. In AD 1022-23 he subdued Gwalior and Kalinjar and in AD 1025, he looted the celebrated temple of Somnath in Kathiawar. The fall of this Vedic temple synchronized with the final extinction of the Shahiya kingdom of the Punjab as well as the beginning of the doom of our sacred literature and religion.

Mahmud's expeditions were mostly in the nature of plundering raids and they resulted not only in the annexation of the Shahiya Kingdom of the Punjab but also in breaking down of the morale of the Indian armies. However, between AD 1030 when Mahmud died and AD 1192 when the Muhammad of Ghur appeared on the scene, the Rajput powers of the Western and the Central India who had divided among themselves the imperial heritage of the Pratiharas remained comparatively immune from foreign invasions though there was occasional harassment by the Ghaznavid Sultans such as the one when one of their generals advanced up to Benares and sacked the holy city. Yet the Ghaznavid occupation of the Punjab not only served as a key to unlock the gates of the Indian interior but also made big cracks in the Indian polity whose fall was simply a question of time. It is true that both the Arabs and the Ghaznavid Sultans could not succeed in adding India to the growing empire of Islam but there is no doubt that they paved the way for the eclipse of the Gangetic kingdoms and of our religion soon.

The successors of Sultan Mahmud were too feeble to maintain their position at Ghazni in the face of the rising power of the princes of Ghur, a small obscure principality to the south-east of Herat in the mountainous region of Afghanistan and of the Ghuzz tribe of Turkmans. The latter captured Ghazni by driving Khusrav Shah who fled to the Punjab, then the sole remnant of the wide dominions of his ancestors. Ghiyas-ud-din Muhammad, cousin and successor of Saif-ud-din who died while fighting against the Ghuzz Turkmans, drove the latter from Ghazni in AD 1173, appointed his younger brother, popularly called Muhammed of Ghur, governor of that province and it was in that capacity that Muhammad of Ghur began his Indian campaigns in AD 1175 which led to the capture of Lahore and the final extinction of the rule of the Ghaznavids in the Punjab. The occupation of the Punjab by Muhammad of Ghur made inevitable a confrontation with the Rajputs, particularly with his neighbour, Prithviraj, the powerful Chauhan King of Delhi and Ajmer.

At that time the political scenario in the Northern India since the invasions of Sultan Mahmud had undergone considerable changes. A part of Bihar was in the possession of the Pala kings who were Buddhists but Bengal had passed under the control of the Senas who were followers of the Vedic religion. The Chandelas still controlled Bundelkhand but the Pratiharas in Kanauj had been replaced by the Gahadavalas. Jaichand, the Gahadavalas ruler of Kanauj, who lived mostly at Benares, was considered to be the greatest king of India at that time.However, he was jealous of Prithviraj and did not ally himself with him when the Muhammad of Ghur appeared on the scene in the winter of AD 1190-91.

In AD 1191 in the first battle of Tarain near Thaneswar Prithviraj with the help of his fellow Rajput princes inflicted a crushing defeat on Muhammed of Ghur who retired to Ghazni. Next year Muhammad of Ghur returned with a strong army, met Prithviraj at the same battle site, defeated him and put him to death along with his brother. This victory of Muhammad at the second battle of Tarain was a decisive one—it did lay the foundation of a Muslim dominion and religion in India and the subsequent attempts of the relatives of Prithviraj to recover their lost power ended in fiasco.

Qutab-ud-din Aibak

After the battle of Tarain in AD 1192, Muhammad of Ghur left Qutab-ud-din Aibak who began his career as a slave and who rendered valuable services to him during his Indian expeditions, in charge of his conquests. Qutab was left, infact, "untrammelled not only in his administration of his conquests but also in his discretion to extend it, " and within the next few years, with the help of lkhtiyar-ud-din Muhammad, he was able to conquer a considerable portion of India, extending from the Indus in the West to the Ganges in the East. In 1206, after the assassination of Muhammad of Ghur on his way back from Lahore to Ghazni, his provincial viceroys established their own authority in their respective jurisdictions as there were no male heirs to succeed to him. Thus, Taj-ud-din Yildiz, Governor of Kirman, ascended the throne of Ghazni while Qutab-ud-din Aibak assumed the title of Sultan and was acknowledged as the ruler of the Indian territories by the Muslim officers in India like Ikhtiyar-ud-din of Bengal and Nasir-ud-dih-Qubacha of Multan and Uch.

Qutab belonged to the Ilbari Turks

The kingdom of Delhi under the dynasty of Qutab belonging to Ilbari Turks popularly known as the Slave Dynasty, "was not a homogeneous political entity" though they ruled India for about eight decades till AD 1290.The Khaljis ruled India from AD 1290 to 1320, followed by the rule of the Tughluqs , which continued upto AD 1413. The Tughluqs were replaced by the Sayyids who ruled India till 1451 and were followed by the Lodis till 1526. From 1526 onwards began the rule of the Mughals which after going through a period of ascendancy began to decline in the eighteenth century and lingered on in some form or other till 1857 when the Mughals were replaced by the British Crown.

The Delhi Sultanate

The rulers belonging to the several dynasties before the Mughals, assumed the title of "Sultan" and owed their allegiance to the Caliphs of Baghdad and of Egypt, the successors of the Prophet Muhammad. The authority of the Sultans was normally recognized in the territory roughly corresponding to the United Provinces of Agra and Oudh, Bihar, Gwalior, Sind and certain parts of Central India and Rajputana. The Muslim Governors of Bengal were mostly inclined to remain independent of their control and the imperial hold over the Punjab by the Delhi Sultans was occasionally threatened by the Mongols from Central Asia. The chiefs on all sides of Delhi were indeed the nuclei of Muslim influence though there were many independent local chieftains and disaffected inhabitants always inclined to defy the authority of the Central Government. It was under Ala-ud-din that the imperial period of the Delhi Sultanate began when the Muslim dominion over the different parts of India witnessed a rapid expansion. Gujarat was conquered, so were the Rajput strongholds of Ranthambhor, Chitor, Malwa, Ujjain, Mandu, Dhar and Chanderi. The whole of Southern India including the Yadava kingdom of Devagiri, the Kakatiya kingdom of Telingana, the Hoysala kingdom of Mysore and the Pandya kingdom of Malabar came to be included in Ala-ud-din Khalji's empire by 1312. The reign of Ala-ud-din Khalji indeed represented the apogee of the Delhi Sultanate as well as of the Islam for the Muslim arms in India were always accompanied by the spread of the message of the Allah. The Muslim rulers faithfully followed the Quranic instruction of converting the Dar-ul-Harb or the land of the unbelievers into Dar-ul-Islam or the land of the believers. And one can still find today dilapidated and often broken mosques, dargah and khanqua to facilitate worship of the Allah spread all over India from Kashmir to Kanya Kumarika and from Gujarat to Assam.

Dismemberment of the Delhi Sultanate

However, dismemberment of the Delhi Sultanate began with Muhammad-bin-Tughluq. Endowed with extra-ordinary intellect and industry, he lacked the essential qualities of a constructive statesman. His ill-advised measures and stern policy enforced in disregard of popular will sealed the fate of his empire of 23 provinces. Under his successor Firuz Shah, the process of disintegration further accelerated by such measures as the revival of jagir system, the extension of the institution of slavery, the persecution of the heretical Muslim sects and the imposition of the Jizya on the non-Muslims. While the impact of such administrative measures had been eating into the vitality of the Delhi Sultanate, the invasion of Timur in 1398 destroyed its coherence and increased the selfish intrigues of the nobility, who like the feudal baronage of later medieval Europe, plunged the whole kingdom in disorder and confusion. It was beyond the capacity of the weak Sayyids and the unsagacious Lodis to restore order and discipline in the kingdom. As soon as the central authority grew weak, the centrifugal tendencies, so common in the history of India, made headway. And a number of independent Sultanates like Bengal in the East, Jaunpur, Malwa, Gujarat and Kashmir in the North-West, Khandesh, Berar, Ahmadnagar, Bijapur, Golkunda and Bidar in the South arose on the ruins of the Delhi Sultanate. Among the non-Muslim kingdoms which appeared on the scene were the Vijayanagar, Orissa, Mewar, Kamarupa and Assam and Nepal in the Himalayas.

Babar

It was the internal dissension in the court of Ibrahim Lodi who succeeded Sikander Lodi in November 1517 that led to an invitation to Babar who represented Timur on his father's side and Changiz Khan on his mother's side to invade India. Babar who had inherited in 1494 from his father at the age of eleven the small principality of Farghana in Turkestan cherished the desire of recovering the throne of Samarquand but was thwarted by his kinsmen and by the rivalry of the Uzbeg chief, Shaibani Khan. Having been deprived of his own patrimony of Farghana, he spent his days as a homeless wanderer for about a year when he formed the bold design of conquering India like his great ancestor, Timur, the story of whose Indian exploits he had heard from an old lady of 111 years, mother of a village headman who had once given him shelter. Taking advantage of a rebellion in another part of the dominions of the Uzbegs, whose rising power had kept off the Timurids from their principalities, Babar occupied Kabul in 1504. With the help of Shah Ismail Safavi of Persia, he tried to grab Samarquand for the third time in 1511 but the Uzbegs under Shaibani' s successor finally defeated him in 1512. When therefore, the invitation from Daulat Khan Lodi, the most powerful noble in the court of Ibrahim Lodi, reached Babar, he at once accepted it, entered the Punjab and occupied Lahore in 1524. When Daulat Khan and his ally, Alam Khan saw that Babar had no desire to give up his conquests, they turned against him and compelled Babar to retire to Kabul.

The First Battle of Panipat

Within a year Babar came back with reinforcements, captured the Punjab, and defeated Ibrahim Lodi, the nominal ruler of the shrivelled Afghan empire in the historic battle of Panipat in 1526. It is true that this victory did not at once give Babar the virtual sovereignty of the country because there were other strong powers like the Afghan military chiefs, and the Rajputs under Rana Sangha aspiring after political supremacy, who were sure to oppose him. But the victory at Panipat did enable him to set his foot on the path of empire building in the country and thereby marked the foundation of the Mughal dominion in India and is therefore a turning point in the history of India.

As a matter of fact, there were three phases in the history of the Mughal conquest of India. The first phase which began with Babar was occupied till 1530 with the subjugation of the Afghans and of the Rajputs under Rana Sangha. The second phase which lasted till 1540 commenced with the reign of Humayun in 1530. Humayun made unsuccessful attempts at subjugating Malwa, Gujarat and Bengal, but was expelled by Sher Shah, the Afghan, which meant the revival of the Afghan power in India for fifteen years. The final phase began in 1555 with the restoration of the Mughal dominion by Humayun and its expansion and consolidation by Humayun's son and successor Akbar who ascended the throne of India after Humayun's death in 1556.

Babar who formed the link between Central Asia and India, between predatory hordes and imperial government, between Changiz Khan and Timur, brought to his descendants the energy of the Mongol, the courage and capacity of the Turk, the culture and urbanity of the Persian and thus laid the foundation of the first stone of the splendid fabric which his grandson Akbar completed.

Akbar

An intrepid soldier, a benevolent and wise ruler, a man of enlightened ideas, and a sound judge of character, Akbar launched himself on an annexationist career immediately after his accession to the throne at Agra in 1556 till 1601 when unforeseen and uncontrollable circumstances prevented him from carrying it further. "A monarch", he once observed, "should be ever intent on conquest, otherwise his neighbours rise in arms against him." He brought under his control the whole of Northern and Central India and guided by the traditions of the past imperial governments as those of the Mauryas, the Guptas, the Khaljis and the Tughluqs as well by his own desire to drive the Portuguese out to the sea as he did not think it wise to allow them a share in the economic resources and politics of India, he sought to bring the Deccan Sultanates, Ahmadnagar, Bijapur, Golkunda and Khandesh under his hegemony. However, Akbar did not ignore the feelings of the conquered and trample on their rights and privileges with an eye only to self-aggrandisement. He correctly realized the hollowness of ill-treating his non-Muslim subjects, who formed the overwhelming majority of the population, of relegating them permanently to a position of inequality and humiliation, thereby showing his transcendental ability of Akbar as a statesman. He not only meted out fair treatment to them and appointed them to high posts but also attempted to remove all distinctions between them and the Muslims. Thus he abolished the pilgrim tax in the eight year(1564) and the Jizya in the ninth year(1565) of his reign, and inaugurated a policy of universal toleration and attempted the introduction of a new religion, Din-i-Ilahi, which was a combination of elements extracted from all the existing religions in his empire.

Decline of the Mughal Empire

Akbar, thus, built up and consolidated on his policy of religious tolerance a vast empire which continued in full glory till the end of Shah Jahan's reign. However, reversal of Akbar's policy by Shah Jahan's successor, Aurangzeb, a great grandson of Akbar, contributed to the decline of the Mughal empire, which was further hastened by a succession of weak rulers after the death of Aurangzeb in 1707, followed by the invasion of Nadir Shah in 1739 and of Ahmad Shah Abdali's four invasions, the first of which took place in 1748. In1757 when the battle of Plassey which marks the beginning of the modern India was fought in Bengal, the Mughal empire had virtually shrank into a district around Palam as in the last days of the disintegration of the Delhi Sultanate. And the great grandson of Aurangeb, Aziz-ud-din, who had succeeded the Mughal emperor, Ahmad Shah in 1754 under the title of Alamgir 11, was desperately fighting to free himself from the control of his ambitious and unscrupulous Wazir, Ghazi-ud-din Imad-ul-Mulk, a grandson of the deceased Nizam-ul-Mulk of the Deccan.

11

Nature of the Muslim Rule in India

It is now necessary to have a look at the nature of the Muslim rule in medieval India under the Delhi sultanates and the Mughal emperors to understand its real impact on the religion of the conquered subjects. The Muslim state in India was a theocratic one and its existence was theoretically justified by the needs of religion as revealed in the Quran.

The Islamic theocratic state did not permit the existence of any religion other than Islam within its boundaries. Among the unbelievers who were Ahle Kitab or those who possessed or at least those who resembled the possessors of "some sort of revealed literature, " that is, Quran, were allowed to stay, as were the Jews, Christians and later Zoroastrians who werc initially allowed to stay in the territorial jurisdiction of an Islamic state created by the Prophet Muhammed, in lieu of a payment of a poll tax called "Jizya," "as a sign of humiliation and compensation for security of life and property in a Muslim state" as well as of "compensation from military service" from which they were kept exempted as "being unbelievers." The rest among the unbelievers who did not fall in this catgory were called "Kaffers" or "idolaters" and, as per the Suras 8 and 9, Verses 29, 38 and 39 of the

Quran as translated by Hashim Amir Ali (Charles E. Tuttle Company, Japan, 1974), they were denied the right of existence in an Islamic state. The three schools of Islamic thought, Malakite, Shaffite, and Hanbalite named respectively after their founders, Malik ibn Anas (715-95), Ash Shafi (767-820) and Ahmad bin Hanbal (780-855) offered no other alternative but death to the idolaters on their refusal to embrace Islam. It were only the exponents of the Hanifah School named after Abu Hanifah (699-766) who permitted their existence in an Islamic state as "Zimmis" on payment of "Jizya". In the words of Jadunath Sarkar, the term, "Zimmis", connotes "political inferioty and helpnessness like the status of a minor proprietor under a guardian; such protected person could not claim equality with the citizens of the Muslim Theocracy."

The unbelievers who fiercely resisted conversion to Islam in our country were allowed to remain as "Zimmis" on payment of Jizya but despite the loss of freedom almost in all walks of life, they were often persecuted by the Muslim nobles and the rulers. The religious persecution carried out by Malik Kafur, a convert from the Vedic religion, who carried Ala-ud-din's arms to the South across the Vindhyas, by Firuz Tughluq, another convert from our religion (through his mother, a daughter of Rana Mall, the chief of Abuhar, who was married to Ghiyas-ud-din's younger brother, Rajab) who looted the temple at Jwalamukhi and obtained a booty including a rich haul of Sanskrit manuscripts, as well as , by Sikander Lodi who, paradoxically enough, ordered the translation of one of our Ayurvedic treatises from Sanskrit into Persian, was well-known, as was well-known later Aurangzeb's persecution of the Sikh religious leaders.

The Muslim rulers in India were foreign victors with no roots in the soil of the country. They had established their rule by force, led by the armies of Islam and depended heavily on the foreign ruling elite as well as on their own soldiery for the protection of their newly founded state in the teeth of stiff and bitter opposition from the unbelievers including the Rajputs. As the unbelievers who were dubbed as Zimmis could not be trusted, the Muslim rulers tried to multiply the number of their community in the country and strove for the extension of their presence by various means including forced conversion of the unbelievers into Islam. The spread of the Mongol sway which cut off the Turkish sultans from their own ancestral lands in the Central Asia proved indirectly very helpful to them for the purpose, as hordes of Muslim immigrants including military nobles and soldiers and intellectuals came to Delhi in search of protection, and settled down under the patronage of the Delhi sultans. The military nobles among them were often planted as "Iqtadars" or "Muqtas" in the far off regions of their vague and undefined Islamic dominions in the midst of the hostile unbelievers. The Delhi Sultans, beginning with Qutab-ud-din Aibak and Iltutmish, as pointed out by K.A. Nizami in his work on religion and politics in Medieval India, pp.128-30, used this system "as an instrument for liquidating the feudal order of the Indian society" of unbelievers "and linking up the far-flung parts of the empire to one Centre." The system also satisfied the cupidity of the Turkish governing class, solved the urgent problem of the maintenance of the law and order and of the collection of revenues in the newly conquered territories.

Muhammad of Ghur who laid the foundation of the

Muslim state in India found it absolutely impossible with the support of a handful of Arab soldiers either to compel the mass of the conquered unbelievers "to choose between Islam and death" particularly when the latter were "armed to the teeth" and offered stiff resistance to their forced conversion to Islam. He, therefore, secured the status of "Zimmis" for them from the Caliphs of Baghdad and Egypt and accorded protection to their lives and property on payment of Jizya. This became a momentous decision followed by the Turko-Afghan sultans and the Mughal rulers later, except the great Akbar who abolished Jiziya, of Delhi and Agra in dealing with the vast multitude of the unbelievers in medieval India.

However, it must not be construed from the example of Muhammad of Ghur that the Muslim rulers of Delhi always acted under the guidance of the Caliphs of Bagdad and Egypt. As a matter of fact, the heads of the Muslim dominions in India paid only a ceremonial allegiance to the Caliphs of Baghdad and Egypt but they never owed their power and position to them nor to the will of the people of the conquered lands, which rested on their military strength. And this was understood and acquiesced in, not merely by the unthinking rabble but also by the soldiers and the intellectuals – the poets and the philosophers, and the Ulemas of the age. They had to be constantly on their guard against the hostility of the non-Muslim states, the non-Muslim communities and the foreign invaders through the North-West. This required a strong centralized government, which gradually made itself despotic, in the absence of a hereditary Muslim aristocracy which was conscious of its own rights and privileges and eager to assert these against royal despotism, of popular assemblies keen about constitutional liberty and of public opinion strong enough to oppose autocracy.

The Ulemas who excercised much influence in the state had not the courage to openly oppose the activities of the heads of the state though the heterogeneous Muslim nobility sometimes played its cards in the choice of a successor as the succession to the deceased head of the state in Muslim India was not regulated by any recognized law or any definite principle of inheritance. He was the chief commander of forces, he was also the chief lawgiver and the final court of appeal. In theory his authority in religious matters was limited by Quran but in practice he was a perfect autocrat, unchecked by any restrictions—his word was law binding upon all. He was the Caesar as well as the Pope—both combined in one person.

The Muslim Administration

However, autocratic a ruler could be, it was difficult to manage the affairs of a large and unwieldy empire which rose to its apogee first under the Delhi sultans, Ala-ud-din and Muhammad-bin-Tughlaq and then under the Mughal emperor, Akbar and his successors. He had to devise an administrative machinery with a regular hierarchy of officers in charge of various departments, who, however, did not in any way check his authority but rather carry out their respective duties according to the former's orders. In matters of administration both the Delhi sultans and the Mughal emperors could consult their trusted friends and officers who formed a sort of advisory body or council but the latter's advice was not binding upon the former who selected their own personnel for administration.

Under the Delhi sultans as under the Mughal emperors

the highest office in the state was the Wazir who had control over the other departments such as those of Risalat or Appeals; Arz or Military; Insha or Correspondence; Bandagan or Slaves; Qaza-i-Mamalik or Justice, Intelligence and Posts; Amir Kohi or Agriculture (created by Muhammad-bin-Tughluq); Mustakhraj or Collection of arrears of revenues (created by Ala-ud-din Khalji); Khairat or Charity (created by Firuz Shah Tughluq); Istihqaq or Pensions as well as those of the Mint, Charitable Institutions and the Karkhanas.

The chief departments of the state under the Mughals were (a) the imperial household under the Khan-i-Saman, (b) the exchequer under the Diwan, (c) the military pay and accounts officer under the Mir Bakshi, (d) the judiciary under the Chief Qazi, (e) the religious endowments and charities under the Chief Sadr or Sadr-us-Sudur, and (f) the censorship of the public morals under the Muhtasib. The Diwan or Wazir was usually the highest officer in the state, being in sole charge of revenues and finance.

Every officer of the Mughal state held a Mansab or official appointment of rank and profit, and as such, was bound theoretically to supply a number of troops for the military service of the state. Thus, the Mansabdars formed the official nobility of the country and this system was "the army, the peerage, and the civil administration, all rolled into one." Each of the chief officer of the department was assisted by a number of subordinate officials. Thus, the Quazi-ul-Quazat or the principal judicial officer in the realm appointed Qazis in every provincial capital, who made investigations into, and tried, civil as well as criminal cases of both the Muslims and the non-Muslims; the Muftis expounded Muslim Law; and the Mir Adls drew up and pronounced judgements.

In the days of the Delhi sultanate the number of provinces rose from 20 to 25. The head of the province was the Naib Sultan who exercised his executive, judicial and military functions, like a despot, subject only to the control of the central government, which varied according to the strength or weakness of the latter. The Naib Sultan sub-divided his province into smaller portions which were placed in the charge of the Muqtas or the Amils. These were further sub-divided into smaller units under Shiqdars, whose jurisdiction did not often extend beyond a few miles.

Similarly, the number of provinces under the Mughals rose from 12 in the time of Akbar to 21 in the time of Aurangzeb. The head of the province often styled as the Sipah Salar or the Commander-in-Chief, Sahib Subah or Lord of the Province or simply Subahdar was officially described as the Nazim who was the head of the civil and military administration, assisted by a staff of subordinate officiers like the Diwan, the Bakshi, the Faujdar, the Kotwal, the Quazi, the Sadr, the Amil, the Qanungo, the Bitikchi, the Potdar, and the Waqa-i-navis. The provincial head was paid from the revenue of the province and after meeting the expenses of his administration, he had to remit the surplus to the central exchequer. He main-tained a local militia and had to render military aid, at times, to the centre. Normally members of the ruling families were appointed to the provinces as their governors or viceroys. Thus, the administration of the provinces under the Delhi sultans as well as under the Mughal emperors "was an exact miniature of the central government" or "a replica of the empire."

Impact of an Extensive Empire on Our Religion

The building up of a vast empire by the Delhi sultans under Ala-ud-din Khalji and Muhammad-bin-Tughluq as well as by the Mughals under Akbar and his successors and that of a vast bureaucracy both at the centre and in the provinces needed to administer it, has far-reaching socio-religious consequences often overlooked by those who concentrate mainly on the politico-economic impact of the nearly more than 650 years of Islamic rule in the country.

In the first place, this long period of Islamic rule in the country means putting into oblivion the non-Muslim kingdoms and their ruling dynasties who were patronisers of the Vedic, the Jain and the Buddhist religions in the country.With their disappearance also disappeared the sustenance of our religions continuously reeling under the destruction of the temples and the Buddhist viharas—a process initiated by the first Muslim invaders of our country. Secondly, quite in keeping with the Quranic extortions, the Muslim rulers were out to establish their own religion as the dominant religion in the country by converting the Dar-ul-Harb into Dar-ul-Islam and this they sought to achieve in three ways: First, they destroyed the visible symbols of the religion in the form of temples and viharas of the conquered people and built in their places their own religious organizations such as mosques and khanquas. Second, where ever possible they tried, either by force or by persuasion, to convert the conquered subjects into their own religion and in this they were largely successful as many from the oppressed and the depressed classes of the Aryan society opted for the new religion which was the religion of the ruling class, where they hoped to find their own freedom and comforts. These converts formed the bulk of the Muslim armies and helped the rulers to hold their own countrymen in perpetual subjugation. There were also instances of the converts from the higher classes who aspired for a higher position either in the army or in the civil administration of the Muslim rulers. The examples of Malik Kafur, a convert from unbelievers, who became the most trusted military commander of Ala-ud-din-Khalji and of Firuz Tughluq who succeeded Muhammad-bin-Tughluq as the Delhi sultan, are well-known. Third, taking advantage of the Quranic injunction of having four wives, the Muslim officials and soldiers who came to India, largely and mostly, unaccompanied by their women, married Indian women after converting them into their own religion. Here again, the women came mostly from the depressed classes of the Aryan society though there were more frequent instances as in the case of Akbar and his successors when they either married or put in their harem the queens and the daughters of the vanquished non-Muslim rulers. And, as later events show, this single act of marrying a converted unbeliever woman became the most important factor in increasing the number of the Muslim community in the country and largely explains a very recent (2011) observation by a Dar-ul-Uloom Deoband Islamic scholar, Maulana Wahiduddin Khan that nearly "95 per cent of Indian Muslims have Hindu ancestors." (*The Times of India*, 4 December 2011).*

With the increase in the number of the Muslims through local converts, it now became extremely necessary to initiate them as well as their children to the Islamic religion. Coupled with this, the migrant Muslim community in the country also needed initiation of their religion to their children born here. This could only be done through a study of the Quran and it began at the maktab usually attached to a mosque which the Muslim ruling class built at every possible place within their conquered territories.

*Maulan Wahiduddin's observation can also be accessed through the Internet: http://articles.timesofindia.indiatimes.com/2011-12-04/special-report/30474274 1 sufism-wahabism-suffi-shrines. Accessed on 01 August 2012.

12

Islamic Education as an Indoctrination for the New Converts as well as for the Children of the Muslim Settlers

Maktab represents the lowest rung in the Muslim education system to meet the needs of the Muslim administration and of the Muslim community. Maktab played an important role in the scheme of the followers of Islam who were exhorted by the Prophet Muhammad to convert the Dar-ul-Harb or non-Muslim lands into Dar-ul-Islam or realms of Islam.While the initial stages could be completed by the Jihad or the holy wars, the final stages required the transmission of the knowledge of the Prophet or the Quran to the newly converts. As a matter of fact, a course at the maktab was never completed for one who was not able to read the Quran and utter the prayers at the Namaz.

Madrasah

At the higher level there was the madrasah set up not only to meet the needs of a growing Muslim administration but also of the Muslim intellectual community at large. The Muslims were called upon to rule in an alien environment, people belonging to another religion and culture, people who far outnumbered them. Unless and until they had adequate number of personnel with qualifications in Islamic education, theology, law and jurisprudence, art of war and of administration, the foundations of their empire in India would rest on quicksands. It was a chain of madrasahs which every ruler was keen to create that supplied the necessary qualifications needed for the required personnel of the Muslim administration. And until the days of Akbar, these madrasahs set up in the provincial cities or the capitals and often attached to mosques or the vice-versa, were the close preserves of the Muslim community, though occasionally instances could be found of a non-Muslim with a knowledge in Persian or Arabic acquired privately serving the army or the administration at a higher level under a tolerant ruler like Sher Shah or Akbar.

A Parallel with the British System of Education and Administration

The education system introduced by the Muslims offers an interesting parallel with the one introduced later by the British who virtually began to rule parts of India from 1757 onwards. The British ruled India with their own personnel recruited and trained in their own education at home though reluctantly from 1853 onwards they began to admit a few qualified Western educated Indians as members of their covenanted civil service. However, the difference between the British and the Muslims lies in the fact that while the former regarded India as a colony and looked upon themselves as mere birds of passage, the Muslims never did so. The latter accepted India as their own homeland and the rich among them were never allowed to remit wealth out of the country. Secondly, while the British discriminated the Indians mainly on the basis of colour and race, the Muslims never did so and we all know that one of the wives of the Prophet

Muhammad was a coloured one. Finally, while the British liaisons with the Indian women from 1757 onwards gave birth to the Anglo Indian community who were not accepted by the British nor by the Indians as members of their own societies, there was no such hybrid community that came into existence in the long span of nearly 650 years of Muslim rule in the country simply because of the Quranic allowance of upto four wives that a Muslim could take legally. And they liberally used this allowance by adding an Indian woman after her conversion into Islam to their household to fill the Quranic quota.

However, the British, despite the presence of the Christian missionaries in large numbers, never officially interfered with the religion of the Indians which the Muslims did to fulfill the goals of Islam. The Muslim rulers looked upon themselves as Ghazis or Holy Warriors and the Mughal emperors from Jahangir onwards officially affixed Ghazi to their royal titles. As a matter of fact, the early years of the Islamic rule in India concentrated on increasing the number of converts from other religions often by force, coercion or persuasion and there is no doubt that a large number of people suffering from various disabilities and restrictions of their own religions embraced the new faith which was the faith of the new rulers. And they did so certainly not without any material advantages such as the exemption from the payment of the Jizya tax imposed by the Muslim rulers except Akbar on "unbelievers" in Islam. For these new converts as well as for the offsprings of the inter-marriages, maktabs were more important than the madrasahs, where, as we have already said, introduction to the knowledge of the Quran was made. Maktabs were always attached to the mosques which could be seen, even today, dotting the different parts of the Muslim dominions, including villages where the Muslims often outnumbered the followers of other religions.

Construction and the Maintenance of the Maktabs and the Madrasah

While maktabs with mosques could be constructed and maintained by the local Muslims or by the rich among them for congregational prayers, the construction and maintenance of a madrasah which called for more expenses was usually done by rulers, members of the ruling families and by the wealthy officials and nobles not excluding the prosperous merchants and traders, petty landlords and chieftains. The contemporary Muslim chronicles are often strewn with references to the constructions of madrasahs by these people and the usual sites for these were the imperial and provincial capitals, new cities and towns built by the rulers, and important trading and commercial centres. It was to these institutions that students would often come from faraway places and would reside on the campus, attending instructions by distinguished teachers in advanced Islamic learning in the morning and in the evening with a break at noon, for several years, before they could empower themselves for a better life and prospect.

Courses offered were not at all Relevant to the Conquered Subjects and their Country

There is no doubt that the Islamic education catered only to the needs of the rulers and its people and was largely geared to the fulfillment of its religion by spreading the message of Allah as revealed in the Quran and the Hadith. The courses offered and the themes taught were all Islamic and they hardly reflected the interests of any religions other than Islam. The texts were Arabic and Persian and their authors were also Arabic and Persian though later Muslim authors from Amir Khusrav onwards, with family connections in Central and Western Asia, who composed their works in India, gradually came to be studied in the madrasahs. Yet, the subjects the latter composed in India, particularly in history and *belles* letters, had little to do with interests outside their own rulers and communities and were therefore largely irrelevant to the needs of the non-Muslims or the society at large. It was as if a bit of Arabia and Persia was transplanted in the Indian soil through the maktabs and the madrasahs. And though Akbar tried to broaden the courses by including Vedic learning, they continued to have little impact as the basic character of the Islamic education was not much altered. And if Bernier were to be believed, Aurangzeb was the first Muslm ruler of medieval India to question the relevance of an education which did not enlighten one about history, geography, politics, religions, culture and languages of the people of one's adopted homeland, that is, India. To put in a nutshell, Islamic education was basically a religion oriented education which took care only of the interests of the Muslim communities and its rulers in the medieval India.

Islamic Education was not an Indigenous One

There is no doubt that the Muslim system of education was not rooted into the soils of India but its strength lies in the fact that the Islamic education was imparted not through the mother tongue of the Muslim rulers, which was Turki, but through Arabic and Persian which formed the medium of instruction of all Islamic institutions set up by the Muslim conquerors in their conquered territories including India and this contributed to a feeling of an Islamic brotherhood among the Muslims of the world and fostered the mobility of learned persons and scholars from one part of the Islamic world to another, thereby enriching the culture and the learning of both. A host of Muslim scholars from Central and Western Asia attracted by the wealth and the munificence of the Muslim rulers in India came to reside at their courts and ultimately made India their homeland, some of them acquiring non-Muslim women as their wives, following the examples of their patrons among the Delhi sultans and the Mughal emperors.

Impact of the Islamic Education on the Vedic Religion and Education

The reason why we have entered into a brief but critical analysis of the Islamic system of education in medieval India is to understand its impact on the existing Vedic religion in the country. The Vedic religion depended for its sustenance on its patrons who were normally and usually the kings and nobles and on the Vedic schools where Vedic religious scriptures were studied and commentaries written and on such religious functions as the yajna or sacrifices which formed the nuclei of the Vedic religious life. With the disappearance of the non-Muslim kingdoms and their ruling dynasties who were generally the followers of the Vedic religion also disappeared their patronage to the Vedic schools as well as to the various religious sacrifices. The priestly classes who managed these schools and were hitherto supported by the royalty in the form of moveable and unmoveable gifts and bequeaths could no longer support themselves and the students who lived with their teachers for many years for the completion of their courses in the Vedic religion. Thus, studies in the Vedic religion were not only disrupted but in a sense the continuity of the Vedic schools were also seriously affected, for it was the students at a Vedic school who after completion of their courses branched out to different parts of the country they came from and set up their own schools to impart lessons in the Vedic religion to a new group of students. The priestly class including those who often served the royalty as purohitas or advisers became unemployed and many of them migrated either to the bordering non- Muslim kingdoms across the Vindhyas or the Himalayas or to those areas where despite the penetration of Muslim rule the non-Muslim chieftains were left undisturbed in their day to day rule on timely payment of yearly tribute to the Muslim rulers.

Sanskrit

However, the most serious casualty of this change was the language of the scriptures, that is, Sanskrit. Sanskrit was the language of the royal courts and the priestly classes who used to speak in Sanskrit among themselves, and orally transmitted the knowledge of the scriptures in Sanskrit. And, it was only after the fifth century AD following the example of the Buddhist viharas which used to impart their instructions from written Buddhist religious scriptures that the Vedic religious scriptures began to be written in Sanskrit. However, overall transmission of the knowledge of the scriptures from a guru to a shisya continued to remain oral as before. Sanskrit was, however, used as a vehicle of non-religious literatures much earlier and the earliest evidence of written Sanskrit words could be traced to the days of the Mauryas.

Over the years, Sanskrit which had become as a language of our religious scriptures and of the royal courts an index of our civilisation now came to be replaced by the Persian language with the coming of the Muslim invaders and conquerors. And deprived of royal patronage and priestly support, it gradually began to languish and wither in the middle ages in India under the Muslim rule.

Rare and Academic Interests of the Islamic Rulers in Sanskrit

It is interesting to note that some Muslim scholars came to possess a knowledge of Sanskrit who had helped Firuz-Shah Tughluq in arranging for the translation of the Sanskrit works captured at the temple of Jwalamukhi—Elliot mentions the translation of a Sanskrit work, on astrology as well as another on veterinary science entitled Salotar in Persian, which he saw in the library of Nawab Jalauddaulah at Lucknow. Such interest in Sanskrit language and literature which received a boost under Zain-ul-Abidin of Kashmir in the early fifteenth century and later under Akbar who not only arranged for the translation of many Sanskrit works into Persian and included Sanskrit in the curricula at the madrasahs as well as Dara Shukoh who himself undertook the Persian translations of the Upanishads, the Bhagavat Gita and the Yoga Vasishtha Ramayana had been, as a matter of fact, growing ever since the days of the Arab occupation of Sind, when the Arab astronomer Abu Mashar went to Benares and studied astronomy there for ten years.

Such Academic Interest among the Muslim Rulers and the Scholars had little Impact on the Masses

However, such interest in Sanskrit and its allied literature were very rare and purely academic–and the ordinary people other than the priestly classes had over the years ceased to be drawn to it, for, not only, it did not enjoy the status of language of the court, of the administration and of the learning institutions after having been replaced by the Persian but also it faced a formidable rival in the rise of the vernacular languages and of a new language called Urdu, the genesis of which could be traced to the use of Kharoshthi scripts introduced by the Persian invaders in ancient India.

Challenge of the Rising Vernaculars to the Sanskrit

The process of the withering of the Sanskrit language under the Muslim rule was further hastened by the development of the vernacular languages in the different parts of India. Hindi in the North, Bengali in the East, Tamil, Telegu and Malayalam in the South and finally Marathi in the West posed a stiff challenge for the survival of the Sanskrit language even among the priestly classes who now became accustomed to it. The significance of the development of the vernaculars, particularly Hindi in the North and the Bengali in the East as well as the rise of the Dravidian languages in the South vis-à-vis the Sanskrit must not be lost sight of. The development affected Sanskrit the most. Already deprived of royal support and patronage and without any further opportunity for its cultivation as a language of learning and teaching in the Vedic schools which were doomed to gradually disappear under a hostile Islamic rule, Sanskrit remained confined to the small groups of the priestly families who had to keep learning the language to have access to the religious scriptures. This also meant for the vast majority of the growing non-Muslim population a gradual ignorance of the existence of Sanskrit and of the religious literatures composed in it since the days of the Guptas. What survived through the priestly families was mostly a knowledge of some of the works of the Sutrakaras needed to cater to the needs and requirements of the pious non-Muslim families in Muslim India on their socio-religious functions often performed at home.

With regard to the survival of the original religious texts as well as the works of the Sutrakaras and their commentaries, we have to look for them in the Vedic schools that continued to function in the neighbouring non-Muslim kingdoms across the Vindhyas in the South, in the West and in the Himalayas in the North at the time of the degeneration of the Delhi Sultanate and of the decline and fall of the Mughal empire.

The tragic impact of a withered Sanskrit, of a depleted priestly class and of a non-existent Vedic school prepared the ground for the dominance of the Quran and the disappearance of the Vedas and allied religious scriptures. This happened not in a single day, month or a year under the rule of a particular Muslim ruler but in successive days, months and years over the centuries of Islamic rule in the country. And the process started with the Persianisation of our country which began with the Delhi sultans from 1206 onwards.

13

Persianisation of the Muslim India and Confirmation of the Loss of Our Religious Identity

Persian was the language of the royal courts of Egypt and of Baghdad and in the contemporary Islamic world, it stood as a language of culture, polite manners and refinement. We have already seen that the Muslim rulers adopted this language as the medium of instruction in their institutions of higher learning from the very beginning of their rule in India and soon they adopted it as their language of their royal court and administration also.

The growth of Persian influence in India began with the beginning of the reign of the Delhi sultans who were well-versed in Arabic and Persian and was certainly influenced and abetted by the ravages of Changiz Khan in Central Asia which led to an influx of noted Persian scholars who took refuge in the Delhi court. Thus, the famous Persian poet and philosopher Amir Kuhani who fled from Bukhara came to the court of Iltutmish, followed by Nasiruddin known for his popular collection of historical anecdotes in Persian and Fakhr-ul-mulk, formerly Wazir of the Caliph of Baghdad for nearly thirty years, who was now appointed Wazir by Iltutmish. The Persian influence further increased when the celebrated

Persian, Minhaj-us-Siraj, the author of Tabaqat-i-Nasiri, made the court of Nasir-ud-din Mahmud his home. However, it was during the reign of Ghiyas-ud-din Balban (1266-87) that the Persian influence at the Delhi court rose to great heights helped by the ravages of Changiz Khan of Khurasan and other places in Central Asia which sent some fifteen princes including some of the most illustrious men of learning of the time to seek refuge in Balban's court. Balban assigned the uprooted princes suitable positions and allowances and prided himself on his generosity towards them. Balban was always on the look out for scholars and learned men who could be a source of strength for his empire and in this context the advice given by him to his son, Muhammad, is indeed remarkable: "Spare no pains to discover men of genius, learning and courage. You must cherish them by kindness and munificence that they may prove the soul of your councils and instruments of your authority."

The example created by Balban was followed by the successive Muslim rulers and the influence of Persian scholars and learned men in the Delhi court and in the courts of the provincial capitals continued unabated till the days of the last Mughal emperor. They composed poems and wrote prose, *belles* letters, memoirs and biographies of the Muslim rulers and together they created the core groups in Persian in the country and backed by the Muslim rulers' love for the Persian language and culture, Persian became synonymous with the Muslim rule in the medieval India.

An Extensive Empire helped the Spread of the Persian

For the first time since the fall of the Guptas, the Muslim rulers from Qutab-ud-dib Aibak through Ghiyas-ud-din Balban, Alauddin Khalji, Muhammad-bin- Tughluq,

Akbar and Aurangzeb built up an extensive empire from Kashmir to Kanya Kumarika and from Gujarat to Bengal with a centralized administration where the officials took orders from Delhi and Agra in Persian which was also the medium of instruction in the Islamic higher education institutions. Persian was not merely the language of the court and the administration, of public business and polite society, Persian tastes and ideas came to profoundly influence arts and letters in contemporary India.

Non-Muslim Interests in the Persian

Non-Muslims from the vanquished ruling and the affluent classes began to learn Persian from the sixteenth century onwards for a foothold in the Muslim administration and in the membership of the *nouveau riches* and the ruling elite. And with a common language, a common tastes in arts and letters, a common etiquette, they formed together with the Muslim officials trained in the madrasahs, one of the invisible pillars of the Muslim rule in the medieval India.

Essence of the Impact of the Persian

In the dominance of the Persian language and culture in the court and in the administration in the medieval India under the Muslim rule for more than 650 years lay almost buried our ancient civilisation and culture as well as our religion and religious scriptures. Our social manners and customs began to be governed by Islamic manners and customs while our relationship with the Muslim state began to be governed by the Islamic laws and jurisprudence. We were the conquered subjects and we became as "Zimmis" second-class citizens in our own country. As such our freedom was restricted in many areas and we had to carry the stigma of a subjugated people. Our freedom to practice our religion was suppressed and we had to pay a tax called Jizya imposed on the non-Muslims by all Muslim rulers except Akbar to proclaim our degraded status of "Zimmis" in our own country. As payers of Jizya, we carried the stigma of a subjugated people without any freedom and were known as Kaffers, infidels or idolaters. And this continued for more than 650 years till the Muslims were replaced by the British.

Revival of the Use of the Term, "Hindu" and Confirmation of the Loss of our Religious Identity

In the wake of the Persianisation of the medieval India also came the use of the term "Hindu" to refer to the non-Muslim conquered subjects in India. We have already said earlier that when the Persians first came to India around 519 BC, occupied the North-West and stayed there for nearly 200 years till they were replaced by the Greeks around 326 BC, they used the term "Hindu" to refer to the Aryan people who lived on both sides of the river Sindu which the Persians pronounced as "Hindu". The use of the term was confined only to their conquered subjects and as we have said earlier, it was very likely that the latter knew that they were called "Hindus" by the Persians occupiers and the conquerors. For, 200 years of the Persian occupation of the North-West, some 2500 years ago from now, despite the absence of any technology which usually leads to rapid changes in the society as it is happening now, were nevertheless a scene of a very slow but substantial pace of progress and development in the North-West.

There is no doubt that the "Hindu" term continued to be used by the Persians even after their dislodgement by the Greeks from the North-West in scattered Indian territories which remained under the control of some branch of foreigners like the Sakas, the Pahlavas and the Kushanas who spoke an Iranian or Persian language. When the Arabs came in the early eight century and occupied the lower valley of the Indus, they found themselves in the midst of the descendants of the ruling families of the Brahmanised foreign immigrants of the Hunas and the Pratiharas, now known among the thirty-six clan of the Rajputs, who had found a place as the degenerate Kshatriyas in the Aryan society. They were known to the Arabs as "Hindus" as could be evident from the observation of the Arab scholar, Al-Beruni in his "An Account of India of AD 1030" edited by Edward C. Sachau(Delhi edition, 1964). Al-Beruni was the travelling Arab scholar who possessed the most intelligent and outstanding intellect among his contemporaries and he described these inhabitants living in the lower valley of the Indus as "Hindus" but he had hardly any time and patience to verify whether the term was actually in circulation among them as a mode of address amongst themselves.

The lower valley of the Indus was inhabited mostly by the usurpers of the successors of the imperial Guptas and they became known as "Hindus" after accepting the Vedic religion. It was very natural for the Arabs who conquered and later occupied these areas to continue to refer the conquered residents on the both sides of the Indus as "Hindus." It is, however, doubtful whether the use of the term "Hindu" was ever extended to the vast areas of the country which were under the control of the Guptas, their successors and other Indian powers in the Northern India. And, in all probability the Indians in these areas, not to speak of the people beyond the Vindhyas, were not aware of the term.

With the Muslim rulers who built up an extensive empire spreading from Kashmir to Kanyakumarika and from Gujarat to Bengal in the middle ages from 1206 onwards also came the Persianisation of the whole of our country, and with the Persianisation also came the use of the term "Hindu" everywhere in their extensive dominions, now under a new garb and with a new significance. The new garb was the Islamic religion which the Muslim invaders and the conquerors had earlier bestowed on Persia, hitherto predominantly a follower of the religion of Zoroaster, Zoroastrianism which recognized the dual principle of both good and evil, when they conquered that country and the new significance lay in the fact that unlike the Persians who used the term to describe the people living on both sides of the river Sindu, the Muslim rulers now used it to denote all the non-Muslms who followed a different religion from theirs and were frequently called Kaffers or unbelievers in the Islam.

With the gradual increase of the boundaries of the Muslim dominions in the country, the use of the term also increased and was extended to cover the conquered non-Muslims so that by the time Babar came and occupied Delhi and Agra, India was already known in the Middle-Eastern and the Central Asian countries as "Hindustan" or the Land of the Hindustanis much in the same way the British introduced the use of the term "India" and described her people as "Indians", obviously inspired by the name "Indus", given by the Greek occupiers in the past to the river Sindu.

Babar always referred to India as "Hindustan" and the people living there as "Hindus" in his "Memoirs" written in his own mother tongue, Chaghatai Turki. In p. 518 of A.S. Beveridge's translation of *Babarnama* from Chaghatai Turki, there is a very significant observation by Babar on the people of Hindustan, which confirms our view. He observes: "Most of the inhabitants are pagans; they call a pagan Hindu. Most Hindus believe in the transmigration of souls. All artisans, wage-earners, and officials are Hindus. In our countries, dwellers in the wilds [nomads] get tribal names; here the settled people of the cultivated lands in villages get tribal [caste] names. Again, every artisan there follows the trade that has come down to him from forefather to forefather."

It is quite clear from Babar's observation that the non-Muslims were known to each other by castes and groups they belonged to as was the case in ancient India. And the term "Hindu" was generally used by the Muslim rulers and the Muslims only on occasions when its use did not carry any slur. It is, however, doubtful whether the term "Hindu" was frequently used by the Muslim rulers. The latter preferred to call them Kaffers, idolaters or infidels and in contemporary Persian works, when they had the occasions to use the term, "Hindu", they always did it with the religious connotation to describe them as the group of idolaters.

With Islam becoming the dominant religion as the religion of the rulers and with the Vedic schools replaced by the Islamic institutions of learning and Sanskrit by Persian, and the unbelievers losing their freedom as the Zimmis, there was little hope for the religion that emerged out of the Vedas, the Brahmanas, the Aranyakas and the Upanishads to remain alive and breathing as Vedic and Upanishadic and it gradually began to move almost into oblivion in the minds of our ancestors living in the domains under the control of the Muslim rulers. There is no doubt that such a development was further sealed by the gradual withering of the Sanskrit language which holds the keys to the gateway of our religious scriptures, in the face of the rising vernacular languages. We have already seen that in such a scenario, while many of the priestly classes migrated to the non-Muslim kingdoms across the Vindhyas and the Himalayas, there were still many who remained at their places of birth catering to the needs of the faithful on the occasions of their birth, marriage and death. We have also said earlier that there were no external manifestations of the performance of the Vedic religion as these were either simply banned, suppressed or prohibited by the Muslim rulers.

When the Vedic schools were not functioning, the priestly classes as teachers were not teaching the religious scriptures and the students who came from far and wide to learn them were not coming, the awareness of the Vedic religion as it pervaded the minds of the Aryans in ancient India gradually and naturally began to disappear. Non-Muslim people at large gradually began to forget their own religious scriptures and to get accustomed to their description as "Hindus" or Kaffers or worshippers of idols as gods and goddesses. And how the priestly classes who were presumed to keep alive our religious traditions and practices accepted and adjusted themselves, without any knowledge of the roots of their own religion, with the term "Hindu" could be seen in the action of Baji Rao, son of Balaji Vishwanath, a Chitpavan Brahmana from Konkan. Balaji Viswanath was the Peshwa or Prime Minister of Shahu, the son of Shivaji. When Balaji died and his son, Baji Rao I became Peshwa in 1720, he dreamt of establishing an empire by driving out the weak successors of Aurangzeb from Delhi after securing the sympathy of the non-Muslim chiefs who were followers of the Vedic religion. He, thus, told his master Shahu, "Let us strike at the trunk of the withering tree. The branches will fall of themselves. Thus, should the Maratha flag fly from the Krishna to the Indus." To evoke the sympathy and secure the support of the non-Muslim chiefs, he preached the ideal of an empire which he described as "Hindu-Pad- Padshahi."

This means what it appears to mean to us—identification of the term, "Hindu", with the national and the political unity of the intended Marathi empire, "Hindu-Pad-Padshahi." And from that time onwards there had been no going back to the roots of our religion—Vedic and Upanishadic. Baji Rao I as a member of an esteemed priestly class from the Maratha kingdom—a region which had striven hard to keep our threatened religion alive from extinction under the impact of Islam could not have done otherwise as the term, "Hindu", had already become synonymous with our religion by his time.

Long before Baji Rao I, the non-Muslims had accepted Persian as a language of opportunity and in the seventeenh and the eighteenth centuries non-Muslim scholars vied with the Muslim in enriching Persian literature and thought in prose and poetry. The entire range of Muslim dress, social customs and food habits, indoor and outdoor games, manners and social behaviours, superstitions and taboos were absorbed by the multitude of non-Muslims without demur except that they would not touch beef or eat with the Muslims. The non-Muslims changed their architecture to Muslim influence to such an extent that even their temples "could not remain immune from the influence of the Mughal architectural forms." The Rajput princes freely patronized

Mughal art and architecture and transmitted the cultural trends of the Imperial court at Delhi and Agra to their own chieftains and the aristocracy.

As a matter of fact, in the midst of the forceful imposition of the Islamic religion and Islamic culture under Persian garb by the Muslim rulers on the non-Muslims which later led to the birth of many new regional social habits and practices as well as the birth of a new language called Urdu which could be traced to Kharoshthi in the North-West under the Persian occupation before the beginning of the Christian era, the non-Muslims in India began to forget the genesis of their religion and culture over the centuries and felt content to live as "Hindu" through its outward manifestations in the form of religious functions and performances as on the occasions of their birth, marriage and death as well as to worship their gods and goddesses at home and often to visit a temple if a temple which had survived the wrath of a tolerant Muslim ruler was available in the locality.

To put in a nutshell, following the example of the Persian rulers who came to the North-West India around 519 BC and who used the term for the first time to refer to the conquered subjects as "Hindus" who lived on the both sides of the river, Sindu, the Muslim rulers in the midst of the Persianisation of India also described them as such and extended the use of the term, "Hindu", to the different parts of their extensive empire. And the conquered subjects being fully unaware and unconscious of their own religious past, accepted this description, without a murmur, as idolaters or worshippers of gods and goddesses and followers of religious practices and customs remarkably different from the religion of their new Muslim rulers. Such a thing happened, as we have already said before, not in their one generation but in their many succeeding generations covering a period of more than 650 years of the rule by the Muslims till they were replaced by the British. With the loss of our sovereign rights and responsibilities as Zimmis, we also lost our religious identity in the use of the Persian term, "Hindu", under the garb of Islam, which has nothing to do with our religious scriptures and our religion over the centuries till date.

The use of the term with religious connotation was continued later by the British who found it advantageous to rule a vast country with a handful of British military and civil officials. As we have already said much earlier in the Preface, that the East India Company officials, Hastings, Cowper and Malcolm, confirmed this religious connotation at the very begitming of their rule in the early nineteenth century while opposing the despatch of the Christian missionaries to India on the eve of the passing of the Charter Act of 1813, on the ground that it would harm the interest of the Company by uniting the two religious groups, "Hindus" and "Muslims" against any attempt at proselytising them. The shrewd advice of the officials of the East India Company in the early nineteenth century was meticulously followed by the British administrators in India and guided most of their actions after the transfer of the power from the Company to the Crown following the revolt of the sepoys in 1857. Thus, the British administration in India shrewdly and tacitly supported Syed Ahmed Khan's theory of two nations, the Hindus and the Muslims, from 1875 onwards through the foundation of the Muhammedan Anglo-Oriental College in Aligarh to his foundation of the United Patriotic

Association to oppose the Indian National Congress in 1886, indulged in the Partition of Bengal with the segregation of the Muslim community in the larger part in 1905, supported the formation of the Muslim League at Dacca in 1906 in the wake of the Partition, provided for the separate electorates for the Muslims in the Act of 1909, helped the establishment of the Hindu University at Benares (1916), the Muslim University at Aligarh (1920) and finally gave the necessary support to the Muslim League which eventually led to the bifurcation of our country on the basis of Syed Ahmed's and later Jinnah's theory of two nations in 1947.

On our part our religious pundits and national leaders looking for an identity of their own accepted the use of the term, "Hindu", without any murmur as its use no longer carried with it the earlier humiliation which their ancestors and forefathers had suffered as "Zimmis" under the Muslim rule for nearly 650 years. One very interesting example of how our past leaders and intellectuals of the society in the early nineteenth century got used to the use of the term, "Hindu" could be seen in the setting up of an indigenous and pioneering English medium school at Calcutta under the name "Hindu" School, in 1817, which a decade later became a "Hindu" College and still later in 1855 came to be known as the Presidency College as Dalhousie thought that this premier college should be open to all religious groups.

In the late nineteenth century when Syed Ahmed Khan (1817-98) propounded his theory of two nations, the "Hindus" and the Muslims, and set up in 1875 the Mohamedan Anglo-Oriental College at Aligarh to uplift the social and educational backwardness of his community, not much attention was perhaps paid to it. However, soon the militant nationalist leaders like Bal

Gangadhar Tilak, Lala Lajpat Rai and Bipin Chandra Pal were quick to grab the significance of Syed's theory of two nations and hijacked the term "Hindu" with its religious connotation to find our national identity and ideology. The moderate nationalist leader Pandit Madan Mohan Malaviya followed suit and set up a political organization, "Hindu" Maha Sabha in 1909 to promote our ancient religious ideals and values and soon started a movement for the establishment of a "Hindu" University at Benares on a "Hindu" model provided by the Central "Hindu" College set up by Annie Besant in 1898 to restore the values and ideals of our ancient religion, which came into existence in 1916, four years before the Muslim University at Aligarh in 1920.

As a matter of fact, our Western educated national leaders of the Freedom Movment like Nehru and Patel who were most influenced by the idea of an European Nation State fell an easy prey to the use of the term "Hindu" as denoting our national identity simply because a nation state could not be formed without a national identity and ideology. And, so when the Muslim League first set up at Dacca in the early 1906 and became politicized later in the same year at Simla in the wake of the Partition of Bengal, came forward with the idea of a separate homeland for the Muslims in India, some of our national leaders also began to think of such a nation state with a national identity and ideology and they quickly appropriated the term "Hindu" for the purpose and moved towards the idea of "Hindutva", which redefined the "Hindus" as a nation and "Hindutva" as their national ideology. And, this happened years before Muhammad Ali Jinnah actually spoke of "Hindus" and Muslims as two separate nations in the closing years of the Freedom Movement in the country. V.D. Savarkar who was a very strong member of Malaviya's "Hindu" Mahasabha, had no qualms in making a honest admission on the matter: "I have no quarrel with Mr. Jinnah's two-nation theory. We, Hindus are a nation by ourselves and it is a historical fact that Hindus and Muslims are two nations." Savarkar's comments were very important as he was an avowed atheist and had scant regards for any religion. This only shows the desperateness of our national leaders for the search of a national and political identity, which they ultimately found in the term "Hindu".

And in our acceptance of the term "Hindu" from the days of Baji Rao I to describe our national and political identity, we have not only lost our religious identity but also our keys to the unlocking of a glorious and prosperous civilisation and culture that dominated the lives of the people in the days of the Mauryas and the Guptas in ancient India. And we had to wait until the British Orientalists in the late eighteenth and the early nineteenth centuries followed by the French and the German Indologists in Europe came forward to our rescue, rediscovered our Sanskrit language, our religious scriptures and our religion based on the Vedas and the Upanishads.

PART THREE

Survival of Our Religion

14

The Priestly Classes in Muslim India and in the Bordering Non-Muslim Kingdoms

The loss of our religious identity as the followers of the Vedas and the Upanishads, in our description as "Hindus", happened progressively almost every day, every month and every year of the 650 years of the Muslim rule in the country. Yet, our religion survived in fragmentation almost everywhere in our country in and outside the Muslim India despite the loss of our religious identity. It survived mainly because of the survival of the priestly classes from the sabres of the Muslim arms. The knowledge of the scriptures was transmitted from one generation of the priestly classes to a succeeding one through guru-shisya parampara. It was often difficult to identify a priestly family holding school at the residence than to identify and destroy a matha or a monastery housing the Buddhist monks and learning by an invading Muslim army. This actually happened when the Muslim invaders first came to India. They found it easier to destroy and demolish the Buddhist viharas on their path. The unarmed non-violent monks living in these monasteries either perished or somehow managed to flee to the kingdoms in the Himalayas and they stayed there even after replacement of the Muslim rule in the country by the British. This partly explains why there is still a large presence of the Buddhists monks and the Buddhist viharas or the monasteries in Nepal, Tibet, Ladakh, Sikkim and Arunachal while in their own heartland in the eastern part of the country in Bihar, they could be found now only in and around the newly constructed Buddhists viharas which are liberally patronized by the neighbouring countries in Asia professing Buddhism.

The priestly classes were therefore, the central point in the story of the survival of our religion. While in the Muslim India their activities were much restricted having deprived of royal patronage and support, in the non-Muslim kingdoms across the Vindhyas and in the Himalayas as well as later in Maharashtra, Rajasthan and the Punjab they were able to keep the flag of our old Vedic religion fluttering.

The survival of our religion took many a subtle form—first, in the performance of the Vedic ritualism by the depleted priestly classes in and outside the Muslim India on the occasions of birth, marriage and death as well as on other religious functions held at the residences of the non-Muslims, second in managing the Vedic schools in the non-Muslim kingdoms which emerged behind the Vindhyas, the Himalayas, and in the western, northern and the eastern borders of the Muslim empire; third, in the Sanskrit commentaries composed by the surviving Vedic schools both in and outside the Muslim India which defended the Vedic religion against Islam and finally, in the translation of the Sanskrit religious works into the rising vernacular languages of the contemporary India, which made the Vedic religious ideas and beliefs easily accessible to the literate and the semi-literate non-muslims all over the country. It must be said here that the work of translation of Sanskrit treatises was often done by a sympathetic and interested provincial Muslim ruler and assisted by persons who were not members of the priestly classes.

The Surviving Priestly Classes

The Vedic ritualism was carried on by the depleted priestly classes through successive generations because it was their profession from the past and in the medieval India under the Muslim rule it had now become the only livelihood after being thrown out of work at the Vedic schools which had almost ceased to exist in the capital cities and the villages as well as from the jobs of acting as advisors to the kings and monarchs who were now dethroned by the Muslim rulers. Most of the priestly classes, as said earlier, migrated to the bordering non-Muslim kingdoms across the Vindhyas and in the Himalayas where with support from the kings, chiefs and nobles, they could set up new Vedic schools or joined the existing ones.

Such migration was possible because of the earlier precedents created by the Southern kingdoms where the learned Brahmanas from the North were invited by the former to come and settle down around the temple colleges they had built for the furtherance of the cause of the Vedic learning and religion. The most powerful among such kingdoms were the Cholas of Kanchi and Tanjore, the Hoysalas of Mysore and the revived Pandya dynasty of Madura. Thus, the scenario in the South was one of a very flourishing Vedic religion before the Muslim invaders came and settled down in the North.

We have already said that the Vedic religion earlier had never believed in the external and mechanical methods of organization and was left to be dealt with between the guru and his disciple in their personal relationship from which the whole world was excluded. Nevertheless, in the wake of the emphasis laid by Jainism and Buddhism upon organized brotherhoods in rock-cut caves and halls, viharas and monasteries, the Brahmanical religion followed suit with similar organizations like the mathas and regular colleges as centres of learning and religion from tenth century onwards following the revival of the Vedic religion by Sankaracharya.

In Southern India the extent of such temple colleges was widespread as could be gathered from the various inscriptions describing the deeds of endowments for their upkeep by such dynasties as those of the Rashtrakutas, Cholas, Pallavas, Hoysalas and Pandyas. Besides, the establishment of such temple colleges often equipped with hospitals to take care of the health of the teachers and the students, arrangement was often made by some specific endowment as can be seen in *Epigraphica Indica* in an inscription dated 1122 AD which records the magnificent gift of 44 villages to a temple for the purpose of giving food and clothing to Vedic students, religious teachers and ascetics.

Such public benefactions establishing temple colleges often provided for the setting up of colonies of pious and scholarly Brahmanas in select areas for the pursuit of knowledge for its own sake. Such learned settlements were centres of light and life, showing how theory and practice should go together, how precept should be supported by example, ethics by conduct and how learning was to be lived and truth of religion was to be realised in the activities of daily life.

Once the Islamic rule settled down in the North, the

Muslim arms crossed the Vindhyas in the reign of Ala-ud-din Khalji (1296-1315) under his eunuch general Malik Kafur, a convert from the Vedic religion and for a time a Muslim sultanate was even set up in the extreme South at Madurai. And this Muslim occupation of the South certainly delivered a crushing blow to the Vedic religion which till now had escaped the wrath of the Muslim rulers of the North.

The Vijayanagar Empire

However, the Dravidians were not finally subjugated. Within a few years of Malik Kafur's raids, in 1336, an independent kingdom was founded at Vijayanagar, on the Tungabhadra river, which after desperately resisting the Bahamani sultans in the Northern Deccan, established its hegemony over the whole peninsula from the Krishna river southwards. Learning something of military strategy from their Muslim enemies, the kings of Vijayanagar maintained their independence until the middle of the sixteenth century, and in a reduced form even later.

It is the kingdom of Vijayanagar which for well nigh three centuries stood for the Vedic religion and culture of the country and saved these from the rush of new ideas and forces generated by the Islamic arms. Sayana, the famous commentator of the Vedas, and his brother, Madhava Vidyaranya, the celebrated Brahmana sage and scholar of the day, described as "the supreme light incarnate" in an inscription of Harihara II, flourished in the early days of Vijayanagar. And it was at their advice that Harihara and Bukka, two of the five sons of Sangama, laid the foundation of the city and kingdom of Vijayanagar, on the southern bank of the Tungabhadra river facing the fortress of Anegundi on the northern bank.

All the emperors of the Vijayanagar empire were patrons of the Vedic religion. They were either Saiva or Vaishnava. Yet what marks them out was their liberal attitude not only to the Buddhists and the Jainas but also to the alien creeds—Christian, Jewish and Moorish. As Edoardo Barbosa who was present in Vijayanagar in 1516 writes about the greatest among them, Krishnadeva Raya of the Tuluva dynasty: "The king allows such freedom that every man may come and go and live according to his own creed without suffering any annoyance, and without enquiry whether he is a Christian, Jew, Moor, or Hindu." Known for his munificent gifts of land and money to poets, philosophers and religious teachers, Krishnadeva Raya built the famous Hazara temple which, according to Longhurst, is "one of the most perfect specimens of Hindu temple architecture in existence." The Vithalasvami temple, also a fine example of Vijaynagar style, "shows the extreme limit in florid magnificence", in the opinion of Fergusson, to which the style had advanced by the time of the king.

Fall of the Vijayanagar Empire

The Vijayanagar empire was severely jolted by its battle of Talikota in January 1565 at the combined hands of the Deccan sultanates of Bijapur, Golkunda, and Ahmadnagar but the empire continued to exist till the early part of the seventeenth century under the rulers of the Aravidu dynasty, "before it got weakened and dis-membered—weakened by the constant invasions from the north and dismembered by the dissatisfaction and rebellion of the viceroys within." The "insane pride, blind selfishness, disloyalty and mutual dissension" of the feudatories of the Vijayanagar empire largely facilitated the conquest of the Vedic Deccan by the Muslim states of Bijapur and Golkunda, while the subordinate viceroys like the chiefs of Seringapatam and Bednur and the Naiks of Madura and Tanjore carved out independent kingdoms for themselves.

Kingdoms other than Vijayanagar in the North and the East

Besides the Vijayanagar empire in the South, Vedic religion received its royal patronage from the non-Muslim kingdoms which emerged at the time of the disintegration of the Delhi sultanate. And among such kingdoms were Orissa, Kamrupa and Assam in the East and Mewar in the North.

In the North, the break up of the Mughal empire after the death of Aurangzeb in 1707 saw the emergence of two more Rajput kingdoms besides Mewar. These were Marwar (Jodhpur) and Amber (Jaipur) which tried to throw off the allegiance of the Mughal emperors and became the champion of the Vedic and Jain religion and faith in the post-Aurangzeb years.

The Maratha Country

In the West, the rise of the Marathas introduced an important factor in the Indian political scenario in the second half of the seventeenth century, as that of Vijayanagar had done in the previous age. In ancient India, the Marathas had brilliant traditions of political and cultural activities when they upheld the national causes under the Yadavas of Devagiri. They lost their independence with the fall of the Yadava Ramachandra in the time of Ala-ud-din, but in forty years they began to play again an important part in the Bahamani kingdom and subsequently in the succeeding sultanates. The Maratha country, enclosed on two sides by mountain ranges like the Sahyadri running from north to south, and the Satpura and the Vindhya running from east to west, protected by the Narmada and the Tapti rivers and provided with numerous easily defensible hill forts, remained the bastion of the Vedic religion and culture long before Shivaji organized the Marathas into a national state. The Marathi religious reformers like Ekanath, Tukaram, Ramdas and Vaman Pandit, preaching through successive centuries, the doctrines of love and devotion of God and equality of all men before him, without any distinction of caste or position, and the dignity of action, had sown in their land, the seed of a renaissance or self-awakening which is generally the presage of a political revolution in a country. Ramdas Samarth, Guru of Shivaji, exerted a profound influence on the minds of his countrymen and inspired them with ideas of social reform and national regeneration through his disciples in the mathas and his famous work known as *Dasabodha.* The devotional songs of religious reformers were composed in the Marathi language and consequently a forceful Maratha literature grew up during the fifteenth and the sixteenth centuries to inspire the people of the land with noble aspirations. "Thus," observes Sir Jadunath Sarkar, "a remarkable community of language, creed, and life was attained even before political unity was conferred by Shivaji. What little was wanting to the solidarity of the people was supplied by his creation of a national state, the long struggle with the invader from Delhi under his sons, and the imperial expansion of the race under the Peshwas."

Shivaji

The Vedic religion found a champion in the person of Shivaji. Sincerely religious from his early life, Shivaji did not forget the lofty ideals with which he had been inspired by his mother and Guru Ramdas, in the midst of political and military duties. He sought to make the Vedic religion a vital force in the uplifting of the Maratha people. "Religion remained with him", remarks a modern Marathi writer, "an ever fresh fountain of right conduct and generosity; it did not obsess his mind or harden him into a bigot." Tolerant of other faiths, he deeply venerated Muslim saints and granted rent free lands to meet the expenses of illumination of Muslim shrines and mosques, and his conduct towards the Capuchin fathers (Christian monks) at Surat, during its first sack by him, was respectful. Even his bitterest critic, Khafi Khan writes: "But he [Shivaji] made it a rule that whenever his followers were plundering, they should do no harm to the mosques, the Book of God, or the women of any one."

Successors of Shivaji

The Vedic religion remained a strong force with the successors of Shivaji who died a premature death at the age of 53 only and we all know how a Chitpavan Brahmana from the Konkan, named Balaji Viswanath, helped Shahu, the son of Shambuji and the grand son of Shivaji to come out successful out of a protracted civil war with Tara Bai, the widow of Rajaram, the younger brother of Shambuji and to ascend the Marathi throne. Shahu appointed him Peshwa or Prime Minister in 1 713. By virtue of his superior talents and abilities, Balaji Viswanath and his illustrious son and successor Baji Rao made the Peshwa thc real head of the Maratha empire and thereby relegated the Chatrapati or the king to the background in a course of a few years. Baji Rao who became Peshwa in 1720 followed a policy of expansion beyond the Narmada with a view to striking at the root of the imperial power. The Peshwaship came to be hereditary in the family of Balaji Viswanath and aimed at supremacy on the dismemberment of the Mughal empire preaching the ideal of Hindu Pad- Padshahi or a Hindu empire which ended disastrously at the third battle of Panipat in 1761.

Nepal

Another important kingdom which was the seat of the Vedic religion was Nepal in the Himalayas. Nepal was the refuge of not only of the fleeing Buddhist monks but also of many a member of the priests of the Vedic religion who took shelter in the country to escape the fury of the Islamic invaders. For more than two hundred years (1097-1326) the Karnataka king Nanyadeva and his successors claimed, from their capital at Simran, a sort of loose sovereignty over the local princes of Nepal.

In Defence of the Vedic Religion

As we have said earlier, in the territories directly under the Muslim rule, the Vedic religion survived through the priestly classes who could not make it to the bordering non-Muslim kingdoms. They stayed behind and kept alive the rituals of the Vedic religion. In ancient India besides serving as gurus in the Vedic schools, many of their numbers also held royal assignments often as advisors to the kings and monarch. These formed their sole occupations and livelihoods. And now deprived of these under a new religion and a new administration which replaced Sanskrit by Persian, they had to keep their knowledge and trade alive to cater to the needs of the non-Muslim households on the occasions of various socio-religious functions such as birth, marriage and death. The financial incentives involved in such assignments were sufficient to maintain them as they gradually came to be deprived of royal patronage under the Islamic rulers. This explains the presence of the Vedic schools in the form of tols and chatuspathis , as had been seen later and reported by the British officials in various parts of Muslim India.

And these schools including those which flourished under the patronage of the Vedic kings across the Vindhyas, the Himalayas and elsewhere in Assam, Orissa, Maharashtra, Mewar, and Marwar were the scenes for a considerable number of compositions in Sanskrit before the advent of the Mughals. Such acounts were mostly in defence of the Vedic religion, against the onslaught of Islam which reminds us of the Sutrakaras like Manu, who prepared elaborate treatises in defence of Brahmanism to ward off the influences of the Mlecchas as well as to check the spread of Buddhism in ancient India.

Commentaries on Religion in Sanskrit

As the proselytizing zeal of Islam gradually increased, conservatism in the orthodox circles of the non-Muslims also strengthed itself to fortify its position against the spread of the Islamic faith by increasing the stringency of the caste rules and by formulating a number of rules in the Smriti works. Thus, Madhava of Vijayanagar wrote his commentary on one of the Smriti works of Parasara, entitled Kalanirnaya in between 1335-60 and Visvesvara wrote another Smiriti work entitled Madanaparijata for king Madanapala in between 1360-70. The other famous

Smriti works were by Kulluka, a Bengali author belonging to the Benares school by domicile, who wrote his famous commentary on Manu and by Raghunandan, a contemporary of Shri Chaitanya in Nadia. As a matter of fact, not only Smriti but also grammatical literature flourished not only in Bengal but also in Mithila in Bihar and the most famous writers of these subjects were Padmanabha Datta, Vidyapati Upadhayaya and Vachaspati. Parthasarathi Mishra wrote in1300 several works on Karma Mimansa, of which Sastra Dipika was studied most widely. The period which saw the birth of some works expounding the doctrines of the Yoga, Vaiseshika and Naya systems of philosophy also saw a tremendous spurt in the production of a mass of Jaina religious literature.

Non-religious Literature in Sanskrit

Sanskrit, the language of the religious scriptures, got a new leash of life in non-religious literatures like Sanskrit dramas and poems which stole the limelight and the most important among them were Gita Govinda by 12th century Bengali poet Jayadeva; Hammirmadamardana by Jay Singh Sufi in between 1219-29; Pradyumnabhyudaya by the Kerala prince Ravivarman; Pratap Rudra Kalyan by Vidyanath in 1300; Parvati Parinaya by Vamana Bhatta Bana in 1400; Gangadasa Pratapa Vilasa, celebrating the fight of a prince of Champner against Muhammad II of Gujarat, by Gangadhar, and Vidaghda Madhava and the Lalita Madhava, written in 1532 by Rupa Goswami, a minister of Husain Shah of Bengal, and author of no less than twenty-five works in Sanskrit.

Impact of the Rising Vernacular Languages under Patronization by the Muslim Rulers

However, it is not the compositions in Sanskrit in religious and the non-religious subjects alone but the rising vernacular languages which had begun to receive the patronage of some Muslim provincial rulers and their descendants that acted as a great conduit for the spread of the religious messages and ideas of the Vedic religion to the literate, semi-literate and illiterate non-Muslim population of the country. The Muslim provincial rulers and their families as well as those who came along with them became after a couple of centuries almost Indianised with an interest in Indian religion and culture. Far away from Delhi and Agra, the seats of imperial power and position, and consequently therefore from the routine influence of Arabic and Persian, they began to commission translation of Vedic religious scriptures and Sanskrit literatures into provincial languages spoken and understood by them instead of Arabic and Persian as had been done by the imperial courts at Delhi and Agra under Firuz Shah Tughluq and Akbar and as late as Dara Shukoh. Among such provincial governors the most notable one was Zain-ul-Abidin of Kashmir whose ancestors came from Swat. Abidin ruled Kashmir from 1420 to 1470 and could understand and converse in Hindi. It was he while arranging for the translation of the Mahabharata and the Rajatarangini into Persian also got several Arabic and Persian works translated into the Hindi language. Similarly, the Muslim rulers of Bengal engaged scholars to translate the Ramayana and the Mahabharata from Sanskrit into Bengali. It is widely believed that Krittivas whose Bengali version of the Ramayana has been hailed as the Bible of Bengal worked under the patronage of the Sultan Ghiyas-ud-din Azam who ruled Bengal from 1383 to 1410 and later eulogized by the Bengali Poet Vidyapati. Sultan Husain Shah who reigned in Bengal from 1493 to 1518 patronised Maladhar Vasu who translated the Bhagavata into Bengali and conferred on him the title of Gunaraja Khan in recognition of Vasu's work. Husain Shah's general Paragal Khan attempted a translation of the Mahabharata into Bengali by the Bengali scholar Paramesvra also known as Kavindra. Paragal's son, Chuti Khan who became governor of Chittagong, continued his father's work with the help of the Bengali poet Srikarna Nandi who translated the Asvamedha Parva of the great epic. It is Husain Shah's son, Nasir-ud-din Nusrat Shah who succeeded his father in 1518 and ruled Bengal till 1533 had the great epic completely translated under his orders.

Non-Muslim Princes and Chieftains

It is not merely the provincial rulers, their higher officials and petty chieftains who encouraged translations of important and popular works from Sanskrit into a language which they spoke and understood. Following their examples, many non-Muslim princes and chiefs also did the same. Thus, Vidyapati Thakur, who though a native of Mithila, is regarded as a poet of Bengal and whose memory is still venerated by the Bengalis, was the court poet of a non-Muslim chief named Siva Simha. His contemporary, the famous Vaishnava poet, Chandidas who was born, probably towards the end of the fourteenth century, in the village of Nanur in the Birbhum district of Bengal, composed devotional songs, poems and lyrics which are still popular among the common folk of Bengal.

Vernaculars at Delhi and Agra

Around Delhi and Agra it was Hindi which received the imperial patronage. Akbar's keen interest in, and patronage of Hindi poetry gave a great stimulus to Hindi literature which saw some of our ancient Sanskrit treatises translated into Hindi. The peace and order secured by Akbar and the cosmopolitan ideas of the religious movements of the period, preached by a band of saintly teachers in a language, "understanded of the people" stimulated genius of the latter, which unfolded itself in manifold petals; consequently the sixteenth and the seventeenth centuries became "the Augustan age of Hindustani literature." However, with the withdrawal of the court patronage, the growth of Hindi literature received a setback during the reign of Aurangzeb.

Nevertheless, Aurangeb's successors like Bahadur Shah and Muhammad Shah revived royal patronage of men of letters who seemed to flourish more in the provincial capitals than in the imperial as could be seen in the patronization extended to the devotional songs of Ramprasad by the Raja Krishnachandra Dev of Nadia in Bengal.

Vernaculars in the South

While the vernaculars in the North had not found any literary expression at the time of the Muslim invasion, the Dravidian languages had been flourishing in the South for centuries in the past. Four of these languages had distinctive script and written literatures—Tamil, Kanarese, Telegu and Malayalam. Of these Tamil was spoken in the South from Cape Comorin to Madras, Kanarese in Mysore and parts of Hyderabad, Telegu from Madras northward to the borders of Orissa and Malayalam in Malabar. Tamil is certainly the oldest of these languages with a literature going back to early centuries AD. The earliest Tamil literature contains few Sanskrit-loan-words, and those it does contain are generally adapted to the Tamil phonetic system. As Aryan influence penetrated the whole of the Tamil land by sixth century AD and her kings and chiefs worshipped and supported the gods of Brahmanism, Jainism and Buddhism, many words often in their correct Sanskrit form were borrowed by the Tamil literature. Telegu and Kanarese, which were spoken further North were actually even more influenced by Sanskrit. While Malayalam, very closely akin to Tamil, became a separate language in the eleventh century, Telegu did not appear as a literary language until the twelfth century and only became really important under the Vijayanagar, of which it was the court language.

Ascetics

However, the real significance of the rising vernacular languages in the North and the South could be seen in their uses by a continuous band of ascetics who appeared on the scene spreading over a period of more than 650 years. They spoke and preached in their local languages, wrote poems and verses in them and immediately made an impact on the growing number of their disciples who were becoming increasingly disillusioned with the things as they were existing in the country as well as in their own society. The ascetics, without any fail, spread the Vedantic message of one god and one soul, which they did despite the official ban by the provincial and local Muslim chiefs and rulers against an open demonstration of the faith of the Kaffers or the non-believers. And most of them except a few were the worshippers of the Siva, Vishnu or Rama and their followers were known as the Siva-bhaktas, the Rama-bhaktas and the Vishnu-bhaktas. We shall now make a brief analysis of some of the ascetics who appeared on the medieval scene as well as of the works by their followers and disciples in vernacular languages which carried the Upanishadic message of love and devotion and identificaion of the Brahman with the Atman to the hearts of all, literate, semi -literate or illliterate as the gate-way to their liberation from the cycle of birth and death. It will be most appropriate if we analyse the contribution of these ascetics who contributed to the survival of our religion in a separate chapter now.

15

Ascetics

The ascetics who were as old as the four Vedas often appeared at a very difficult time of hisiory to rescue the people from distress, disbelief and superstition and showed them the correct path to their religion and the way to the liberation of their souls from the cycle of death and birth. They carried the messages of the Upanishads in varying forms and degrees and often made a lasting impact on their followers. They are the reincarnations of the Lord Krishna who has said in Chapter 4, Slokas 7 and 8 in the Bhagavad Gita: "Whenever there is a decay of Dharma [righteousness] and an ascendancy of unrighteousness, I manifest Myself; and for the protection of the virtuous, the destruction of the vicious, and for the establishment of righteousness, 1 manifest myself in age after age."

We have already seen that in ancient India how the Siva-Baghavat and the Krishna-Bhagavat movement spread the message of love and devotion among people, irrespective of castes and creeds and generated a tremendous support particularly from those who were affected by the contemporary political instability and turbulence and gradually gathered a large number of followers from the believers in the traditional Vedic ritualism. We have also seen how the ranks of many a Buddhist monk in the Buddhist viharas included the members of the priestly classes and it was because of their influence that Sanskrit, and not Pali as originally advocated by the Buddha as the language of preaching, became from fifth century onwards the written language of the Buddhist scriptures as well as the medium of instruction in the Buddhist viharas.

In the medieval India with the dominant and the aggressive Islam attempting to encroach into the fabric of the Vedic religion through conversion either by force or by persuasion and with the latter withdrawing into a state of rigidity to protect itself from the Islamic onslaught, almost all the ascetics who were, with some differences in details, exponents of the liberal Bhakti cult, strongly advocated reform of the existing religion. Most of the ascetics in medieval India came from the priestly classes. And confronted with the dominance of the Islamic religion of the rulers and an almost continuous exodus of the lower castes to embrace the religion of the rulers to save themselves from the religious disabilities imposed on them by the Vedic religion, they preached before the unlettered masses themes like the fundamental equality of all religions, the unity of god head, the dignity of man depending on his actions and not on his birth, protested against excessive ritualism and formalities of religion and domination of the priests, and emphasized simple devotion and faith as the means for salvation for one and all. The underneath current of Saivaism and Vaishnavism, that is, devotion and love, which characterizes the history of religion since the Upanishadic days in ancient India, continued its subtle flow in medieval India. And a host of religious reformers preaching Bhakti, that is, love and devotion, as a means to salvation, appeared on the scene.

Ramananda

Among these religious reformers, the first in point of time was Ramananda though there are differences of opinion regarding the dates of his birth and death. Born in a Brahmana family of Kanyakubja or Kanauj at Allahabad, Ramananda travelled through the holy places of Northern India. A worshipper of Rama, he preached the doctrine of Bhakti in Hindi to members of all classes and both sexes. Among his twelve principal disciples, one was a barber, another a cobbler and the third a Muslim weaver.

Vallabhacharya

The next in point of time was the famous Vaishnava saint, Vallabhacharya who was an exponent of the Krishna cult. Born in 1479 of a Telugu Brahmna family near Benares where the latter had come on pilgrimage, he showed signs of a genius in his early life. After finishing his education, he travelled to the court of Krishnadeva Raya of Vijayanagar where he defeated some Saiva pandits in a public discussion. He advocated renunciation of the world and insisted on "the complete identity of both soul and world"—clearly a refletion of the teachings of the Upanishads. His monism was known as Suddha-Advaita or pure non-deity, which was abused later by his followers to such an extent that Monier-Williams does not hesitate to assert that "Vallabhacharyaism became in its degenerate form the Epicureanism of the East."

Chaitanya

However, the greatest and the most popular of the Vaishnava saints was Chaitanya, 1485-1533. Born in a learned Brahmana family of Nadia in Bengal, Chaitanya displayed a wonderful literary acumen in his early life and his soul soon aspired to rise above the fetters of this world. At the age of 24, he renounced the world and spent the rest of his life in preaching the message of love and devotion—eighteen years in Orissa, and six years in the Deccan, Brindavan, Gaur and other places. Krishnadas Kaviraj, the author of *Chaitanyacharitamrita,* the famous biography of Chaitanya, thus brings out the essence of Chaitanyaism. "If a creature adores Krishna and serves his Guru, he is realeased from the meshes of illusion and attains to Krishna's feet, and leaving these [temptations] and the religious system based on caste, [the true Vaishnava] helplessly takes refuge with Krishna."

Thus, he was opposed to priestly ritualism and preached faith in Hari. He believed that through love and devotion, and song and dance, a state of ecstasy could be produced in which the personal presence of god would be realized. His gospel was meant for all, irrespective of caste and creed, and some of his disciples were drawn from the lower strata of both from the non-Muslim as well as the Muslim members of the contemporary society.

Namadeva

In Maharashtra, the religion of devotion was preached by Namadeva; and among his followers a few were Muslim converts to Brahmanism. Namadeva, who belonged to a caste of tailors or calico printers, flourished probably either during the later half of the fourteenth or the first half of the fifteenth century. With his faith in the unity of the god head, he did not set much store by idol worship and external observances of religion. He believed that salvation could be attained only through love of god: "As the love between a child and his mother/So is my soul imbued in the god."

Kabir

Kabir made the most earnest efforts to foster a spirit of harmony between Brahmanism and Islam. His life is shrouded in a good deal of obscurity, and the date of his birth and death are uncertain. He flourished either towards the close of the fourteenth century or in the first quarter of the fifteenth century. A legend tells us that he was born of a Brahmana widow, who left him on the side of a tank in Benares, and was then found and brought up by a Muslim weaver and his wife. He is represented by a tradition to be a disciple of Ramananda. Though, as Carpenter puts it "the whole background of Kabir's thought is Hindu, " he was influenced to a great extent by the Sufi saints and poets with whom he came in contact. Thus, he preached a religion of love, which would promote unity amongst all classes of creeds. To him "Hindu and Turk were pots of same clay: Allah and Rama were but different names. It is needless to ask of a saint the caste to which he belongs. The Hindus and the Mussalmans have the same lord. A saint has no caste and god is accessible to all—barber, washerman, carpenter, Raidas and Rishis. Hindus and Moslems have achieved that end where remains no mark of distinction." Kabir did not believe in the efficiency of ritual or external formalities, either of Brahmanism or of Islam; to him the true means of salvation was bhajan or devotional worship, together with the freedom of the soul from all sham, insecurity, hypocrisy and cruelty. As he says: "It is not by fasting and repeating prayers and the creed/That one goeth to heaven;/The inner veil of the temple of Mecca/ Is in man's heart, if the truth be known." He, therefore, preaches: "Make thy mind thy Kaaba, the body its enclosing temple,/Conscience its prime teacher;/ Sacrifice wrath, doubt and malice;/Make patience thine utterance of the five prayers./The Hindus and the Mussalmans have the same Lord."

Nanak

Another great preacher of the time was Nanak, the founder of Sikhism and the reviver of the pure monotheistic doctrine of the Upanishads. He was born in a Khatri family of Talwandi, about thirty-five miles to the south-west of Lahore in 1469, and spent his whole life in preaching his gospel of universal toleration, based on all that was good in Brahmanism and Islam. As a matter of fact, his mission was to put an end to the conflict of religions in the country.

Like Kabir, he preached the unity of god head, condemned with vehemence the formalism of both Brahmanism and Islam. As he writes: "Religion does not consist in mere words, in wandering to tombs or places of cremation or sitting in attitudes of contemplation or in wandering in foreign countries or in bathing at places of pilgrimage. The way to religion is to abide by the pure amidst the impurities of the world and to look upon all men as equal."

While advocating a middle path between extreme asceticism and pleasure seeking, Nanak exhorted his followers to discard hypocrisy, selfishness and falsehood: "Make continence thy furnace, resignation thy goldsmith/

Understanding thine anvil, divine knowledge thy tools, / The fear of god thy bellows, austerities thy fire, /Divine love thy crucible, and melt god's name therein. In such a true mint the Word shall be coined. This is the practice of those on whom god looked with an eye of favour." Nanak's religion being a proselytising one, several Muslims were converted to it, and it gathered momentum under his successors.

It must be mentioned here that probably the original intention of Nanak was not so much the idea of setting up a religion separate from ours but to enlighten the people about the true religion and to reform and do away with the absurdities of ritualism of the contemporary Vedic religion groaning under the dominant Islamic religion of the rulers. The Upanishads remained his base for his teachings and in all probability Nanak's religion could have been one of the many sects within Saivaism or Vaishnavism as had been the case with most of the religious reformers of the time. However, the subsequent gurus confronted by the Mughal persecution developed it into an well-organised religion with the adoption of some innovative commandments to fight it out.

The Ascetics in Action

While the orthodox scholars in the Vedic schools both in and outside the Muslim ruled territories continued to write in dying Sanskrit, the ascetics who talked about the reform of the existing Brahmanical religion, wrote and spoke in a medium which could be easily understood by the uneducated and illiterate masses. Thus Ramananda and Kabir both preached and wrote in Hindi. The Dohas and the Sakhis of Kabir which were permeated with devotional fervour, are now brilliant specimens of Hindi literature.

Mira Bai and some other preachers of the Radha- Krishna cult sang in Brajabhasa while Nanak and his disciples encouraged Punjabi and Gurumukhi and the Vaishnava saints and teachers preached and wrote in Bengali, thereby tremendously enriching the growth and development of the Bengali language and literature. Similar is the case with the ascetics in Maharasthra. All of them beginning with Namadeva and including Ekanath, Tukaram, Ramdas and Vaman Pandit wrote and preached in the Marathi language. Ramdas Samarth preached his disciples in the monasteries in the Marathi and also wrote "Dasabodha" in the same language which besides carrying the message of the Upanishads, exerted a profound influence on the minds of his countrymen and inspired them with the ideas of social reform and national regeneration.

In some varying form and degree, almost all the religious reformers in their preachings and writings echoed the Upanishadic message of the oneness of god, of love and devotion and of the identification of the soul of the self, that is, Atman, with the soul of the Universe, that is, Brahman. Since they preached and wrote not in Sanskrit but in the regional languages, Hindi, Bengali, Marathi, Punjabi, as well as in Tamil, Telugu and Malayalam, the message of the Upanishads quickly and easily filtered into the hearts of the both literate and illiterate masses.

Most of the religious reformers appeared on the scene in the fourteenth and the fifteenth centuries which saw the disintegration of the Delhi sultanate which had earlier supplanted the rule of the Brahmanical and the Buddhist monarchs.People of both the older religion of Brahmanism, Jainism and Buddhisim as well as of the newer faith, Islam, suffered from a feeling of social and political insecurity and disillusionment and sought shelter in the religion of love and devotion and of the oneness of god.

16

Disciples of the Ascetics in the Sultanate Period kept up their Gurus' Work Alive in the Succeeding Centuries

The spread of the message of the Upanishads did not end with their preachers in the fourteenth and the fifteenth centuries. The disciples and followers of these religious reformers, in the subsequent centuries, joined the sects of their gurus or founders, kept up their work, wrote on their life and teachings and produced biographies and commentaries.

As a matter of fact, as in the fourteenth and the fifteenth centuries, so in the sixteenth and the seventeenth centuries, a crop of religious poetical literature, marked by the exposition of either Krishna worship or Rama cult kept the Upanishadic message of love and devotion not only alive but also carried it to the hearts of the millions of unlettered and uneducated people in and outside the Muslim India.

Writers in the Brajabhumi

Many writers of the former faith flourished in the Brajabhumi, which corresponded roughly to the Yamuna valley, and exerted an influence of the Rama cult beyond its borders. Among the eight disciples of Vallabhacharya and his son Vithal Nath, grouped under the name of

"Astachap", the most notable was Surdas, "the blind bard of Agra," who, writing in Brajabhasa, described in his Sursagar the sports of Krishna's early life, and composed many verses on the charm of Krishna and his beloved Radha. The other important poets in this school were Nanda Das, author of the *Ras-Panchadhyayi*; Vithal Nath, author of *Chaurasi Vaishnava Ki Varta* in prose; Paramananda Das, Kumbhan Das, and Ras Khan who was a Muslim disciple of Vithal Nath and wrote *Prema Vartika.*

Tulsi Das

Among the writers of the Rama cult, the most illustrious was, however, Tulsi Das (1532-1623), who lived in Benares, "unapproachable and alone in his niche in the temple of Fame." He was not merely a poet of a high order, but a spiritual leader of the people of the country where his name had become a household word and his memory is worshipped by the millions of his countrymen. He was a Rama-bhakta and the most famous of his work, known as *Ramacharitamanas* or "the Pool of Rama's Life," has been justly described by George Grierson as "the one Bible of a hundred million people" of the country. Growse also observed in his translation of the *Ramayana* of Tulsi Das that "his book is in everyone's hands, from the court to the cottage and is read and heard and appreciated alike by every class of the Hindu community, whether high or low, rich or poor, young or old."

Vaishnava Writers in Bengal

In Bengal, a brilliant outburst of Vaishnava literature including its various branches such as the Karchas or notes, the Padas and songs and the biographies of Chaitanya Deva kept alive in the minds of the people not only the Upanishadic message of love and devotion but also served as a mirror of the social life of the province of that age. The most prominent among the Vaishnava writers were chronologically: Brindaban Das, born in 1507, the author of *Chaitanya Bhagavata*; Jayananda, born in 1513, the author of *Chaitanya Mangal*; Krishnadas Kaviraj, born in 1517 of a vaidya family of Jhamalpur in Burdwan, the author of *Chaitanyacharitamrita*; Trilochan Das, born in 1523, the author of a biography of Chaitanya Deva also titled as *Chaitanya Mangal*. Narahari Chakravarty's *Bhaktiratnakar*, a voluminous biography of Chaitanya Deva written in fifteen chapters, is considered to be next in importance to the works of Krishnadas Kaviraj.

This period in Bengal also witnessed the production of numerous translations of the two great epics, the *Ramayana* and the *Mahabharata*, the *Bhagavata Gita*, and the books in praise of Chandi Devi and Manasa Devi. The most important of these works were the *Mahabharata* of Kasirama Das and the Kavikankan Chandi of Mukundaram Chakravarti, both of which enjoy to this day as much popularity in Bengal as the *Ramayana* of Tulsi Das in the Uttar Pradesh and Bihar.

Essence of the Survival of Our Religion

In the ultimate analysis, what survived of our religion in India under the Muslim rule is not so much of the orally transmitted and later written manuscripts of the four Vedas, the Brahmanas and the Aranyakas which were no doubt continued to be cultivated in the Vedic schools across the Vindhyas or in the Himalayas but of the Upanishads which speak of the Brahman and the Atman, of the Absolute and the Self and of love and devotion as the gateway to the achievement of salvation or liberation from the bondage of the cycle of birth and death. Brahman is represented in all the gods and the goddesses worshipped by the generations of the Aryans and among the two deities that hold the most prominent place are the Siva and the Krishna. The cult of the Siva and the Krishna as well as the story of the Ramayana and the Mahabharata represent the essence of the Upanishads. And while the Sanskrit version of the two great epics remained a close preserve of the priestly classes of the Vedic schools, their translation into regional languages reached the core of the hearts of the non-Muslim masses, often through the Kathak or the Reader or the Speaker of the sacred scriptures to the illiterate and uneducated who were the majority among them, and kept the flames of our religion burning in their hearts.

It must be admitted here that the survival of our religion in the medieval India under the rule of Islam was more by an accident than by any determined effort of the non-Muslim subjects. An accident because of the inability of the Muslim rulers to penetrate the remote areas where the non-Muslim chiefs remained independent and could patronise the Vedic schools and their managers, the priestly classes. In some remote areas the subjugated non-Muslim chiefs almost remained independent after sending regular tributes and gifts to Delhi and Agra and they could follow their religion without any hindrance or intervention from the ruling class. Secondly, the emergence of the vernacular languages and the presence of some tolerant provincial Muslim rulers who took an interest in some of the Sanskrit treatises including the two great epics, the Ramayana and the Mahabharata and got them translated into the vernaculars and thereby provided an access to a few literates among the non-Muslims, mostly members of the priestly classes, who could read them out at the gathering of villagers at the village temple or at the residence of the village headman. And finally, the appearance of the ascetics and the religious reformers was not a guaranteed one. They appeared sporadically and occasionally and were mostly based in a particular region or a province and could hardly interact with other places and people who spoke a different vernacular language despite the fact that many of them travelled widely on foot either in search of a guru, or for debates on religion and for enrichment of personal knowledge and experience. We may describe the chanced survival of our religion under a persecuting Islam, which did not even spare the ascetics who led a detached life, of more than six hundred years as a feat which is nothing short of a miracle.

Part Four

Revival of Our Religion

17

Rebirth of Sanskrit

The keys to the revival of our religion lay in the revival of Sanskrit. We know that our religious scriptures were orally composed and transmitted in Prakritas later refined as Sanskrita and only from fifth century onwards following the Buddhist example, they were put into writing. We have also seen that in the middle ages, Sanskrit lay buried under the impact of thc Persian which was the language of the courts and institutions and received further blows at the hands of the rising vernaculars and a new language, Urdu. Its use remained mainly confined to the dwindling number of the priestly classes who were called upon to perform the Vedic rituals of the pious non-Muslims as well as to the few Vedic schools that managed to survive the wrath of an intolerant Muslim ruler. In some of the neighbouring kingdoms under non-Muslim rulers, the language did flourish in the Vedic schools but only for a short period as they were also gradually brought under the control of the Muslim rule. By the time of the Mughals, it was scarcely used except in the Vedic schools in the Maratha kingdom, Rajasthan, Punjab and Nepal. When the keys to the understanding of our religious scriptures were rusting and fast falling into disuse, it could hardly be expected that the knowledge about our religious scriptures would remain alive.

Yet almost a miracle happened and it happened with the coming of the East India Company to Bengal in 1690. In 1757 the East India Company in alliance with the rebels against Siraj-ud-daula, the ruling Nawab of Bengal, defeated the latter in the legendary battle of the Plassey, put Mirjafar on the throne of Bengal and in 1765 acquired the Diwani rights of Bengal, Bihar and Orissa and thereby became the de facto ruler of these provinces. In the early 1770s some of the officials of the East India Company including Warren Hastings, despite their pre-occupation with administration and trade of the Company, took an interest in the past history of their newly occupied territories and stumbled upon the dying literary language of the country, that is, Sanskrit.

There is, no doubt, that Sanskrit was known to the Arab scholars, some of whom travelled as far as Benares to learn it and that the Jesuit fathers like Hanxleden who during his stay in Malabar from 1699 to 1732 compiled the first Sanskrit grammar in a European tongue and Coeurdoux mastered the language much before the East India Company officials took an interest in it. Father Coeurdoux was also the first student to recognize in 1767 the kinship of Sanskrit and the languages of Europe and suggested that the the Brahmanas of India were descended from one of the sons of Japhet, whose brothers migrated to the West. However, the British officials were the first to make an organized attempt to diffuse the knowledge of Sanskrit and the literatures written in Sanskrit in and outside India and thereby not only brought to the knowledge of the contemporary non-Muslims their almost buried and lost religious scriptures but also an insight into their glorious past history, culture and civilization which existed in the country before the coming of the Muslim invaders and conquerors.

In 1783 William Jones(1746-94), a Persian scholar and a linguist genius at Oxford was appointed a judge of the newly founded Calcutta Supreme Court and in that capacity he founded in 1784 the Asiatic Society of Bengal with thirty elite English members to investigate into the arts and sciences of Asia. Jones learned Sanskrit from the friendly Bengali pundits and a fellow official, Charles Wilkins(1749-1836) who published the first English translation of the *Bhagavad Gita* in the journal of the Asiatic Society, *Asiatick Researches,* in 1784 and of the *Hitopadesha,* in 1787 respectively. In 1789 Jones translated Kalidasa's Sakuntala which later went into five English translations in less than twenty years. When Goethe of the *Faust's* fame read the German translation of the *Sakuntala* by George Forster, sent to him by Johann Gottfried Herder, a leader of the Romantic Movement in German literature, in 1791, he wrote a poem on it in *Deutsche Monatsschrift,* which is quite famous now. Meanwhile, Jones followed his work on *Sakuntala* by translating the *Gita Govinda* of Jayadeva in 1792 and the *Dharmashastras* of Manu which was published posthumously under the title, *Institutes of Hindu Law* in 1794.

Jones and Wilkins were followed by Henry Colebroke (1765-1837), H.T. Prinsep (1792-1878) and Horace Hayman Wilson (1789-1860). Sanskrit was first taught in 1805 at the training college of the East India Company at Hertford while the first chair of Sanskrit, the Boden Professorship, was created at Oxford and conferred on Horace Hayman Wilson in 1832. Across the English Channel it was the French scholar, Anquetil-Duperron who published in 1786 a translation of four Upanishads from a seventeenth century Persian translation by Dara Shuko. The translation of the whole Persian manuscript of the 50 Upanishads under the title, *Oupnek'hat*, in Latin was completed in 1801 and thereby Europe was introduced for the first time to the Indian religious thought and philosophy and attracted a host of European scholars and philosophers in the nineteenth century.

As a matter of fact, it is not merely in translating the Upanishads but also in acquainting the European scholars with Sanskrit that France took the lead. In 1795 was founded *École des Langues Orientales Vivantes* where Alexander Hamilton(1762-1824), one of the founding members of the Asiatic Society of Bengal, now held a prisoner on parole in France at the end of the Peace of Amiens in 1803, became the first person to teach Sanskrit in Europe. It was from Hamilton that Friedrich Schlegel of Germany learnt the language and he was the first German to learn it. France also took the lead in establishing a university chair in Sanskrit at Collège de France in 1814 and the first Sanskrit scholar to hold it was Léonard de Chézy.

Germany soon followed France. In 1816, Franz Bopp (1791-1867), a Bavarian, succeeded in very tentatively reconstructing the common ancestor of Sanskrit and the classical languages of Europe on the basis of the hints of William Jones and thus, comparative philology became an independent discipline. And from 1818 onwards the country began to establish university chairs in Sanskrit in almost all leading and larger universities including Leipzig where the great Sanskrit scholar MaxMüller (1823-1900) was a student between 1841 and 1843. It was MaxMüller who first edited the Rigveda and the great series of authorative annotated works on the *Sacred Books of the*

East in fifty volumes in 1879-1900. However, his interest in our religious scriptures arose mostly as a secondary interest to Sanskrit which bore a striking resemblance to the classical European languages, Greek and Latin, and like most other European scholars of the time in Sanskrit, was set out to identify its roots with them. We all know that he spent the major part of his working life as the Professor of Comparative Philology at Oxford, England.

In 1821, Société Asiatique was founded in Paris, followed two years later by the Royal Asiatic Society in London. From these beginnings the work of the editing and study of ancient Sanskrit literature went on apace throughout the nineteenth century. Probably the greatest achievement of the Indological scholarship in the nineteenth century Europe was the enormous Sanskrit-German dictionary known as the St. Petersburg Lexicon, produced by the German scholars, Otto Böhtlingk and Rudolf Roth, and published in parts by the Russian Imperial Academy of Sciences from 1852 to 1875.

While the work of these European scholars in translating our religious scriptures as well as in commenting on them led to an awareness in the minds of the interested scholars in countries other than Europe, say, the USA and Canada, about the existence of a religion much older than Christianity and Islamism, whose genesis could be traced back to the hymns of the sages dated some 1500 years before the beginning of the Christian era, in India it led to a rebirth and reawakening of a dying religion and culture among a community long used to living in subjugation as Kaffers or Zimmis under an alien rule and religion, without any religious freedom of their own, for more than 650 years.

However, the small group of the researchers of the

Asiatic society whose work had led to this discovery soon began to lose its importance in the face of the rising utilitarianism at home which now began to send young officials in the employ of the East India Company imbued with the ideas of James Mill and Jeremy Bentham to modernize India, which meant an introduction of Western education, ideas and values. In the General Committee of Public Instruction formed in 1823, twenty years after the Charter Act of 1813 had sanctioned Rs. one lac for the education of the people of the country, to disburse the amount, they began to increasingly oppose the work of the Orientalists till they came out successful with the support from Macaulay, who came to India as a Law Member of the Governor-General's Council in 1834, in his Minute on education dated 2 February l835. The Governor-General Bentinck who had been greatly under the influence of the philosophy of James Mill and Jeremy Bentham and who had been waiting for an opportunity to carry forward his twin objectives of a gradual replacement of Persian by English in all official works as well as the spread of the English language in all educational institutions was actually waiting for an expert advice to proceed further. He now found it in Macaulay's Minute and so immediately, without waiting for an approval of his action from London, he passed a resolution on 7 March 1835, stating that "the great object of the British Government, ought to be the promotion of European literature and science amongst the natives of India and that all funds appropriated for the purposes of education would be best employed in English education."

The resolution thus, practically ended the honeymoon of the British Orientalists, atleast officially, with further scholarly works in Sanskrit but they were allowed to retain the existing Oriental institutions and the expenses involved in supporting them. Fortunately for us, by that time, a Sanskrit College in Benares in 1791 and another in Poona in1821 and still another in Calcutta in 1824 had come into existence as well as two more Oriental colleges at Agra and Delhi in 1824 and 1825 respectively had started functioning; provision for financial assistance to some tols and madrashas had been made and Oriental scholars had been employed to translate English books containing useful knowledge into Arabic, Persian and Sanskrit and had undertaken the task of printing and publication of Oriental manuscripts. All these activities of the Orientalists had now made the learned people at large in and around Calcutta aware of a glorious religion, civilisation and culture in ancient India and made them really proud of their past heritage and heralded the dawn of a Renaissance, which first began in Bengal.

18

Back to the Vedas and the Upanishads

The Anglicists in the General Committee of Public Instruction who had opposed the work of the Orientalists also derived support, apart from Macaulay and Bentinck, from a group of young men in and around Calcutta who saw a knowledge in English as a passport to the employment opportunities offered by the various official and non-official establishments in the country. The English education in the country had already been fuelled by a number of missionary schools opened in and outside Calcutta which attracted mainly the students from the lower castes of the society. In 1815 David Hare, a watch maker by profession in collaboration with some of the leading intellectuals of the country including Rammohan Roy drew up a plan for an institution at Calcutta, which came into existence, despite the withdrawal of Roy at the last stage for his bold views on religion which were opposed by the orthodox section of the society, in January 1817, with 20 scholars receiving tuition in English, Bengali and Persian. This was followed by the creation, through the combined efforts of the Indians, Europeans and the missionaries, of the Calcutta School Book Society in 1817 and of the Calcutta School Society in 1819. By 1821 the latter had under its umbrella some 115 vernacular schools with a total strength of 3, 328 pupils.

However, in the late 1820s the excesses committed by the missionaries in making converts from the lower castes of the society as well as by some of the students of the school set up in 1817 and now known as the Hindu College, who, under the leadership of Derozio (1809-1831), went to the extreme of denouncing their own religion which, over the past centuries under the Muslim rule without any current of new philosophical thinking and ideas, like a pool of stagnant water which attracts weeds and insects, had now grown many vices and abuses into it. These came under attack by the Western educated students of the Hindu College. While some of them violated the religious code in food and drinks, others went to the extreme of denouncing it further by embracing Christianity. This really created some kind of trend among the contemporary Western educated students of other metropolition cities like Bombay and Madras, who began to denounce and ridicule their own religion.

This greatly alarmed the priestly classes of the orthodox section of the society which had now become aware of a glorious religious past, culture and civilisation. Freed from the shackles of a suffocating Muslim rule and now breathing a free and fresh air in religious matters under the British Raj which, as a matter of policy, hardly interfered with the religion of the people, they now attempted to tighten their grip on our religion. However, the most enlightened among them differed from the orthodox group and gave a call to the people of the country for a return to the Vedas. As against this, there were other enlightened reformers among the Western educated elite who had gone through our religious scriptures very deeply as well as had studied other religious literature very critically and they now wanted to proceed forward more cautiously along the line of least resistance in giving our religion a progressive, reformed and modern outlook.

Rammohan Roy (1772-1833) and the Brahma Samaj

Rammohan Roy belonged to the last group of the religious reformers we have mentioned above. Born in 1772 in an aristocratic and affluent Brahman family in Calcutta, Roy began his career in the service of the East India Company. He was the first among the Western educated enlightened Indians who was greatly affected by the prevalent state of the religion when a sati took place in his own family. Roy delved deep in our religious scriptures to find evidences of such an act and found none. In the process he was greatly impressed by the works of our sages and thought of reviving the Brahmanical or the Vedic religion based on the teachings of the Upanishads, after its years of depression under the Muslim rule. Well-versed not only in Sanskrit but also in Arabic and Persian, he was the most learned man of his times. He was the founder of the first vernacular newspaper in India, *Samachar Darpan*, in 1818, in association with the Serampore missionaries, Carey, Marshman and Ward. By his deeds and writings, he was to herald the dawn of a Renaissance in the country, which first began in Bengal.

Rammohan Roy attempted an assimilation of the Eastern religious ideas with the Western ones to get rid of our society of the existing vices and superstitions like sati, child-marriage and infanticide. For this purpose, he delved deep not only in the study of our sacred literature but also in those of Christianity and Islam and came forward with a strong belief in the unity of god-head preached by all religious scriptures, including our Rigveda and the Upanishads. This conception of true god formed the basis of the Vedanta College he set up in 1826 as well as later, of his Brahma Sabha. In the trust deed of 8 January 1830, he directed that the house which was constructed for the Brahma Sabha was to be used as a place for "public meeting of all sorts of descriptions of people without distinction" for the worship of one god only and there would be no worship of any images with rituals.

From the Brahma Sabha to the Brahma Samaj

This Brahma Sabha later formed the basis of his Brahma Samaj. There is a ridiculous belief among many of us that Rammohan's Brahma Dharma which forms the basis of his Sabha and Samaj is different from our Vedic religion. Absolutely not. It is the Brahman of the Upanishads, the Vedanta or the end of the Vedas which inspired his ideas and he attempted through the creation of the Brahma Dharma to purify our religion by stripping it many of the vices and superstitions it had acquired over the centuries under the rule of Islam and adjusting it to the needs and the requirements of the time created by an inflow of the Western ideas and values in the metropolitan cities of the country. It is easy to see why the idea of the Brahma Samaj and the Brahma Dharma is usually and generally limited to the Western educated families. It is true that Rammohan Roy discarded the worship of images which he felt probably not necessary to invoke the spirit of the Brahman but he never gave us any indication that he was setting up an order different from the religion of his father and fore- fathers. He remained a Brahmana, wore the sacred thread as did his contemporary Brahmanas till his death and never allowed any non-Brahman to enter the room of the Brahma Sabha where the Vedas were recited by the orthodox Brahmanas.

Rammohan Roy's Successors

Rammohan's successor Devendranath Tagore at the Brahma Samaj went further in declaring the Vedas which were the basis of the organization as a divine revelation. When this evoked a strong protest from the younger members of the Samaj under Akshay Kumar Dutta, Devendranath Tagore made a compilation of select passages from the Upanishads indicating the idea of one god and replaced the Vedantic covenant with a new one embodying the principles of universal theism.

Keshab Chandra Sen (1838–1884)

It was the fervent devotion, passionate enthusiasm and wonderful power of eloquence of Keshab Chandra Sen that made the Brahma Samaj popular. Keshab joined the Brahma Samaj in 1857 and Devendranath Tagore was quick to appreciate the services of Keshab in introducing an element of devotional fervour in the organization. However, when the young members under Keshab's leadership began to advocate and openly celebrate inter-caste marriages and widow remarriage and to insist that the Brahmana ministers wearing sacred threads should not be allowed to preach from the pulpits, the relationship between Devendranath Tagore and Keshab Chandra Sen became strained. Since Devendranath Tagore did not want the Samaj to move away from the path as laid down by Rammohan Roy, he dismissed Keshab and his followers from all offices of trust and responsibility. Keshab accepted this challenge and started a separate organization in 1865 consisting of members who chafed at the use of Sanskrit texts and at the performance of Vedic rituals on the occasions of socio-religios functions of the non-Muslim community.

Under Keshab's inspiration the Brahma Samaj introduced women as members and adopted a moderate programme of social reform including abolition of child marriage and polygamy and sanction of widow remarriage and inter-caste marrIages.

Sadharan Brahma Samaj

However, Keshab's moderate views about female education and female emancipation as well as the practice of prostrating, *à la mode de Vaishnava,* at each other's feet, particularly at the feet of Keshab who came to be regarded as a divine incarnation caused a further schism when he performed the marriage of his fourteen year old daughter with the Maharaja of Coochbihar in March 1878. The seceeders now formed a different Brahma Samaj under the name of the Sadharan Brahma Samaj. Thus, within twenty years since 1857 when Keshab joined the Brahma Samaj, it went through a deviation not only from the path of Rammohan Roy but also a transformation in line with the progressive ideas of its succeeding young members.

Parthana Samaj

In Maharashtra, in 1867, was set up under the guidance of Keshab Chandra Sen the Parthana Samaj which reflected the activities of the Sadharan Brahma Samaj in Bengal and under the guidance of the justice Mahadev Govinda Ranade the latter turned out to be the centre of many activities for social reform in the Western India. However, thc members of the Parthana Samaj as followers of Namdev, Tukaram, and Ramdas were devoted theists and never "looked upon themselves as adherents of a new religion or of a new sect, outside and alongside of the general Hindu body, but simply as a movement within it."

Swami Dayananda Saraswati(1824-1883) and the Arya Samaj in the Punjab

In the Punjab, the Brahma Samaj movement started at Lahore in 1863 but was subverted by Swami Dayananda Saraswati who was at first attracted to the former and actually held a meeting at Calcutta in 1869 to come to terms with it. However, nothing came out of it and the Arya Samaj ultimately overwhelmed and absorbed the Brahma Samaj movement in the Punjab.

A great Sanskrit scholar without any English education, Dayananda's motto was "Go back to the Vedas" and asserted that "any scientific theory or principle which is thought to be of modern origin may be proved to be set forth in the Vedas." Founder of the Suddhi movement for the conversion of the persons belonging to the non-Brahmana religion to Brahmanism, he set up in 1876 at Kathiawar the Arya Samaj with a similar social reform programme of the Brahma Samaj in Bengal. Like Rammohan Roy he believed in one god and decried the worship of images. He did not confine his teachings to an intellectual elite but directly appealed to the masses in a very plain and simple language. His appeal to the masses was a tremendous success in the Punjab and the Uttar Pradesh and the Arya Samaj movement gathered considerable momentum in these two places.

Split in the Arya Samaj

However, as in the case with the Brahma Samaj in Bengal,

a new generation of leaders led by Lala Hansraj and Lala Lajpat Rai sprang up within the Arya Samaj movement who saw the value of English education and set up in 1885 the Dayananda Anglo-Vedic College at Lahore. This was certainly contrary to the wishes of the founder of the Arya Samaj movement and soon in 1892 it splitted itself into two groups—one led by Lala Hansraj who advocated modern education as a progressive force for social reform and the other by Munshi Ram, later known as Swami Sradhananda who "endeavoured to be not modern but Vedic and harkened back to the traditional Brahman ideal of ascetic Sanyasis."

In 1902, Munshi Ram founded a remarkable educational institution known as the Gurukul, based on the ancient tradition of a Vedic school, in Hardwar. As the name suggests, the students from faraway places came here at the age of seven or eight to reside for not less than sixteen years with their gurus with vows of poverty, chastity and obedience. Sanskrit was the common language and the most important discipline was the Vedas. However, English and courses on modern sciences were also included.

Ramakrishna Paramahansa (1836-1886)

The question of incompatibility of worship of thc images of the gods and the goddesses with the belief in the existence of one god or one supreme power found its answer in the preachings of Ramakrishna Pramahansa, a poor priest from a rural village in Hooghly in a temple at Dakshineswar near Calcutta. And despite being without any formal education, he had a deep faith in the inherent truth of all religions, Brahmanism, Islamism and Christianity. According to him, "all the different religious views are but different ways leading to the same goal." He further says that as different words in different languages denote the same connotation, so also Allah, Hari and Christ are but different names under which we worship the same god. He is both one and many, with and without forms, and may be conceived either as a great universal spirit or through different symbols.

In his own life Ramakrishna demonstrated not only the compatibility of the worship of the goddess Kali with the highest spiritual life seeking Brahman or the universal soul but also proved that worship of images could be utilized as an excellent means of developing spiritual fervour in human beings. Ramakrishna's broad catholicity, mysticism and ardent spiritual fervour attracted a small number of occasional visitors, mostly from Calcutta, who heard his views in short pithy sayings and parables, many of which were collected by Mahandra Nath Gupta and published before his death as *Ramakrishna Kathamrita.*

Vivekananda (1863-1902) and the Ramakrishna Mission.

Among the visitors was a young graduate from Calcutta University and though initially highly critical of Ramakrishna, later became his most trusted and beloved disciple. He was Narendranath Dutta, later known as Swami Vivekananda (1863-1902). Narendranath's learning, eloquence, spiritual fervour and wonderful personality attracted a band of followers including prince and peasant who helped him to attend in 1893, after untold sufferings, the "Parliament of Religions" at Chicago. In his speeches, for the first time in the history of modern India, he boldly asserted the superiority of the Vedic religion, culture and civilization, the greatness of her past and the hope for the future. His speeches at the Chicago Parliament of Religions won him friends and fame and from that day, the teachings of Ramakrishna as interpreted by him came to be recognized as a force behind the formation of Ramakrishna Mission and monasteries which came into existence first in the USA and then in India since 1898.

In Swami Vivekananda the patriotic and spiritual impulses mingled and blended in a supreme desire to uplift the people of India and to restore them to a proper place among the nations of the world. As Valentine Chirol has correctly described him as "the first Hindu whose personality won demonstrative recognition abroad for India's ancient civilization and for the new-born claim to nationhood."

Both Ramakrishna and his disciple, Vivekananda are ascetics of the first order who have renounced the world. While Ramakrishna realized the Brahman in the goddess Kali he worshipped at the Dakshineswar temple, Vivekananda realized his, further in the souls of the deprived and the down-trodden people of the country. In words and deeds, he tried to uplift them from the position they had been assigned to for centuries past and it is specially for them that he endeavoured to set up the Ramakrishna Mission.

The Ramakrishna Mission

The Ramakrishna Mission, as set up by Vivekananda, has therefore no intention of developing into a sect like the Brahma Samaj of Rammohan Roy or the Arya Samaj of Dayananda Saraswati. It holds up the Vedantic philosophy as interpreted by Vivekananda as its ideal and aims at the development of the highest spirituality inherent in human beings. And this highest spirituality can only develop out of the Upanishads which are, according to him, "the great mine of strength. . . . Freedom, physical freedom, mental freedom and spiritual freedom are the watch words of the Upanishads." At the same time the Ramakrishna Mission emphasises the value and the utility of the worship of the images as manifestations of the Brahman or the universal soul. It remains to this day a monastic order disseminating the reforming ideas among the masses without violently uprooting them from their socio-religious moorings. It has set up many schools, colleges and dispensaries and has rendered ungrudging help to the people in distress caused by famine, flood or any other natural calamity. It remains a strong force rejuvenating Vedic and Upanishadic ideas and values among the people of the country.

Vivekananda and Sankara (788–820)

Vivekananda's organization of the Ramakrishna Mission reminds us of Sankara's organization of the Vedic mathas and temples. Both died very young—Sankara at the age of 32 and Vivekananda at the age of 39. Both left behind them an impeccable and indelible record in the interpretation of the Vedanta and in the revival of our religion at a very critical time of our history.

Theosophical Society and Annie Besant(1847-1933)

Another organization which contributed to the revival of our religion was the Theosophical Society set up by Madame H.P. Blavatsky and Col. H.S. Olcott of the United States at New York in 1875. They moved to India in 1879 and set up their headquarters at Adyar near Madras in 1886 and began publishing materials on our religion and

Theosophy. The West came to know more about our religious ideas and practices from these and attracted noted Western intellectuals like W.B. Yeats who helped Tagore's translation of Gitanjali which later fetched Rabindranath his Nobel prize, Aldous Huxley and Christopher Isherwood. The Society later opened many branches all over India and became an important factor in socio-religious reform in South India.

However, the contribution of the Society was mainly through Annie Besant(1847-1933), an Irish lady, who after joining the Society in 1887 settled down in India at the age of 46. Besant held the current problems of India could be solved by reviving the ancient ideals and institutions. As she wrote in her autobiography in 1893: "The Indian work is, first of all, the revival, strengthening, and uplifting of the ancient religions.This has brought with it a new self-respect, a pride in the past, a belief in the future, and, as an inevitable result, a great wave of patriotic life, the beginning of the rebuilding of a nation." And with that end in view she started, in 1898, with her own resources the Central Hindu School in Benares which gradually developed into a college and ultimately into the "Hindu" University in 1916. Besant trained a young man, Jiddu Krishnamurthi who was educated in England, to take over from her the society's leadership. She declared him as the Messiah of the newly founded "Order of the Star in the East." However, Jiddu rejected the idea and became a teacher of the doctrine of Pure Awareness derived from Sankara's Advaita Vedanta.

In India and abroad, there were, however, many who considered the old usages and beliefs supported by the Society as retrograde in character and disliked its occult mysticism and in our opinion, however, it did send abroad a firm confirmation of our description as "Hindus" and our religion as "Hinduism" and this exportation from the Theosophical Society which was in touch with the Western intellectuals came now to be widely circulated in the West.

Aurobindo (1872-1950)

An almost a near contemporary of Annie Besant, who unconsciously found himself transformed from a Western educated militant nationalist to a dynamic path-breaker spiritualist deriving inspiration from our religious scriptures was Aurobindo. Born on 15 August 1872, he was taken to England with his two elder brothers with the express idea of grooming him for Indian Civil Service. In 1890 when he was at the King's College, Cambridge on a senior classical scholarship, he passed the ICS but at the end of the probationary period of two years he was disqualified for his failure to clear the riding examinaion. In 1893, Aurobindo left England with an appointment in the service of the Gaekwar of Baroda. It was at Baroda that Aurobindo transformed himself from an Occidentalist into an Orientalist, learning Sanskrit and acquiring a deep and critical knoweldge of our religious scriptures, civilisation and culture.

A great part of the last years of his service from 1902 onwards at Baroda was spent on leave in preparing for a Swadeshi Movement and in 1906 he left Baroda to fully participate in the Anti-Partition Movement that had began with Curzon's partition of Bengal in 1905. Faced with sedition charges in 1907 and next year implicated in the Alipur Conspiracy Case, he spent a year in jail as an undertrial and after his release, he brought out an English weekly, *Karmayogin* and a Bengali one, *the Dharma*, to revive the now disorganised nationalist movement but soon realised that his ideas were not matured for the time. In February 1910, he secretly withdrew to Chandernagore and from there next month sailed for Pondicherry, the capital of French India and settled down there. At Pondicherry, he severed his connection with natonalist politics and remained exclusively devoted to his spiritual work and yoga which he had begun earlier during his stay in the Alipur jail.

For four years he practised his yoga silently and in 1914, he started publishing a monthly philosophical journal, the *Arya,* where he gradually serialised most of his important works, *The Life Divine, The Synthesis of Yoga, Essays on the Gita* and *The Isha Upanishad.* At Pondicherry he at first lived a life of retirement with four or five disciples but afterwards when more came to join his spiritual search, a community of sadhaks who believed in Aurobindo' s spiritual ideas had to be organized for those who had left every thing behind them.

And the task of organizing them in an Ashram was left to the Mother, who joined Aurobindo soon. The Mother who was born as Mirra, on 21 February 1878, in Paris, had gone through between the ages of 11 and 13 "a series of psychic and spiritual experiences about the existence of God and man's possibility of uniting with Him, of realising Him integrally in consciousness and action, of manifesting Him upon earth in a life divine." She first came to Pondicherry at the age of 36 and on 29 March 1914, she met Aurobindo and at once she realised that he was the guru who for many years had inwardly been guiding her spiritual development. She had to leave Pondicherry after 11 months because of the War but came back on 24 April 1920, resumed her work with Aurobindo at the Ashram, which she continued to do after Aurobindo's death in 1950. She left her mortal beings on 17 November 1973, at the age of ninety-five.

Aurobindo's Yoga, known as "Integral Yoga", attempted at uniting and harmonising the two ends of existence, Spirit and Matter. Most Yogas are paths to the Beyond leading to the Spirit, and in the end, away from life; Aurobindo rises to the Spirit to redescend with its gains bringing the light, power and bliss of the Spirit into life to transform it into a Life Divine. Aurobindo's "Integral Yoga" is based on his four realisations: the first was that of a silent, spaceless and timeless Brahman; the second was the realisation of the cosmic consciousness and the vision of the Divine as all beings; the third was the Supreme Reality with the static and dynamic Brahman as its two aspects and finally the higher planes of consciousness leading to the Supermind. Aurobindo continued the process of ascent into the higher planes of consciousness and of bringing down the power of these planes into the physical consciousness and his effort was crowned with success on 24 November 1926 when he experienced the descent of the "Godhead of the Overmind", the highest of the planes between Mind and Supermind, into the physical. This descent was preparatory to the descent of the Supermind itself by which the highest perfection in human mind could come.

Aurobindo worked towards this descent till 1950 when he left his human body. His legacy now lives in the Pondicherry Ashram created and developed "not for the renunciation of the world but as a centre and a field of practice for the evolution of another kind and form of life which would in the final end be moved by a higher spiritual consciousness and embody a greater life of the spirit." A new township near Pondicherry, Auroville, has also come into existence to perpetuate the memory of the Rishi Aurobindo.

The Return Journey and the Social Reform

The return journey to the Vedas and the Upanishads was often tuned to the requirements of the contemporary society and invariably led to an era of social reform. Some of the programme of the social reform as advocated by the ascetics in medieval India to arrest the exodus of the socially oppressed people to Islam, also figured in the preachings of those who attempted a revival of our religion in the nineteenth and the twentieth centuries. This reform programme laid emphasis primarily on the improvement of the position of our women who had suffered most since the occupation by the pre-Islamic Persian of the North-West in 519 BC, which led Manu to promulgate child-marriage. Under the rule of Islam women were affected not only by the incidence of child-marriage, but also by sati and infancticide which became a frequent occurrence in the country. The British rule added to their misery further when dowry as a social institution travelled from England to India. Every year shipload of young British damsels was dispatched by their parents to find husbands among the young officials of the Company (and later of the Crown) to escape the exorbitant dowry for them at home. (I have discussed this in detail while analyzing the development of the Anglo-Indian Community in my doctoral thesis at London later published by E.J. Brill at Leiden in 1971. See Bibliography).

19

Ascetics and their Contribution to the Saga of Revivalism in the British India

All the organizations that came into existence, after the knowledge of our past scriptures and heritage was unlocked by the European scholars, were either based on the Vedas or on the Upanishads or on both as modified by the teachings of their founders. We have already seen how the ascetics in the middle ages based their teachings mainly on the Upanishads to counter the increasing rigidity of the Brahmanical religion under the dominant and the suppressing influence of the Islam. In the British India, Ramakrishna's teachings represent a classic blend of what all the ascetics in the middle ages had tried to impress upon the common people—that god is one and the same in all the religions and whatever names a god in any religion may assume, he is the same and open to all who seek him through love and devotion. What Jesus is in Christianity, is Allah in Islam and Hari or Krishna in Brahmanism. We have seen at the very beginning of our work that the concept of one god as the supreme power is suggested towards the end of the Rigveda and is later fully developed in the Upanishadic concept of the Brahman or the Absolute. All the gods and the goddesses who are identified with the different forces of nature in the Rigveda are the manifestations of the same and the one Brahman, the Cosmos or the Universe as realized by Ramakrishna and his disciple, Vivekananda.

As a matter of fact, the British policy of non-intervention in religious matters created a fresh breeze which blew over our religion and many a mystic and saint flowered in the different parts of the country under their rule, who based their teachings on the Vedas and the Upanishads. Thus, to name a very few among them, there were Swami Narayan from Uttar Pradesh who set up his ashram in Gujarat, Loknath who after spending most of his years in the Himalayas came back to his place of birth at Burdwan in Bengal, Tailangaswami from Andhra Pradesh who stayed at Benares in Uttar Pradesh, Ramdas from the Punjab who set up his ashram as Kathiyababa at Brindaban in Uttar Pradesh, Balananda from Madhya Pradesh who lived in his ashram at Deogarh in Jharkhand, Mirabai in Rajasthan and Yashodabai in Uttar Pradesh—all preached about the existence of one god and one soul and emphasized the identification of the latter with the former only through love and devotion as the gateway to the path of salvation from the sufferings of the world.

Similarly, the Tamil mystic Ramana Maharishi (1879-1950), a contemporary of Aurobindo, taught Advaita at Tiruvannamali and attracted a large number of disciples including Westerners; the Paramahansa Yogananda (1890-1952) of Himachal Pradesh wrote a fascinating biography of his spiritual journey and founded the Self-Realization Fellowship in India and was later instrumental in founding another abroad at California and the Sant Sawan Singh (1903-48), the mystic of the Sant tradition from the Punjab, the founder of the Radhasoami Satsang at Beas taught "god-realization" instead of "self-realization". His teachings influenced a Protestant preacher, Dr. Julian Johnson to such an extent that she carried his ideas to the West. And there were many others at a lower level who by their teachings and deeds revived the Vedic and the Upanishadic ideas of our religion amongt us.

Many of these ascetics were either the followers of the Lord Siva or of the Lord Krishna (Vishnu) and still a fewer among them were the followers of the Goddesses Durga or Kali as the worshippers of the Sakti. They mostly came from the priestly classes with a background of the Vedic learning though a few among them often belonged to the classes other than the former. Most of them left their families and homes at the very early stages of their lives, began their search for the gurus across the countries for initiation to the Sannyas or renunciation from the world, and while some of them returned to their places of birth, others stayed behind either at their places of initiaion or elsewhere where they set up their own ashrams.

There are many among these ascetics of the British India like Loknath in Bengal, who are worshipped today by their own communities as divine incarnations and some among them across all the communities all over our country. We may cite here the examples of two such ascetics who are regularly worshipped in the temples dedicated to them by their devotees. The first in point of time in the Colonial India is Swami Narayan of Gujarat.

Swami Narayan (1781-1830)

Born as Ghanshyam in April 1781 in the rustic village of Chhapiya in Northern India of a Sarvaria Brahman pandit, Hariprasad Pande and his wife, Premvati, Swami

Narayan commenced Sanskrit studies under his father also known as Dharmadev at the age of seven and mastered the four Vedas by the age of ten and next year at the age of eleven, after his parents' death, he left Ayodhya for the Himalayas to begin his life work of establishing Ekantik Dharma. His mendicant garb consisted of a loin cloth only and his possessions included an image of Bal Mukund or Sri Krishna and a diary full of wise notes from his teacher-father, Dharmadev.

After travelling for seven years a distance of some 12,000 kms and visiting some 187 places, he settled down at Loj, a village near Mangrol in Southern Kathiawar in Gujarat as a disciple of Swami Ramanand, an eminent sadhu and exponent of the Vishishtadvait philosophy (qualified non-dualism) of Ramanujacharya of Shrirangam, in Saurashtra. And for the next thirty years after succeeding his guru Ramanand in 1801, he taught the Vishishtadvait philosophy and spearheaded a socio-religious renaissance in Gujarat attacking and eradicating animal sacrifices in yagnas, re-establishing the extinct *Brahmacharya Ashram*, enlightening the renunciate order which had become uncontrolled and wanton, laying down the ideals of self-control of the gurus and acharyas who had lapsed, attacking the custom of sati and giving women a well-defined status in the society. He taught purity of character to the shudras and subjugated the looting instincts of the Kathis and the Kolis. He admitted followers of other faith, Islam and Zoroastrian, into his order, advocated its members a purely vegetarian and non-alcoholic diet, boosted literature, music and fine arts.

To put in a nutshell, he was a proponent of the paths of pure bhakti and pure jnan, was a teacher of Bhagavat Dharma and extoller of the principles of the Vedas.

People adored him and worshipped him as an Avatar of Vishnu and his successor, Aksharbrahma Gunatitanand Swami, spread his glory and continued his mission of character-building and uplifting mankind. As Monier-Williams observed in 1887: "What I saw of their whole system, it convinced me that the Swami Narayanis are an energetic body of men and their sect an advancing one, without doubt the tendency of their doctrine is towards purity of life, which is supposed to be affected by suppression of the passions and complete devotion to the Supreme Being. In an honest desire to purify the Vaishnava faith this sect has done and is doing much good." In 1907 was set up, by Brahmaswarup Shastriji Maharaj, the Bochasanwasi Shri Akshar Purushottam Swaminarayan Sanstha, that is, BAPS, based on he Vedic teachings as propagated by Swaminarayan. It was intended to be a global socio-political organization committed to the moral and spiritual upliftment of the human-beings.

Sai Baba of Shirdi (—1918)

Each one of these ascetics since the days of the Upanishads including those who appeared in medieval and modern India were either a Sivabhakta, a Ramabhakta or a Vishnubhakta. Such an ascetic usually began with a small band of followers who shared his teachings and philosophy, which often gradually grew to a large number and develop into a particular sect reflecting the teachings and the ideals of its first guru or its founder. But the one among them who had never intended to do so and was quite satisfied with the well-being of his immediate neighbours, maintaining harmonious relations among them as his devotees, has now perhaps the largest number of the followers spread all over the country. And this great ascetic who led a very simple and detached life among the humble villagers and who was, in his mortal existence on the earth, easily accessible to all, irrespective of the castes and religion, classes and races, colours and creeds, and now lives in the heart of the million of us, is the Sai Baba of Shirdi.

The date and the place of his birth as well as his parentage are not known and he came to Shirdi as a teenager of sixteen years and one day the villagers found him in deep meditation under a neem tree. He made the place his home for the rest of his life except for a short time when he disappeared in the forest of the Aurangabad district and returned to Shirdi again with the marriage party of Chand Patil of Dhoop. And as he was alighting from the bullock cart at the foot of a banyan tree, the young Fakir was welcome as "Ya Sai" by Bhagata Mhalsapati, the owner of the land where the cart carrying the marriage-party had anchored. And thus, every body in the village began to address him as "Sai" at Shirdi where he achieved his mahasamadhi on the Vijaya Dasami day or Dussehra, on 15 October 1918.

Shirdi was inhabited by the poor people, peasants, artisans, craftsmen and cultivators who belonged to both Islam and the Vedic religion and the young mendicant who was accidentally given the name "Sai" became "Sai Baba" who looked after the well-being of the people who lived around him and took care of the latter in their sufferings and distress and often miraculously cured some of them of their diseases and illness by making himself suffer for their past and present sins. His love for them knew no bounds.Yet he could fly into a violent temper, raving and beating his disciples and often shocked them with conventional ideas of a guru by asking for money, which he never kept for himself but distributed it among the poor and the needy. And though we have no knowledge about his schooling, he could recite verses from the Gita and interpret these to the village folk who came to listen to him. With his frequent utterance of the words of "Allah Malik" and "Sab ka Malik ek hai" and with his emphasis on love and devotion, faith and patience for the attainment of the liberation of soul, Sai Baba echoed the philosophy of the Upanishads. He became a god to the villagers during his life-time and the latter erected for him who spent most of his living years in a dilapidated masjid, a Samadhimandir at Shirdi, now both a tourist and a pilgrimage center and attraction.

Ramakrishna and Sai Baba

There is, no doubt, Sai Baba resembled Kabir in his approach to create a bondage in his neighbourhood among the followers of Islam and the Vedas. Yet, there are striking similarities between the teachings of Sai Baba and Ramakrishna. Both taught in small examples or sayings, in symbols and stories and both never tried to propagate their own beliefs and ideas through a band of devotees and create a religion separate from the religion of his own followers. On the other hand, both tried to emphasise upon their followers the uniqueness of all religions and of all gods, for, the lord of all things, living or non-living, great or small, is one and the same. While Ramakrishna visited Church and Masjid, Sai Baba combined the celebration of Urs and Ram Navami in Shirdi. Apparently, more in the case of Sai Baba than in the case of Ramakrishna, the object could have been to create harmony among the followers of different religions and to do away with the distrust and misgiving that were then creeping in the contemporary society around Shirdi but they were basically based on the Upanishadic philosophy of one god and one religion, that is, the religion of love and devotion and the identification of the Brahman or the Universal Soul with the Atman or the Individual Soul. When the Self is lost in the Absolute, liberation from the cycle of birth and death is achieved.

The similarities between both Ramakrishna and Sai Baba could be carried further when one remembers that like Ramakrishna, Sai Baba also had a contemporary recorder of his life and deeds in the person of Hemadpant who wrote with Sai Baba's blessings *Shri Sai Satcharita* in Marathi language, later translated in English by Nagesh Vasudev Gunaji in1990. However, while Ramakrishna had a Vivekananda to organize his philosophy tinged with his own interpretation of the Upanishads into a mission called Ramakrishna Mission, Sai Baba did not have one. Yet, the ordinary milieu who came into contact with Sai Baba's deeds and teachings and with his motherly love and care for all carried them further to the people living far and wide and it will be a surprise today not to see a temple dedicated to the worship of Sai Baba in the remotest parts of the country.

While Swami Narayan was an extremely brilliant student of the Vedas and completed the courses in the Vedic school in the earliest possible time, Sai Baba like Kabir and Ramakrisha did not probably have any opportunity to learn them in such a school. Yet, he was aware of the contents of the Vedas and the Upanishads and could explain and comment on the slokas in the Gita to his disciples.

Tailanga Swamy (—1887)

Both Swami Narayan and Sai Baba are the classic

examples of the ascetics representing the Vishnu Bhagavata Sect. Among the Saiva Sect, it is that of Tailanga Swamy which is the most outstanding one. Nobody could definitely say when he was born but when he settled down in Benares at the beginning of the nineteenth cenury, he was said to be older than 200 years. He was said to be born of the second wife of Narasimha Rao, a petty zamindar in village of Holia in the Telengana region of the Andhra Pradesh. Narasimha Rao's second wife Vidyabati was a devout worshipper of the Lord Siva and the child was named Sivaram after the name of the Lord Siva. From his very childhood, he was drawn to asceticism and at the age of 40 after the death of his parents, he left his home and began to live in the cremation ground of the village where he first met Swamy Bhagirathananda Saraswati, an ascetic of a very high order from the Punjab and together they went on a tour of the pilgrim centres of the South and the North India. At Pushkar, Bhagirath Swamy initiated Sivaram to Sannyas with a new name, Ganapati Swamy. Afer ten years, Sivaram achieved his success as a great yogi, and at the age of 80, after the death of his Guru, he started on visiting the various pilgrim centres of the country before he came to Benares and settled down in an ashram in the city.

By that time he had displayed tremendous yogic power at Rameswaram and at the foothills of the Himalayas by bringing life to the dead persons and at Narmada, where he saved a sinking boat full of people from drowning in the river and while at Benares he cured many persons of their non-curable diseases. The people at Benares were mesmerised by his yogic power and looked upon him, as Ramakrishna described him later to his disciples at

Calcutta, "the living god Siva." They called him Tailanga Swamy as he hailed from Telengana. Most of the time he remained naked and floated on the river Ganges near the Dasashamedha Ghat. In his ashram he kept a Siva-Linga which he lifted alone from the bed of the river. It was so heavy that it needed atleast twelve persons to move it.

Many reknown ascetics came to Benares to offer their respects to him. In 1868, Ramakrishna met him at Benares, had discussion with him on the nature of god and affectionately fed him with kheer specially prepared for him. In January1887, he attained his Mahasamdhi and one month before it he allowed his disciple, Mangal Bhatta, to prepare a stone image which was installed in his ashram. As per his wish his body was put in a large box of sandal wood and was placed in the body of the river Ganges.

Ascetics like Swami Narayan, Sai Baba and Tailanga Swamy who continued the trend from the days of the Upanishads down through the middle ages when our Vedic religion was almost eclipsed, had numerous pious followers, and kept the message of the Upanishads alive. They appeared at a time when our society was greatly distressed and looked for a saviour to keep its moral alive. They are indeed the human incarnations of the Lord Krishna who had assured Arjuna in the Bhagavat Gita of his reappearance on the earth at its critical time.

20

Revivalism led to Militantism in Our National Movement and Politics

In the last few decades of the British rule in India the revived Vedic religion contributed to the growth of a militant nationalism in the freedom movement in the country. And extremist leaders both in Bengal and Maharashtra invoked the sprits of the Vedic gods and goddesses not only to provide strength to them in their struggle for freedom but also to rouse the dormant patriotism in the hearts of the masses. Thus, the extremist leader Balgangadhar Tilak introduced the Ganesh festival in Maharashtra which achieved his object of rousing the patriotism of the Marathi people during his own lifetime and after his death the Ganesh festival became extremely popular not only with the people of Maharashtra but also of the whole of India. Similar was the case of the worship of the mother goddess, Kali or Durga, as the embodiment of shakti invoked by the freedom fighters in Bengal and in the post-independent years a Bengali household which does not worship either one of the goddesses is unthinkable.

Madan Mohan Malaviya(1861-1946) and the "Hindu" Maha Sabha

Such religious fervour among political leaders struggling for the freedom of the country from the British rule could often crystallise into the formation of a political party with highly religious motif as it actually happened in the case of the political leader, Madan Mohan Malaviya who presided over the Indian National Congress in 1909, 1918, 1932 and 1933. A staunch orthodox Brahmin, Malaviya was a member of the Arya Samaj of Swami Dayananda. He stood for the revival of our ancient religious ideas and values and with that end in view he started a movement for the establishment of a "Hindu" University at Benares on the model of Besant's "Hindu" College and founded in 1909, a new political party, almost as a reaction to the formation of the Muslim League in 1906. The new political party, called "Hindu" Maha Sabha, opposed the ideas and values of the Congress and put more emphasis on "Hindutva" than on "Hindu" religion and attempted to unite all Indians professing the various sects of the "Hindu" Dharma against all kind of foreign influences. Malaviya's "Hindu" Maha Sabha gave a tremendous push to the description of our country as "Hindustan" and our religion as "Hindu" Dharma.

Revivalism after Independence: Vinayak Damodar Savarkar(1883-1966)

After Malaviya the most outstanding leader of the "Hindu" Maha Sabha was Vinayak Damodar Savarkar who chalked out a socio-religious programme for the new political party but was not much of a success when after the independence the Congress Party both at the Centre and the State level dominanted the governance of the country and pursued a secular policy inherited from the British, in religious matters.

Rashtriya Swayam Sevak Sangha (RSS) and Viswa "Hindu" Parishad

Malaviya's "Hindu" Mahasabha became the mother of two more socio-religious organizations, one formed before independence and the other in the post-independent years. In 1925, one of the members of the Hindu Mahasabha, K.V. Hedgewar (1890-1940), founded the Rashtriya Swayam Sevak Sangha (RSS), as a powerful cultural organization, to promote the interests of the followers of the Vedic religion against those of Muhammad and Christ. In post-independent years this organization has wielded considerable influence upon India's cultural and political life by sponsoring and upholding Vedic institutions and values such as temples, mathas and schools.The credit for building the RSS in its present form of a rigid institution with a para-military style of functioning and emphasis on discipline goes to M.S. Golwalkar, who served as second Sarsanghachalak or the supreme leader for 33 years from 1940 to 1973. Golwalkar remains the ideological guide of the RSS often mentioned in its literature as Shri Guruji. Its Swayamsevakas now spread over approximately 50000 villages and towns in the country. This organization inspired the formation in 1964 of a much broader one whose boundaries cross the geographical limits of the country. This is Viswa "Hindu" Parishad which has similar aims to those of the RSS and is instrumental in injecting a sense of national pride and identity in the followers of the Vedic religion not only in the country but also outside it.

Shyamaprasad Mukherjee(1901-53) and the Birth of Jana Sangh

However, both RSS and VHP soon realised that without political power and patronage, they could not realize their cherished dream of advancing the values and interests of the Vedic religion and culture when the country was dominated by the Congress Party which followed a secular policy left as a legacy of the British Raj's policy of non-intervention in the religious matters of the country. In 1951 Shyama Prasad Mukherjee founded a political party called Jana Sangh to give voice to "Hindu" nationalism and to oppose the dominant Congress Party at the Center. In the 1950s and the 1960s the Jana Sangh tried to become a major political party in the Hindi-speaking areas in the North by stressing policies such as the introduction of Hindi as the national language, a ban on the slaughter of the cows and the recognition of the Jewish State of Israel. All these issues are clearly anti-Muslims and so the Jana Sangh failed to dislodge the Congress Party which continued to capture power by riding on the prescribed programme of the former.

Janata Party

Following Emergency proclaimed by Indira Gandhi, in 1975, the Jana Sangh dissolved itself by joining other anti-Congress groups to form the Janata Party which defeated the Congress in the General Election of 1977, after the Emergency had been lifted in the country. However, the internal squabbles prevented the Janata Party under Morarji Desai to function effectively and the Congress Party under Indira Gandhi returned to power in 1980. The Janata Party fragmented itself after this defeat and in April of the same year the Bharatiya Janata Party was born.

The Bharatiya Janata Party (BJP), 1980

The BJP which came into existence in 1980 stands for the values associated with the Vedic religion as opposed to the secular values derived from the West and supported by the Congress. Inspired and guided by the RSS which has given shape to its programme on "Hindutva", BJP has attracted wide support from India's educated classes who are looking for an alternative to the Congress rule. While the BJP has an all-India appeal, there are other regional parties like the Shiv Sena founded by Bal Thackeray in 1966 in Maharashtra to look after the local interests of the Maharashtrians against the outsiders who though Indians by birth happen to live in Maharashtra. The party is opposed to Muslims as well as to Christians and is often responsible for many a communal violence in the country .

The BJP wanted to restore the glories of the Vedic religion but it acted on an erroneous philosophy, that is, the philosophy of revenge. When the Muslims came first as invaders and settled down as conquerors, they destroyed numerous temples and almost all the Buddhist viharas they came across to make room for their own mosques and masjids. One such mosque was created by the first Mughal invader Babar, the father of Humayun and the grand father of Akbar, the Great, around a place believed to have originally housed a temple dedicated to the legendary hero of the great epic, the Ramayana. The mosque was called the Babri masjid after the name of its creator and on 6 December 1992 this mosque was demolished by near 1100000 volunteers associated with the BJP, RSS and VHP thereby creating not only great social and political tensions in the country but also communal wounds which are yet to be healed. And when the BJP came to power in 1998, the BJP-led government attempted to saffronise the education by such things as the singing of Vandemataram and the Saraswati Vandana in all government run schools .This stirred a hornet's nest and raised loud protests from the minority communities as well as from some of its own allies in the government.

While the Saraswati Vandana could be traced to our religious scriptures particularly to those composed by the Sutrakaras between 400 and 200 BC, Vandemataram was the song composed by the late nineteenth century Bengali novelist Bankim Chandra Chatterjee in his *Anandamath* and was later tuned by Tagore and sung by the freedom fighters who fought against the British Raj. India is now not only a democratic country but also a plural and multicultural society and the government has to maintain, in the face of adopting a secular policy as a legacy from the British Raj, cordial relations among the different communities in the country. There is no denying the fact that in every age and in every country success and prosperity of a religion depends upon the support and encouragement provided by its government and reverse is the case when such actions are withdrawn by the latter which allows the religion to wither into oblivion. However, if such minor and superfluous actions of revivalism of the government as in the case of the last BJP Government in the country, seem to destroy peace and harmony amongst them, the government should better leave them to the non-government organizations to revive and keep alive our religion within certain guide lines as not to hurt the religious sentiments of the other groups and organizations in the country. As a matter of fact, revivalism of our religion on the lines of the Vedas and the Upanishads could best be done by both the visible and the invisible pillars of our religion, which we have delineated briefly in the succeeding chapter.

Nature of the Revivalism

The revivalism of our religion started correctly with Rammohan Roy who had a deep understanding of our religious scriptures, the Vedas, the Brahmanas, the Araynakas and the Upanishads. He set up a Brahma Samaj and not a "Hindu" Samaj and this current of the revealation of our religion also flowed with Dayananda in his setting up of the Arya Samaj and not a "Hindu" Samaj. Similarly, Ramakrishna discovered in his worship of the Goddess Kali a manifestaion of the Brahman, the supreme power and the soul of the Universe. So also did his disciple, Vivekanand, in the worship of the images of the gods and the goddesses, who further found Brahman living in the soul of all living persons and asserted that in a poor country like Bharat the best way to serve God is to serve the poor and the needy. He set up the Ramakrishna Mission in India and abroad to fulfill his object. Aurobindo went further than his predecessors in understanding the depth of our religion and in attempting to recreate it in the form of an "Integral Yoga" amongst us to transform each of our lives into a life divine.

One can say that, however, weak the intensity of the revivalism of our old religion could be, it proceeded on the right track as indicated by our Vedas and the Upanishads. However, when it passed from the hands of the enlightened religious reformers and persons and fell in the hands of our national leaders fighting against the British Raj, it lost its true character. First, Annie Besant and then Malaviya and his followers gave a vigorous push to our desription as "Hindus" and our religion as "Hindu" Dharma in India and abroad. And, despite, the eclipse of our religion which became almost lost and vanquished under Muslim rule of more than 650 years and rediscovered by the European Orientalists as the one of the Vedas and the Upanishads in the late eighteenth and the early nineteenth centuries, we remain till date as the carriers of the term "Hindu", which has nothing to do with the genesis and the evolution of the religious works of our sages who began composing their hymns years before 1500 B.C. to understand the mysteries of the Cosmos or the Universe. The Vedas were born out of this investigation into the mysteries of the Cosmos or the Universe just as the Upanishads were later concerned with the mysteries and sufferings of the human life. The Vedas and the Upanishads are not merely our religious scriptures but also our books of knowledge about our Universe and human life.

21

The Five Pillars of our Religion

After going through a period of revivalism which began with the efforts of the British officials of the East India Company in the late eighteenth century to unlock our past civilisation and culture, we can now assert that we have now a fairly good idea of our religion as it existed in the pre-Muslim days. Our religion has really become global now. As in ancient India, under the Mauryas and the Guptas, when our religion travelled with trade and commerce to the South-East Asian countries including Thailand, Indonesia, Combodia, Sumatra, Java and Borneo, and settled down there, so also in the nineteenth and the early twentieth centuries a bit of our religion accompanied the Indian labour recruited by the British administration in India for work in their projects on plantations, irrigations and railways in their colonies in South and East Africa, West Indies and a number of Pacific islands like Madagaskar and Mauritius. Beginning with Vivekananda who spoke about our religion in the 1893 Chicago Conference on the World Religion and a host of ascetics who have set up their ashrams in Europe and the United States from that date to teach spiritualism based on the Upanishads or the Vedanta to an Western audience since grown sick and tired of materialism, the world at large is now aware of a religion which has emerged not out of the teachings of a single prophet or of a saint but out of the hymns composed by a large number of sages who were engaged in their investigation into the mysteries of the Universe centuries before the beginning of the Christian era. With the awareness of the existence of a religion other than Buddhism, Christianity and Islam (in chronological order) and of its allied sciences on the yogas, jyotishas and ayurvedas, our religion is no longer in the depressing state as it had been for centuries under the rule of Islam before the coming of William Jones in 1783 as one of the judges of the Supreme Court in Calcutta. It will be worthwhile now to examine the basic pillars of our religion and to see how best these can be sustained in the present scenario of a fast changing world to keep our religion alive and vivacious.

Religious Scriptures

The most important among these five pillars are obviously our religious scriptures, the four Vedas, Brahmanas, Aranyakas, Upanishads and the two great epics, the Ramayana and the Mahabharata as well as the work of the Sutrakaras and the commentaries written on our religious scriptures since the beginning of the Christian era.

These religious scriptures composed, preserved and transmitted orally, with the help of a unique memory-power of the priestly classes, till they were put into writing around the fifth century AD, obviously form the first pillar of our religious wisdom which lay almost buried for more than six hundred years under the rule of Islam in India till they were retrieved by the work of the European scholars who were inspired by William Jones who founded the Asiatic Society of Bengal in Calcutta in 1784.

The scriptures were composed and written in Sanskrit which became eclipsed by the Persian in the middle ages and it was through the version of an European language that the Western educated Indians became aware of these treasures of our religion. The Sanskrit version can still be found in some surviving old Vedic schools and in the possession of the priestly families scattered in the different parts of the country. However, given the present status of the Sanskrit language as well as the status of the English language now mainly patronized by the urban professional middle classes, it is absolutely necessary to translate our religious scriptures in all the regional languages to take them to the home of all people who can have direct interaction with them. This way the knowledge of our religious scriptures could not remain a well-guarded monopoly of the priestly classes as well as of the few interested Western educated persons but a treasured object of the ordinary people. It may be argued that since nearly more than 25 per cent of our people are illiterate, according to the provisional Census Report of 2011, what will be the purpose served in preserving our religion by their translation in the regional languages? It will be easier for a Kathak or a Reader without a knowledge of the English and the Sanskrit traditionally associated with the dissemination of our religion to read out a portion of a religious scripture directly to the illiterate audience in its own spoken language and make it easily understood by them.

While the study of the Vedas continue to remain in the monopoly of the priestly classes who perform our socio-religious functions in accordance with the Vedic rituals, the Upanishads are open to all who want liberation from the cycle of death and birth. As we have said before, one is not required to go to a Vedic school to have a lesson from the Upanishads. What one needs is a guru who has achieved Nirvana or extinction of desires to teach a disciple in a secret session how to achieve it.

What is the basic essence of the Upanishads? The basic essence of the Upanishads, as has been agreed and accepted by all sections of the community which has descended from the historic Aryans, lies in the teachings of the Lord Krishna to his disciple, Arjuna which form the subject matter of the Gita, on the eve of the great Mahabharata War. There is hardly an educated family in the country that does not possess a copy of the Gita, either in its original Sanskrit or one in the local or the regional language.

Gita represnts the essence of the teachings of the Upanishads and as we have already seen that unlike the Vedas and the Vedangas which could be learnt in a Vedic school, the teachings of the Upanishads are to be learnt from a guru or a teacher who has realized Brahman. While such teachers are a rarity, most families have gurus to guide their disciples in all earthly and religious matters. A family's contacts with such gurus who may lead a full professional and family life may be few and far between but it can be said that in having a guru *à la mode de Upanishads,* the tradition of our old religion is not only preserved but also continued.

Ascetics

It is also continued in the group of ascetics who have always appeared in all ages, and in all centuries from ancient to modem times that have kept the flames of the Upanishads burning through their teachings of love and devotion, identification of the Atman or the self with the Brahman or the universal soul, to achieve liberation from the cycle of death and birth. They along with their followers could be divided at random in four major groups – Krishna Bhaktas, Siva Bhaktas, Rama Bhaktas and Sakti Bhaktas or the worshippers of the Mother Goddesses, Durga and Kali.

We have already gone through an analysis of a number ascetics who appeared in the medieval India and mentioned a few among them in the British India including a brief outline of the life and teachings of Swaminarayan of Gujarat, the Sai Baba of Shirdi and Tailanga Swamy who were ascetics *extraordinaire.* There are many among the recent ascetics who have given a new interpretation to our religious teachings based on the Vedas and the Upanishads and have carried them to the West. Among them the most important names are those of late Maharishi Mahesh Yogi, the founder of the Transcendental Meditation and the Divine Light Mission; late Bhaktivedanta Prabhupada, the founder of the Hare Krishna Movement; late Swami Muktananda who have founded Siddha Yoga and late Bhagwan Shree Rajneesh (Osho) who have given a new interpretation to the traditional understanding of our renunciation. Sivananda's disciple, Swami Chinmayananda who died recently, has established centres in many places of the world to continue the teachings of the Vedanta as interpreted by Vivekananda and continued by his late guru. Many among them, like the late Mahesh Yogi, Osho, Yogananda, and Prabhupada, have opened their Ashrams abroad and have a large number of Western followers who are taught yogas and Upanishadic philosophies. Our Vedic and Upanishadic religion or

Bharatiya Dharma has indeed now become almost a global religion through the actions and deeds of these ascetics.

However, some of the modern ascetics while practicing detachment lead their lives which are a marked contrast to the lives led by their early predecessors in the colonial India. Backed by affluent disciples, many of them live a life of luxury and comfort, travel by air and by airconditioned railway coach and imported luxury car. They often spend the hot summer of India in preaching and performing religious functions in a cooler climate abroad among the non-resident Indians.

In Independent India, we have a mushroomed growth of such modern ascetics who do not clearly fit in with our knowledge about them in ancient, medieval and colonial India. A few among the metropolitan and capital city-based ascetics have indeed achieved a celebrity status. They are now almost house-hold names in terms of the celeb-shisyas they claim, the T.V. Channels they manage and often the huge wealth they acquire through their profession of asceticism! We all know about the late Dhirendra Brahmachari who was a yoga-guru to Indira Gandhi and Chandraswamy who was, according to the *New York Times,* "the spiritual adviser, political fixer and close friend" of the late Narasimha Rao. Both Swami Nityananda of Karnataka who has Yeddyurappa and Modi as his disciples and Asaram Bapu who have a large following in Gujarat and Madhya Pradesh, recently landed themselves in troubles on some tantric rituals involving rape in one case and murder in the other. Baba Ramdev who is known not only for his yogas but also for his vast ayurvedic business empire and Sri Sri Ravishankar known for his "Art of Living" often dabble in the politics of the country. While Ramdev has among his followers Bhoopendra Singh Hooda and the Late Bhairon Singh Shekawat, Ravishankar is the guru of Rhea Pillai and Leander Paes, Yash and Avanti Birla. We have also Kalki Bhagwan with his wife Padmavati who intend to "enlighten" 64,000 people by 2013 and Mata Amritanandamayi who claims to "heal" a person by a "hug" and possesses Sabeer Bhatia, the Hotmail founder and Yolanda King, the daughter of Martin Luther King, Jr. among her disciples. Sathya Sai Baba who recently died left behind him not ony a controversy about his so-called miracles but also a huge asset of some 40000 crore, now a bone of contention among the members of his Trust. He, however, never dabbled in politics and immortalized his name by providing for the supply of potable drinking water, foundation of school, college and sophisticated hospital for the benefit of the people in his village, Puttaparthi, in Karnataka and such magnificent works will make a Municipal Corporation of any city proud.

At a lower level one often finds almost in every village or at some corner of a city or at a temple or at a pilgrimage centre and often at a cremation ground ascetics leading a detached or secluded life with a small number of followers or disciples who more or less match with our concept about asceticism in ancient, medieval and colonial India. Many of them may not have heard about the Upanishads and have often become ascetics more by chance or accident than by any deliberate intention, desire or tradition. However, one has to be very careful about the fakes among them who often make news either by cheating their gullible disciples or by some other inappropproate and imprudent actions which do not befit a religious mendicant.

Priestly Classes

While the Upanishadic tradition is governing our life in the form of a guru-shisya relationship and in the form of worship of deities as manifestations of the Brahman in every pious house hold, it is the Vedic ritualism that seems to be a casualty in a modern day city-life. With the coming of the British and the introduction of a New Education, new professional opportunities emerged in the British administration in the metropolitan cities. The priestly classes which almost remained eclipsed in the Muslim India took advantage of the situation. There was frequent emigration from traditional villages to metropolitan cities by the young members of the priestly classes to take advantage of the English education and to settle down as clerks or in some other petty jobs either in the administration or in the mercantile houses. While the number of priests who followed the ancestral profession began to dwindle in the villages, they almost became a rarity in the towns and cities. The shift from the traditional profession to a modern one in the background of the socio-economic changes in the country by the priestly classes as well as the withering of the Sanskrit pose a big question mark about the survival of Vedic rituals performed on the occasions of birth, marriage and death and other socio-religious functions.

In Independent India the scenario is not different and so unlike in ancient times group of priests now could hardly be seen living in a particular place in a village or a town. They are scattered all over India in different towns and cities riding mostly on their knowledge in English and on new trades and profession.

Yet, there are many among them who because of poverty or other compulsive factors cling to their old traditional profession for a living and they could be seen catering to the needs and requirements of the society on the occasions of its socio-religious functions. And the most well-versed among them could often be seen serving as the priests of deities in temples situated in large or small metropolitan cities and towns. These groups of priests are the living exponents of our religious scriptures and it must be seen that they do not fall victims to the lure of other modern day non-religious professions and temptations.

They help us not only to discharge our religious responsibilities and obligations but also to keep us on our religious tracks amidst a host of stresses of modern day living. And so by all means they should not only be encouraged to do these tasks but also to provide them necessary support to organize themselves into a viable professional class on a par with other professions in the country. This will not only strengthen their roots but also give a shot in the vitality of our religious scriptures and religion.

Such persons these days mainly concentrate around temples and mathas in cities, towns and villages. The bigger the temples, the larger is such concentration and most of them have inherited and learnt their profession from their fathers and grand fathers without perhaps any opportunity to learn it at a Vedic school. In every province a Vedic school to train such members of the priestly class who want to follow the priestly profession should be created around a big temple and a pool of trained priests in the performance of the Vedic rituals should be created to assign the willing members to their own communities settled outside their own state in discharging the Vedic rituals on socio religious functions. Thus, a Bengali family living outside Bengal could obtain the services of a priest from its own community in Bengal if none is available locally which often happens. The significance of such an arrangement lies not only in keeping our religious traditions and beliefs alive but also in helping us to remain rooted to our own religion. This way the Vedas and the Vedic rituals will be kept alive in their own communities who are domiciled in other states or parts of the country. This way also will be achieved the twin purpose of not only saving the traditional priestly classes from extinction economically but also keeping our Vedas and the Vedic rituals alive and vigorous.

Sanskrit

We now come to the next, and perhaps the most important of the five pillars, that is, the language of the religious scriptures which is Sanskrit. As we have said earlier many times that our religious scriptures were orally composed, transmitted and preserved in Sanskrit which was refined by Panini around 400 BC following the Persian occupation of the North-West. From the fifth century AD following the Buddhist example, Sanskrit was put to writing to compose, transmit and preserve our religious scriptures. Sanskrit enjoyed the patronage of our kings and monarchs as well as of the priestly classes who conversed in Sanskrit.

With the Sanskrit withering in the Muslim India and almost becoming eclipsed under the impact of the New Education in the British India, there was not much discussion and cultivation of the Vedas and and the allied religious scriptures and philosophies except in the few tols and chatuspathis that managed to survive and the few Sanskrit colleges that came into existence enjoying the patronage of the early British Orientalists who dominated the decision making body of the East India Company's government in education in Bengal. In Independent India the continuation of the Brirish system of education finds it relegated to a very low position or no position at all in the courses and programmes of our universities and colleges and is often described as a "dead language" in the changing socio-economic and political situation in the country.

One of our first endeavours towards the revival of our religion should be by resuming teaching of courses on Sanskrit. If Sanskrit is not taught in the schools and colleges, the students will have no opportunity to learn the language and to have an access to our original religious scriptures. While a study of Sanskrit may not be professionally viable except for those who want to follow a teaching profession, it should have particular appeal among those members of the priestly classes who want to continue their ancestral profession. Sanskrit, the language of our scriptures which survived the onslaughts of the Kharoshthi scripts under the Persian rule in the North-West following Panini's grammar but almost put into oblivion under the Muslim rule and eclipsed by the New Education of the British should be made an optional course at the school and the college level along with Arabic and Persian. This way not only the purpose of secularism will be served but also the interested students will have an opportunity to learn a language which will give them access to their own religious scriptures. A knowledge in Sanskrit will also help the interested students not only to have an access to the non-religious literatures of the past but also to understand the development of our vernacular languages in the country. Sanskrit is the root of almost all vernacular languages in India that came into existence with the dawn of the middle ages in the country just as the Greek and the Latin are the roots of most of the langugaes in modern Europe. Above all, Sanskrit courses at the school and college level will create a demand for Sanskrit teachers, a profession hitherto monopolized by the priestly classes.

Religious Festivals

Finally, as is the case with every religion in the world, the vitality of ours is reflected in a regular observance of our religious festivals annually. While the public worship of the gods and the goddesses, like that of the Goddess Durga or Kali, at a particular time of the year or the observance of the birth days of saints and religious reformers like the Buddha, Mahavira, Nanak, Kabir and a host of others annually could be limited to particular states and communities, there are some which are observed all over the country cutting across all communities within our religion. The most important among them are: the observance of the Sivaratri or the wedding night of the Lord Siva which usually falls in the month of March and that of Janmashtami or the birth day of the Lord Krishna which occurs in the month of August, as well as Dussehra which celebrates the victory of Lord Rama over the Rakshasa King Ravana as the triumph of good over evil and a fortnight later, the Deepavali or the festival of light which celebrates the return of the Lord Rama to Ayodhya in the month of October/November. The Deepavali has an astronomical significance also as it signifies the beginning of winter in the country. And the end of winter is marked by the festival of colours or Holi which is observed across the borders of the states heralds the dawn of the Spring.

Religious festivals relating to Saivaism and Vaishnavism are observed almost every where in the country. We have seen much earlier that these two deities, Siva and Krishna, are as old as the Vedas and are the precursors of the two movements, the Siva Bhagavatas and the Krishna or the Vishnu Bhagavatas in the days of the Upanishads which seek to replace the rigid ritualism and strict casteism of our religion by sheer love and devotion for attaining Nirvana or freedom from the cycle of death and birth. The majority of our ascetics belong to either of these two sects. The birth day of the Lord Krishna is observed with a great festive mood. As a matter of fact, the Janmashtami or the birth day of Krishna is to us what the Christmas or the birth day of Jesus, which is observed on 25th December every year, is to the Christians all over the world. The significance of the observance of these religious festivals is tremendous as they hold the followers of our religion living in different states of the country and having different mother tongues together and create among them a brotherly bond and harmony which is revived every year.

There are other festivals which are observed periodically and among them the most important one is the Kumbha Mela. It is held every twelve years when Jupiter enters Kumbha or Aquarius and the Sun Makar or the Capricorn. It lasts for three months till the entry of the Sun in Mesha or the Aries. Devotees come not only from the different parts of the country but from abroad for a dip in the river to achieve "Nirvana" or liberation from the cycle of birth and death. The four sacred places which hold this festival by rotation every twelve years are Haridwar, Allahabad, Benares and Nasik. The last Kumbha Mela was held in Haridwar in January-

April 2010 attended by millions of bathers from India and abroad. For the Indian settlers whose forefathers migrated to the former British colonies such as Mauritius, Kumbha Mela is not only an unique spiritual experience but also an opportunity to "connect with the people, places and culture that are our very own that we greatly miss back home, " as was significantly observed by Ram Prasad who at the age of 37 attended his third Kumbha Mela at Haridwar in 2010 from Mauritius. As a matter of fact, as reported in the *Times of India* of 25th April 2010, the Chief Minister of Uttarakhand, Ramesh Pokhriyal Nishank has pointed out that more than six crore people from 140 countries converged on Haridwar and for the first time in 250 years the sadhus from the akharas as well as people from different religions took a holy dip peacefully. On a single day at the last Shahi Snan on April 14, more than 1.6 crore people bathed in the Ganga at Haridwar, which is a world record and should be included in the *Guiness Book of World Records* as suggested by the Union Cabinet Secretary. Thus, the Mahakumbha which is held every twelve years at a select place serves a very unique purpose of cementing a bond among the co-religionists and acts as an invisible pillar of strength for our religion.

These five pillars represent the three "Vs" of our religion. These three "Vs" are: Vigour, Vitality and Vivacity. Together they form an inner strength. And this inner strength is the essence of our religion just as the energy of the mind is the essence of our lives.

22

A Final Retrospection on Our Religion

In the preceding four parts of the work we have discussed our religion and religious identity; we have shown how we have lost our religious identity and how our religion suffered an eclipse under the rule of Islam for nearly 650 years; we have also indicated how the traces of our religion have survived and finally we have shown how efforts at the genuine revival of our religion by some of our enlightened religious reformers and ascetics have ended almost in a fiasco under the attempts of our political and national leaders taking shelter in the term "Hindu" as a mark of our national, political and ideological identity.

We may now summarise the main points of our arguments to show how ridiculous and absurd it is to carry our description as "Hindus" in the light of the following simple facts:

First, in the post-Independent years there is hardly an educated family which does not know the story of the Ramayana and the Mahabharata or does not keep a copy of the Gita or hardly is there an illiterate person who follows our religion, misses an opportunity to listen to the readings from the epics or the Gita either by a fellow devotee, a Kathak or a pious Reader. In the Gita obviously there is no reference to the term “Hindu” or to the description of the followers of our religion as “Hindu”.

Second, the Gita, as we have said before, represents the essence of the Upanishads and is a part of the Mahabharata. The Mahabharata took several centuries to complete but it first started at a time when after the completion of the four Vedas the sages had begun the oral composition of the Upanishads and the years assigned to the coming of the Upanishads were between 600 and 400 BC. The Persians who described the Aryans living on the both sides of the river Indus in the North-West as “Hindus” were roughly the witness to the composition of some of the Upanishads between 519 and 326 BC. In the Upanishads the “Hindu” term is conspicuous by its absence and so also it is in the Mahabharata and the Ramayana.

Third, in the works of the Sutrakaras who began their work partly as an initial reaction to the occupation of the Persians described by Manu as Mlecchas and partly as a resistance to the inroads of the Buddhism into the Brahmanism, particularly in the East, one can hardly find the use of the term “Hindu.”

Fourth, in none of the commentaries including those of the Sankaracharya before the advent of the Islam there has been a single occasion where our Aryan ancestors have been referred to as “Hindus”.

Finally, the Muslim rulers who Persianised India very rarely referred to their subjects verbally as “Hindus” but frequently used the words, Kaffers or infidels. In contemporary Persian literature and writings the "Hindu" term with religious overtones frequently occurred. This should have been known to the writers of commentaries on our religion composed during the period of Muslim rule and they would have occasions to refer to the term, "Hindu" in their compositions but there is no such reference.

The British rulers who replaced the Muslims, accepted the use of the term with the religious connotation ascribed to it by the Muslim rulers much to their convenience and used it to put us against the Muslim occupiers of the medieval India, which was unhesitatingly accepted by our national leaders and freedom fighters in search of our national, political and ideological identity. The policy of divide and rule pursued by the British by setting the "Hindus" against the Muslims since the beginning of the rule of the East India Company definitely had its impact on the Freedom Movement and ultimately contributed to the Partition of India in 1947.

Independent India has accepted the British legacies including British ideas and institutions in almost all walks of life without any questioning and so we have also accepted our description as "Hindus". And, thus, we are known as "Hindus" all over the world despite the fact that we and our ancestors have never been described as such in anyone of our religious scriptures composed before and after the coming of the pre-Islamic Persians who during their occupation of the North-West India bestowed this term on our ancestors living on both sides of the river Sindu. Our ancestors created through the compositions of the four Vedas and the 108 Upanishads an Arya Dharma, a Bharatiya Dharma, or a Brahmana Dharma based on the revelation of the Brahman or the Universe in the Upanishads. In the use of the term "Hindu" to describe our religion, our true religious identity as the followers of a great religion orally created through hymns by our sages through Tapas or meditation, engaged in investigating the mysteries of the Cosmos or the Universe, more than 3500 years ago, is lost forever.

We have thus lost our own religious identity in the use of the term "Hindu" and since sometimes tradition is more stronger than truth, and fiction is more acceptable than fact, we shall continue to be known as "Hindus" when the most appropriate term to describe us would have been perhaps "Brahmanas" as followers of our sages who spent their lives in realising the mysteries of the Brahma, Cosmos or the Universe to become Brahmanas or possessors of the knowledge of the Brahma. And we all know that the Brahmanas was the term used to describe us and our religion by both Hiuen-Tsang and I-tsing, the Chinese Buddhist scholars who came to India in the seventh century for further study and research in Buddhism and traversed almost the whole of India.

If some among us, because of the ignorance of the meaning of the term, Brahman, object to its use as referring to the priestly classes only, the other two terms emerging out of Bharat and Aryas which describe us as Bharatbasi and Aryas and our religion as Bharatiya Dharma or Arya Dharma, could be universally accepted by us. The use of both these terms to describe our race as Bharatbasi or Aryas and our religion as Bharatiya or Arya Dharma does inject a dose of integrity amongst us who belong to different provinces, speak different languages and follow different social norms, customs, manners and practices. Unless and until this is done we shall continue to suffer from a loss of religious identity accidentally imposed on us first by the pre-Islamic Persian invaders and occupiers of the North-West India and then revived by the Islamic rulers of the middle ages throughout the length and breadth of the country and finally continued by the British as an instrument of administrative expediency till independence. And after independence, its use has been accepted and continued as a mark of our national, political and ideological identity by our national and religious leaders who have meekly surrendered to this British legacy without raising any questions on its relevance to our religion.

There is, however, no doubt that centuries of the brain-washing of our ancestors, first under the rule of Islam for nearly 650 years and then under the British administration for a further period of 190 years from 1757 onwards, in thinking of themselves as "Hindu" and of our religion as "Hinduism" or "Hindu Dharma" does have its impact on us as their descendants. And it will indeed be difficult for us, given the present status of our knowledge on the subject in a secular India and the hold of some of our political parties disinterested in our religion, to do away with this traditional description of us and boldly assert that we are Bharatiyas and our religion is Bharatiya Dharma, which is based on the four Vedas, the Brahmanas, the Aranyakas and the Upanishads—our books of knowledge about the mysteries of the Cosmos and of the human life bequeathed to us by our venerable sages more than 3500 years ago from now.

Yet, we may not grumble about this loss of our religious identity, for, we now have a fuller knowledge about our past civilization and culture, religion and religious scriptures, thanks to the discovery of the British Orientalists and the European Indologists in the late eighteenth and the early nineteenth centuries. In numerous dispatches to Bengal, the Court of Directors used to describe the presence of the East India Company in India as "An Act of Providence". And as far as I am concerned, this "Act of Providence" consists mainly in the act of providing us with a knowledge of our eclipsed religion and religious scriptures. But for this knowledge, we could not have a Rammohan, a Dayananda, a Ramakrishna, a Vivekananda and finally an Aurobindo as well as a place in today's world of religion and spiritualism.

Bibliography

As stated in the *Preface* the work relates more to a critical investigation into our description as "Hindu" and our religion as "Hinduism" than to a full-fledged account of the complexities of our religion from ancient times down to the present days. While my book, *Civilisation, Education and School in Ancient and Medieval India* mentioned earlier in the *Preface* helps me with the formulation of my ideas on the subject, I have freely drawn upon the available standard works on the history of India as well as on our religion. A very short bibliographical list of some of the very important among the works consulted is mentioned below for an interested reader.

Ali, Hashim Amir, *The Quran,* Charles E.Tuttle Company, Tokyo, 1974.

Beveridge, A.S., *Babarnama* (translated from Turki) in 2 vols. London, 1922.

Ali, Syed Amir, *The Spirit of Islam,* London, 1964.

Biardeau, Madeline, *Hinduism: The Anthropology of a Civilization* (translated from the French by Richard Nice), Delhi, 2002.

Dalmia, Vasudha/Malinar, Angelika/Christof, Martin, ed., *Charisma and Canon: Essays on the Religious History of the Indian Subcontinent,* Delhi, 2003.

Dalrymple, William, *Nine Lives: In Search of the Sacred in Modern India,* New Delhi, 2009.

Deussen, Paul, *The Philosophy of the Upanishads,* Edinburgh, 1906.

—, *Philosophie des Veda,* Leipzig, 1894.

Farquhar, J.N., *Modern Religious Movements in India,* London, 1929.

Flood, Gavin, *An Introduction to Hinduism,* New Delhi, 1998.

Ghose, Aurobindo, *The Life Divine,* Pondicherry, 1973.

Ghosh, Suresh Chandra, *History of Education in Modern India,* Third Edition, Delhi, 2009.

—, *The Social Condition of the British Community in Bengal 1757–1800,* Leiden, 1971.

—, *Freedom Movement in India,* Delhi, 2011 (Second edition)

Gautier François, *Arise, Ó India,* Delhi, 2000.

Grewal, J.S., *Muslim Rule in India,* Calcutta, 1970.

Gruber Elmar R. and Kersten Holger, *The Original Jesus,* Shaftesbury, 1995.

Habibullah, A.B.M., *The Foundation of Muslim Rule in India,* Allahabad, 1961.

Hasan, Ibn, *The Central Structure of the Mughal Empire,* London, 1936.

Keith, A.B., *The Religion and Philosophy of the Vedas and Upanishads,* Cambridge (USA), 1925.

Lanepoole, Stanley, *Medieval India under Mohammadan Rule, 712-1764,* London, 1917.

Mehta, J.L., *An Advanced Study in the History of Medieval India,* Delhi, 1987.

MacDonald (Rev.), K.S., *Rammohan Ray, the Bengali Religious Reformer,* Calcutta, 1879.

Macdonell, A.A., *History of Sanskrit Literature,* London, 1900.

Madan, T.N ./Biardeau, Madeleine/Chaudhuri, Nirad/ Brockington J.L..(eds.), *The Hinduism Omnibus,* Delhi, 2003.

Majumdar, R.C., ed., *The History and Culture of the Indian People*, 9 vols., Bombay, 1965.

Mukundcharandas, Sadhu, *Bhagwan Swaminarayan*, Ahmedabad, 2007.

Müller, Friedrich Max, *The Upanishads*, 2 vols. Oxford, 1879–82.

—, ed., *Sacred Books of the East*, 50 vols., Oxford, 1879-1900.

—, *The Six Systems of Indian Philosophy*, London, 1899.

—, *The Origin and Development of Religion*, Oxford, 1878.

Nizami, K.A., *Studies in Medieval Indian History and Culture*, Allahabad, 1966.

—, *Religion and Politics in Medieval India*, Bombay and Delhi, 1961, 1974 and 2002.

Osborne, Arthur, *The Incredible Sai Baba*, New Delhi, 1957.

Panikkar, Raimon, *The Unknown Christ of Hinduism*, Madrid, 1981.

Prasad, Ishwari, *History of the Medieval India*, Allahabad, 1952.

Radhakrishnan, S., *Eastern Religions and Western Thought*, Delhi, 1939.

Rhys Davids, T.W., *Buddhism, its History and Literature*, London, 1926

Renou, L, *Religions of Ancient India*, London, 1953.

Sachau, Edward C., ed., *Alberuni's India, AD 1030*, 2 vols., Delhi, 1964.

Sarkar, Jadunath, *Fall of the Mughal Empire*, 4 vols., Calcutta, 1947–52.

Sharma, Arvind, *Hinduism and its Sense of History*, Delhi, 2003.

Stevenson, S., *The Heart of Jainism*, Oxford, 1916.

Swami Vivakananda, *Lectures from Colombo to Almora*, Twentieth Impression, Kolkata, 2001.

Weber, Max, *The Religions of India*, Glencoe, 1958.

Williams, J.A., *Themes of Islamic Civilisation*, Berkeley, 1971.

Index

Aditi 7
Abhidhamma 72
Abu Hanifah 114
Abu Mashar 129
Achaemenid empire 41-42
Achaemenids 41-42
Acharyas 18, 52, 209
Act of 1909 143
Act of Providence 243
Adhvaryu 12-16, 23
Adyar 200
Afghanistan 4, 71
Agni 7, 9, 16-19, 21, 47
Agnihotra 14
Agnichayana 14
Agra 101, 104, 106, 137, 141, 147, 161-63, 178, 189
Ahle Kitab 113
Ahmad Shah Abdali, 111
Ahmadnagar 110
Ajatasatru 24, 40, 94
Ajmer 104
Akbar 110 -11, 117, 119-21, 123, 125-26, 129, 134-35, 161-63, 220
Akshay Kumar Dutta 194
Aksharbrahma Gunatinand Swami 21 0
Alamgir 11, 112
Alam Khan 101
Alara Kalama 32, 89
Ala-ud-din-Khalji 106-7, 114, 117-18, 120-21, 133-35, 153, 155
Allahabad 168
Allah 101, 107, 125, 170, 198, 206
Allah Malik 212
Al-Beruni 136
Aldous Huxley 201
Alexander 41-42
Alexander Hamilton 186
Aligarh 143-44
Alipur Conspiracy Case 202
Alptigin 102
Amba 35
Amber 155
Amil 119
Amir Kohi 118
Amir Kuhani 132
Amir Khusrav 126
Anandapala 102
Anandamath 221
Andhra/Andhra Pradesh 71, 207, 214
Anegundi 154
Angas 51, 85
Anglicists 190
Anglo-Indian Community 205
Annie Besant 144, 200-202, 217, 222
Anti-Partition Movement 202
Anquetil-Duperron 185
Apala 45

Apara Vidya 24
Apastamba 51
Arabic 122-32, 161, 189, 192
Arabs 101-3, 136
Archika 13
Arjuna 34-35, 215, 227
Art of Divination 59
Art of Living 229
Arthur A Macdonell 6
Arunachal 150
Aryans 3-39, 50-98
Aryas 241
Aryabhatta (Mathematician) 82
Aryabhattiya 82
Arya Dharma 97, 240-41
Aranyakas 22, 91-8, 225-27, 138, 238-43
Arya Samaj 196-97, 199, 217, 222
Aryavarta 4, 64, 97
Arz 118
Asaram Bapu 229
Ascetics 166-78, 206-15, 227-30
Ash Shafi 114
Asiatick Researches 185
Asiatic Society of Bengal 185-86
Asoka 49, 53, 66, 70-72
Asramas, 54
Assam 107-08, 137, 155, 159
Asvamedha 14, 34
Asvaghosa 7 4
Asvapati 77
Asvalayana 38
A.S. Beveridge 138
Atman, 24-28, 31, 68, 94-98, 173
Atri 8
Asthadhayi 38, 48, 50, 53, 63
Astachap 176
Atharvaveda 12, 15, 18, 20-21, 33
Aurangabad 211
Aurangzeb 111, 114, 126, 139, 163
Aurobindo 202, 204, 207, 222, 243
Auroville 204
Ayodhya 37, 57, 220
Ayurveda, 15, 47, 60, 83
Ayurvedic Pharmacopoeia 61
Aziz-ud-din, 111

Babar 108-10, 137, 220
Babarnama 102
Baba Ramdev 224, 230
Babri Masjid 220
Babylon 81
Bactrian Greeks 72-73
Badarayana 88
Badrinath 84
Bahadur Shah 163
Bahur 83
Baji Rao 1, 139-40, 145, 157-58
Bakshi 118
Bakshali Manuscript 82
Balananda 207
Bal Gangadhar Tilak 144, 216
Bal Thackeray 220
Balaji Vishwanath 139, 157-58
Bal Mukund 209
Bandagan 118
Bankim Chandra Chatterjee 221
Baudhayana 51, 53
Benares 73, 103-4, 143, 168, 170, 189, 207, 214
Bengal 10, 71 76-77, 101, 104-5, 107-9, 111, 137, 160-61, 176-77, 181, 184, 189, 196, 217
Bengali (language) 130, 161-62, 176-77
Bentinck 188, 190
Bernier 126
Besnagar Column 74

Bethlehem 3
Bhagavat Dharma 209
Bhgavat Gita 35-36 91-98, 129, 177, 213, 215, 227, 238-43
Bhagata Mhalsapati 211
Bhagwan Shri Rajneesh 228
Bhairon Singh Shekawat 230
Bhaktivedanta Prabhupada 228
Bhaktiratnakar 177
Bharadvaja 8
Bharat (country) 222, 241
Bharat(king) 56, 222
Bharatiya Dharma 97, 240-41
Bharat tribes 4-5, 11, 40, 43, 97
Bharatvarsha 42, 97, 240-41
Bharhut 87
Bhikkhu 78, 93
Bhoopendra Singh Hooda 230
Bhratiya Janata Party 219-21
Bhrigu 26
Bible of Bengal 161
Bihar 37, 88, 104, 106, 150, 160, 184
Bijapur 116
Bimbisara 40
Bindusara 70
Bipin Chandra Pal 144
Bitikchi 119
Bochasanwasi Shri Akshar Purushottam Swaminarayan Sanstha(BAPS) 210
Bodh-Gaya 71
Bodhisatta doctrine 86- 87
Bombay 190-91
Borneo 224
Brahmanas (priest) 5, 10-28, 91-98, 193, 238- 43
Brahman (mystic power) 5, 10-28
Brahman (universal soul) 23-25, 27-28, 30-32, 44-46, 51-52, 68, 91-98, 173, 178, 207, 222, 238-43
Brahma/Brahmana Dharma 97, 193, 240-41
Brahmanas(scriptures) 22-23, 92-97, 240-43
Brahmagupta 82 I
Brahmanapala 102
Brahmacharya 18-19, 25, 52, 54
Brahmacharins 51-52, 55, 90
Brahmyacharya Ashram 209
Brahmasiddhanta 82
Brahmasutras 88
Brahma Sabha 192-93
Brahma Samaj 193-94, 197, 199, 222
Brahmi Script 48
Brahmavarta 5, 42-43, 64
Brahmaswarup Shastriji Maharaj 210
Brajabhasa 176
Brajabhumi 175
Brindaban, 169, 207
Brihadaranyka Upanishad 24, 29, 54
British Orientalists 183-89
Buddha 22, 32, 40, 49, 58, 70-72, 76, 87-90, 93, 97, 235
Buddhist Order 86, 88
Bukhara 132
Bundelkhand 104
Burdwan 177, 207
Burma 87
Byzantium 81

Caesar 112
Calcutta 143, 185, 189-91, 197
Calcutta School Book Society 190
Calcutta School Society 190
Calcutta University 198

Caliphs of Baghdad and Egypt 101, 106, 116, 132
Cambodia 38, 224
Cambridge 202
Canada 187
Canton 62
Cape Comorin 163
Capuchin fathers 157
Census Repot (of 2011) 226
Central Asia 3, 106
Central India 106
Central Hindu School 201
Central Hindu College 144
Ceylon 71, 81
Chach, 102
Chaghatai Turki 136
Chalukas 102
Chandelas 104
Chand Patil 211
Chandra 58
Chandernagore 203
Chanderi 106
Chhanda 16
Chaitanya 169, 176
Chaitanya Bhagavata 177
Chaitanyacharitamrita 169, 177
Chaitanya Mangal 177
China 76, 79
Chandraswamy 229
Chandogya Upanishad 26, 28, 35
Chandi Devi 177
Changiz Khan 108, 110, 132-33
Chandragupta 11, 74-76
Chandragupta Maurya 55, 93
Chanakya 55
Chandidas 162
Chhapiya 208
Charter Act (of 1813) 142, 188
Chatrapati 158
Chaulmugra Oil 60-61
Chatuspathi 159
Chaurasi Vaishnava Ki Varta 176
Chicago Conference on the World Religion (1893) 224
Chittor 106
Cholas 84, 151, 154
Christopher Isherwood 201
Christian missionaries 142
Chuti Khan 162
Coeurdoux 184
Congress Party 219
Curzon 202
Cyrus the Great 41, 93

Dacca 144
Dahir 102
Dakshineswar Temple 198-99
Dalhousie 143
Dara Shukoh 129, 161, 186
Darius 1, 41
Darius III, 42
Dar-ul-Uloom Deoband 121
Dar-ul-Harb 107, 120, 122
Dar-ul-Islam 107, 120, 122
Dasabodha 156, 173
Dasashamedha Ghat 215
Dasas/Dasyus 4, 11
Dasaratha 37
Daulat Khan Lodi 109
David Hare 190
Dayanand Anglo-Vedic College 197
Deepavali 235
Degenerate Kshatriyas 47, 64, 75, 136
Delhi, 4, 101, 104, 106-8, 111, 117, 134, 136-37, 139, 161-63, 178, 189
Delhi Sultanate 106-8
Democritus 60

Deogarh 207
Derozio 191
Deutsche Monatsschit 185
Devendranath Tagore 194
Devagiri 83
Devajani 45
Deva-Jana-Vidya 20
Devaki 35
Dhana Nanda 81
Dhanus 59
Dhar 106
Dharma 16-17, 202
Dharmadev 209
Dharmashastras 185
Dharmasutras 53
Dhata 16
Dhoop 213
Dhritarashtra Vaichitravirya 35
Dhirendra Brahmachari 229
Din-i-Ilahi 111
Divine Light Mission 228
Diwan 119
Doab 5
Doctrine of Karma 29, 30, 36, 70
Doctrine of Samsara 29, 30, 70
Dohas 172
Dowry 205
Dr. Julian Johnson 208
Dussehra 211
Dvija 18

East India Company 60-61, 142, 184-85, 188, 205, 234, 240, 243
Ecole des Langues Orientales Vivantes 186
Edoardo Barbosa 154
Edward C. Sachau 136
E.J. Brill 205
Ekanath 156, 173
Ekantik Dharma 209
Elliot 129
Epigraphica Indica 152
Essays on the Gita 203

Fa-hien 76, 81, 97
Fakhr-ul-Mulk 132
Farghana 108
Faust 185
Faujdar 119
Fergusson 154
Firuz Shah 107
Firuz Shah Tughluq 114, 118, 121, 129, 161
Franz Bopp 186
Friedrich Schlegel 186

Gaekwar of Baroda, 202
Gandhara 40-1, 48, 56, 74
Ganapati Swamy 214
Ganesh Festival 216
Gangadhar 160
Gangadasa Pratapa Vilasa 160
Ganges 4, 20, 29, 39, 56, 76-77, 80-81, 215
Gargi Samhita 54
Garutmat 9
Gaur 169
Gautama (sage) 51
Gautamiputra Satakarnin 74
Gaupayana 45
Gaugamela 42
General Committee of Public Instruction 189-90
General Election (of 1977) 219
George Forster 185
George Grierson 176
Ghanshyam 208
Ghazni 105
Ghazis 124
Ghazi-ud-din Imad-ul-Mulk 112

Ghazni 102-5
Ghaznavid Sultans 103-4
Ghiyas-ud-din Azam 161
Ghiyas-ud-din Balban 133
Ghiyas-ud-din Tughluq 114
Ghosha 45
Ghur 103-5
Ghuzz tribes 103
Gita Govinda 160, 185
Gitanjali 201
Godhead of the Overmind 204
Goddess Durga 81, 208, 210, 216, 222, 228, 235
Goethe 185
Golkunda 110
Greece 56
Greek(language) 187
Greek invaders and occupiers 40-49, 72-3, 136
Grihasthas 25, 90
Grihasutras 15, 38, 53
Growse 176
Gujarat 71, 101, 107-8, 137, 207, 229
Guiness Book of World Records 237
Gunaraja Khan 162
Guptas 34, 75-76, 136, 144
Gurukul 197
Gwalior 102, 106

Hadith 125
Hammirmadamardana 160
Hanbalite 114
Hanifah School 114
Hanuman 32, 37
Hanxleden 184
Harappa 4
Hare Krishna Movement 228
Hari 51, 169, 198, 206
Haridwar/Hardwar 187, 243
Harihara II, 153
Harishchandra 34
Hariprasad Pande 208
Harsha/Harshavardhana 77-78, 80-81, 95
Hashim Amir Ali 114
Hazara Temple 154
Heliodorus 74
Heemadri 45
Hemadpant 213
Henry Colebroke 185
Herakles 38
Heart 103
Hertford 185
Hetu vidya 78
Himalayas 41-42, 84, 128, 139, 149, 151, 158-59, 207, 214
Himachal Pradesh 207
Hinayana 76, 86
Hind 41
Hindi 130, 161-63
Hindu College 143
Hindu Dharma 24, 95, 217, 222-23, 241-42
Hindu Samaj 222
Hindu School 143
Hindu Maha Sabha 144-45, 217
Hindu-Pad-Padshahi 140, 158
Hindu University 143
Hindus 41-42, 91-98, 216-23, 238-43
Hindush 41-42
Hindutva 144, 217, 220
Hindukush 41
Hiranyagarbha 9
Hitopadesha 185
Hiuen Tsang 78, 80-81, 89, 97, 241
H.S. Olcott 200
H.T. Prinsep 185

Holia 214
Hooghly 197
House of Clay 29
Horace Hayman Wilson 185
Hotri 12, 23
Hoysalas 84, 151, 154
Humayun 109, 220
Husain Shah 160, 162
Hunas 80, 136
Hyderabad 163
Hymn of the Primeval Man 10-11

Ibrahim Lodi 108-9
ICS 202
Ikhtiyar-ud-din Muhammad 105
Ikshavakus 34, 37
Ilbari Turks 113
Iltutmish 115, 132
Indian Muslims 121
Indian National Congress 143-4, 217
Indira Gandhi 219
Indonesia 224
Indra 2, 9, 35
Indrani 45
Indus 47, 105, 136-37
Indus Valley Civilisation 4, 44
Insha 118
Institutes of Hindu Law 185
Integral Yoga 204, 222-23
Iran 101
Isha Upanishad 203
Islamic administration 113-21
Islamic education 122-31
Islamic invaders and occupiers, 101-145
Istihqaq 118
I-Tsing 79, 81, 89, 97, 241
Jadunath Sarkar 114, 156
Jahangir 124
Jaichand 104
Jain Order 66
Jaipal 102
J.L. Malcolm, 142
James Mill 188
Jambudvipa 61
Janaka 24, 29, 37-89
Janamejaya 34, 38
Janmashtami 235
Jana Sangh 219
J anata Party 219
Japan 79
Japhet 184
Jarita 45
Jataka Gathas 38
Java 224
Jayananda 177
Jayadeva 160, 185
Jaysingh Sufi 180
Jeremy Bentham 188
Jesus Christ 3, 27, 95, 198, 206, 218, 235
Jewish State of Israel 219
Jharkhand 207
Jiddu Krishnamurthi 201
Jihad 122
Jinnah 143, 145
Jizya 113-14, 116, 121, 135
Juhu 45
Johann Gottfried Herder 185
John Marshall 4
Jyotisha 16-17

Kaffers 113, 135, 137-39, 164, 187, 239
K.A. Nizami 115
Kabir 170-71, 213, 235
Kabul 72, 108-9
Kadru 45

Kailasanatha Temple 83
Kalanirnaya 159
Kali (Goddess) 198-99, 208, 216, 222, 235
Kalidasa 185
Kalinjar 102
Kalki Bhagwan 230
Kalpa 17, 53
Kamrupa 108, 155
Kanchi 83-84, 151, 154
Kanchipuram 78
Kanishka 72, 73-74, 80
Kanarese, 130, 163-64
Kanauj (Kanyakubja) 77, 81, 86, 102, 168
Kangra 102
Kanya Kumarika 107, 137, 155
Kapilavastu 70
Karchas 196
Karkhanas 118
Karkotas 102
Karma of Jaimini 54
Karma Mimansa 160
Karmayogin 202
Karnataka 71, 158, 229-30
Kashi 20, 48, 57, 62
Kashmir 71, 80, 107-8, 137, 155, 161
Kasirama Das 176
Kataka 59
Kathak 178, 226, 238
Kathaka recession 35
Katha Upanishad 24, 29, 39
Kathiawar 71, 74, 77, 80, 84-85, 102, 196, 209
Kathis 209
Katyayana 38
Kautiliya Arthasastra 37, 55-56
Kavindra 162
Kavikankan Chandi 177
Kedarnath 58
Kerala 70, 88
Keshab Chandra Sen 194-95
Ketu 58
Khafi Khan 157
Khairat 118
Khaljis 105, 107
Khandesh 110
Khanquas 109, 120-21
Kharosthi Script 48, 64, 130, 141, 234
Khotan 79
Khusrav Shah 103
Kirman 105
Kishkindya 37
Kolis 209
Korea 79
Kosala 20, 34, 39, 48, 69
Kotwal 119
Krishna/Krishna-Bhagavatas/Cult 26, 35-36, 38, 68, 70, 78, 94, 164, 166, 168-69, 175-78, 206, 208, 210, 214-15, 222
Krishna Chandra Dev 169, 177
Krishna Pakshas 59
Krishnadeva Raya 154, 168
Krittivas 161
Kshatriyas 11, 17, 21-24, 44-46, 83, 91-98, 136, 238-43
Kujula Kadphises 73
Kulluka 160
Kumbhan Das 176
Kumbha Mela 236-37
Kundagrama 70
Kunti 35
Kuru-Panchala (country) 20, 39, 43, 48
Kusha 19
Kusha (son of Sita) 37

Kushanas 73-74, 95-96, 136
K.V. Hedgewar 218

Ladakh 150
Lahore 104-5, 109, 197
Lakshmi 51
Lakshmna 37
Lala Hansraj 197
Lala Lajpat Rai 144
Lalita Madhava 160
Lamghan 102
Land of the Hindustanis 157; Seven Rivers 4; Sons of Bharata 62
Lanka 37
Latin 187
Lava (son of Sita) 37
Leander Paes 230
Leonard de Chezy 186
Life Divine 203
Limbs of the Vedas 17
Lodis 106, 109
Loj 209
Loknath 207-8
London 187
Longhurst 154
Lopamudra 45
Lucknow 129

Macaulay 6, 188, 190
Machiavelli 55
Madagaskar 224
Madanapala 159
Madanaparijata 159
Madame H.P. Blavatsky 200
Madhava Vidyarayana 153, 139
Madhya Pradesh 207, 229
Madrasah 122-26
Madras, 191, 200
Madurai 84, 151, 153-55
Magadha 20, 48, 69, 76
Maktab 121-28
M.G. Ranade 195
Mahabharata 33-39, 40, 91-98, 162, 177-78, 225, 238-43
Mahabhasya 14, 50, 53
Maha Kumbha 237
Maharishi Mahesh Yogi 228
Mahmud 102-4
Mahmud Shah, 163
Maharashtra, 159, 216, 220
Mahavira 32, 49, 66, 70, 80, 90, 93, 97, 235
Mahavira (mathematician) 82
Mahayana 76, 86
Mahendra Nath Gupta 198
Maitreyi 31
Maitrayana Upanishad 26
Makara 59, 236
Malabar 106
Maladhar Vasu 162
Malakite 114
Malik-ibn-Anas 114
Malik Kafur 114, 121, 153
Malayalam, 130, 163-64
Malwa 106
Mandu 106
Manana 31-32
Manasa Devi 177
Mangala 58
Mangrol 209
Mandalas 8
Manu 45, 47, 52-53, 64, 74, 83, 96, 159, 185, 205, 239
Mansabdars 118
Maratha kingdom 140, 183
Marshman 192
Marwar 155, 159
Mata Amritananadamayi 230
Mathura 73, 102

Matrisvan 9
Matter 204
Maukharis 77-79
Maulana Wahiduddin Khan 121
Mauritius 224
Mauryas 70-72, 145
Max Muller 6
Meander/Milinda 75
Mecca 3
Megasthenes 78
Meru 6, 63
Mesha 59, 236
Mewar 108, 159
Middle-East 27
Milinda panha 75
Mimansa 13
Mina 59
Minhaz-us-Siraj 133
Mira Bai 123, 207
Mirjafar 184
Mirra 203
Mithila 57, 162
Mithuna 59
Mlecchas 47, 52, 159, 239
Mohenjodaro 4
Modi 229
Mongols 106, 155
Monier-Williams 168, 210
Morarji Desai 219
M.S. Golwalkar 218
Muftis 118
Mughals, 109-12
Muhammad (Prince) 133
Muhammad Ali Jinnah 144-45
Muhammad II (Gujarat) 160
Muhammad-bin-Kasim 102
Muhammad of Ghur 103-05
Muhammad-bin-Tughluq 107, 117-18, 120
Muhammedan Anglo-Oriental College 142-43
Mukundaram Chakravarty 177
Multan 105
Mundaka Upanishad 26
Munshi Ram 197
Muslim Administration 117-19, 122-23
Mustakhraj 118
Muqtas 115, 119
Mysore 84, 151, 154, 163
M. Winternitz 6

Nadi 14
Nadir Shah 111
Nagasena 71, 75
Nagesh Vasudeva Gunaji 215
Nagri Script 48
Naib Sultan 119
Nala 35
Nalanda, 71, 78-79
Namadeva 169-70, 173, 196
Namaz 122
Nanak 171-73, 235
Nanda Das 176
Nanyadeva 158
Narada 24, 26, 33-34, 94
Narahari Chakravarty 177
Naraka 61
Narasimha Rao 229
Narayana 35
Narayana-Vishnu 87
Narendranath Dutta 198
Narmada 214
Nasir-ud-din 133
Nasir-ud-din Mahmud 133
Nasir-ud-din Qubacha 165
Nawab Jalauddaulah 129
Naya of Gautama 54, 160
Nazim 119
Nepal 79, 108, 158, 183

Nepal Tarai 70
New Education 231, 233-34
New York, 200
New York Times 229
Nididhyasana 31-32
Nirukta 16-7
Nirvana 32, 40, 70-72, 89, 236
Nizam-ul-Mulk 112
Nobel Prize 201

Occidentalist 202
Order of the Star in the East 201
Orientalists 49, 188-89, 202
Origin and Development of Religion 6
Orissa 108, 159
Otto Bohtlingk 187
Oudh 106
Oupenk'hat 186
Oxford 187

Padmanabha Dutta 160
Padmavati 230
Pakistan 50
Pakudha Katyayana 59
Pahlavas 73, 136
Palam 111
Pala kings 86
Pallavas 83-84
Pandus 35, 38
Pandia 38
Pandit Modan Mohan Malaviya 144-45, 217
Pandyas 84-85, 151, 154
Panini 38, 48, 50-51, 56, 63, 234
Panipat 109, 158
Para Atnara 34
Parables 27, 197
Parasara 34, 159
Paramananda Das 176
Paramesvara 162
Paramahansa Yogananda 207, 228
Pargal Khan 162
Para Vidya 25
Parikshit 34
Parliament of Religion 198
Parthasararhi Mishra 160
Partition of India 240
Partition of Bengal 144
Parthana Samaj 195-96
Parthian rulers 73
Parvati Parinaya 160
Patanjali 14, 33, 38, 51-54
Pataliputra 40, 53, 55, 72, 102
Patala 61
Peace of Amiens (1803) 186
Persia 56, 74, 108, 137•
Persian (Language) 122-31, 161
Persian/Iranian invaders and occupiers 40-49, 72-74
Persianisation 132-45
Peshawar/Purushapura 72, 74, 80, 102
Pinda-Pitri-Yajna 14
Plakshadvipa 62
Plassey 117
Plataea 42
Poland 3
Pondicherry/Pondicherry Ashram 83, 85, 203-4
Potdar 119
Prajapati 10
Prajnaparamitasutra 79
Pradyumnabhyudaya 160
Pratap Rudra Kalyan 160
Pratiharas 102-3, 136, 140
Premavati 208
Prema Vartika 176
Presidency College 143
Priestly class 149-66, 231-33
Prithviraj Ghauhan 104-5

Prophet Muhammad 3, 101, 106, 113, 122, 124, 218
Pulakeshin 11, 77
Punjab 4-5, 11, 41, 71, 72, 74-75, 102-4, 109, 182, 196-200, 207
Puri 84
Purus 4
Pushan 7
Puttaparthi 230

Qanungo 119
Qaza-i-Mamalik 118
Quazi 119
Quazi-ul-Quazat 118
Qutab-ud-din Aibak 105, 115
Quran 113-14, 117, 121-25, 131

Rabindranath Tagore 201, 221
Radha 176
Radha- Krishna Cult 173
Radhasoami Satsang 207
Raghunandan 160
Rahasyas 51
Rahu 58
Rajagriha 57, 71-72
Rajab 114
Rajaram 157
Rajasua 20, 34
Rajasthan 7, 41, 106, 183, 207
Rajputana 106
Rajputs 136, 140
Rama/Bhaktas/Cult 37-38, 168, 175-78, 235
Ramananda 168, 170, 172
Ramcharitamanas 176
Ramakrishna Paramahansa 197-98, 212- 15, 222, 243, 286
Ramakrishna Kathamrita 198
Ramakrishna Mission 191-94, 197- 200, 213, 222
Rammohan Roy 181, 192-96, 199, 222, 243
Ramanujacharya (Shrirangam) 201
Ramana Maharshi 207
Ramdas 156, 173, 196
Ramdas (Kathiyababa) 207
Ram Navami 212
Ramprasad 163
Ram Prasad 237
Ramayana 33-40, 91-98, 161-62, 176-78, 220, 225, 235, 238-43
Rameswaram 214
Rana Mall 114
Rana Sangha 109
Rash Khan 176
Ras-Panchadhyayi 176
Rashtrakutas 84, 151, 154
Rashtriya Swayam Sevak Sangha 218, 220
Ratnins 20
Ratnadadhi 79
Ratnaranjaka 79
Ratnasagara 79
Ravana 37, 235
Ravivarman 160
Religious Festivals 235-37
Renaissance 82, 156, 181, 189, 192
Rhinoplasty 60
Rigveda 6, 8-10 12-3, 15, 18-9, 21-2, 27-8, 33, 40, 68, 87, 91, 186, 193, 206
Risalat 118
Romesh Pokhriyal 'Nishank' 237
Rome 81
Royal Asiatic Society 187
Rudra 7-8
Rudolf Roth 187

Rummindei 70
Russian Imperial Academy of Sciences 187
Sab ka Malik ek hai 212
Sabha 20
Sabeer Bhatia 230
Sabuktigin 102
Sabdavidya, 78
Sadharan Brahma Samaj 195-96
Sadr 119
Sahib Subah 119
Sahyadri 156
Safi Ismail Safavi 108
Sai Baba 210-215, 228
Saif-ud-din Muhammad 103
Sakas 72, 95-96, 136
Saka Era 74
Sakhis 172
Sakti 87, 208
Sakuntala 35
Sakuntala 185
Sakyamuni 70
Sa1otar 129
Samarquand 108
Samachar Darpan 192
Samaveda 12, 15, 18, 23
Samabartana 52, 54
Samkhya of Kapi1a 54
Samudra Gupta 75
Samajaguha 79
Samiti 20
Sanchi 87
Sanat Kumar 24, 26, 33, 94
Sankaracharya 63, 83-85, 88-89, 152, 200-201, 239
Sannyas/Sannyasins 25, 36, 89, 197, 208
Sanskrit 48, 50, 64, 78-79, 128-31, 139, 145, 150-51, 159-162, 167, 172-78, 183, 226, 233-35
Sanskrit College 189
Sant Sawan Singh 207
Sapta Sindu 4
Sariraka of Badarayana 54
Sariputta 71
Sarasvati 7, 51
Saraswati Vandana 221
Sassanian dynasty 74
Sastra Dipika 160
Satapatha Brahmana 25, 35
Satavahanas 74
Sathya Sai Baba 230
Satpura 156
Satya 16
Saudi Arabia 101
Savitri 7, 35, 45
Sayyids 107
Serampore missionaries 192
Shaffite 114
Shah Jahan 111
Shahi Snan 237
Shahiya kingdom 102-3
Shahu 139-40, 157
Shaibani Khan 1 08-09
Shambuji 157
Shapur 1, 74
Shivaji 139, 156-57
Shiv Sena 220
Shiqdars 119
Shirdi 210-15
Sivananda 228
Shri Chaitayna 160
Shringeri 84
Shrirangam 209
Shudras 11-12, 21, 25, 44-47, 57, 83, 91-98, 238-43
Shyamaprasad Mukherjee 219
Siam 87
Sibi 35
Siddha Yoga 228

Siksha 16-7
Sikander Lodi 108, 116
Silabhadra, 78
Sind 4-5, 41, 102, 106
Sindu 7, 40-41, 47, 56, 71, 91, 135-37, 141
Sipah Salar 119
Siraj-ud-daula 184
Sita 37
Sivananda 228
Siva/Siva Bhagavatas/Bhaktas/Cult 8, 68, 70, 98, 164, 166, 178, 208, 210, 214, 228
Siva Linga 215
Siva Simha 162
Sivaram 214
Societe Asiatique 187
Socrates 27
Socotra 62
Soma 7-8, 10, 13
Sopara 62
Somnath 102
Spain 101
Spirit 204
Sramanas 69, 93
Srauta Sutras 35, 53
Srikarna Nandi 162
Sri Krishna 26, 166, 215, 228
Sri Sri Ravishankar 229
Sruti 19
Stotras 13
St. Petersburg Lexicon 187
St. Thomas 23
Subahdar 119
Suddhi movement 186
Sukla Paksha 59
Sukra 58
Surya 7, 16, 58
Sulvasutras 53
Sultan Husain Shah 161
Sumatra 224
Supermind 204
Suradas 176
Sutlej 5, 7 11
Sutrakaras 50-58
Sutta 72
Svadhyaya 25
Svetaketu 26-28
Svetasvatara Upanishad 29, 75
Swami Bhagirathananda Saraswati 214
Swami Chinmayananda 228
Swami Dayananda Saraswati 194, 199, 217-222, 243
Swami Muktananda 228,
Swami Nityananda 229
Swami Narayan 207-10, 213, 215, 228
Swami Ramananda 209
Swami Sradhananda 197
Swat 76
Synthesis of Yoga 203

Tabaqat-i- Nasiri 133
Tailanga Swami 207, 213-15, 228
Taittiriya Aranyaka 35
Taj-ud-din Yildiz 105
Taksha 56, 60
Talikota 154
Tamil 71, 130, 163-64
Tamralipti 76, 78
Tanjore 84, 151, 154-55
Tapti 156
Tarabai 157
Tarain 104
Taxila 40, 48 56, 62 80
Telegu 130, 163-64
Thailand 224
Thaneswar 102
Theosophical Society 200, 202

Tibet 88, 150
Times of India 121, 237
Timur 107-8, 110
Timurids 108
Tiruvannamali 207
Tithi 59
Tols 159, 189
Trasadasyu 4
Transcendental Meditation 228
Trilochan Das 177
Trimurti 68, 83
Tughluqs 105
Tukaram 156, 173, 196
Tulsi Das 176-77
Turkestan 108
Turki 126

Uch 105
Uddaka Aruni 28, 88
Uddandapura 86
Udgatri 12-3
Udyana 76
Uluka Kanada 57
United Patriotic Association 143
Upadhyaya 52
Upanayana ceremony 44, 51, 54
Upanishads 23-9, 92, 91-98, 238-43
Upasakas 70, 86
Upasikas 70, 86
Urdu 130, 141
United States 200
U.S.A. 187
Urvasi 45
Uttararchika 13
Uttar Pradesh 196, 207

Vachaspati 160
Vaisampayana 34
Vaiseshika 59
Vaishas 11-12, 21, 25, 44-47, 57, 83, 91-98, 238-43
Vaishali 70
Vajapeya 20
Vajarayana monastery 88
Vajasaney Samhita (Atharvaveda) 46
Valmiki 37
Vallabhacharya 168
Valentine Chirol 199
Vamanadeva 8
Vaman Pandit 156, 173
Vamana Bhatta Bana 160
Vanaprastha 25, 36, 89
Vandemataram 221
Varanasi 40
Varnasramadharma 54
Varuna 7, 9, 19, 26
Vasudeva 8, 35, 74
Vasistha 8, 53-54
Vasistha Samhita 8, 53-54
Vata 7
Vayu 7
Vedas 3-19, 33, 53, 91-98, 238-43
Vedangas 12, 56, 227
Vedanta College 193
Vedic schools 17-19, 25, 33, 46-7, 51-52, 56, 85, 127-28, 138-39, 150-52, 178, 183-87, 189, 232
V.D. Savarkar 145, 217
Vidghda Madhava 160
Videha 20, 37, 48
Vidula 35
Vidyabati 214
Vidyapati Thakur, 162
Vidyanath 160
Vidyapati Upadhayaya 160-61
Vidya 51
Vijaya Dasami 211
Vijayanagar 108, 153-55, 164, 168

Vikramshila 88
Vima Kadphises 73
Vindhyas 95-96, 128, 130-31, 137, 139, 149, 151, 153, 156, 159, 163
Vinya 72, 76
Vis 11
Vishnu 8, 38, 210
Vishnu Bhagavatas (*See* Krishna Bhagavatas)
Vishnu Urukrama 7, 35
Visvakarman 9
Vishvamitra 8
Vishishtadvait 209
Visvavara 45, 159
Visva Hindu Parishad 218
Vithal Nath 175-76
Vithalaswami Temple 154
Vivekananda 198-201, 203, 222, 245
Vratyas 22
Vrischika 59
Vrishabha 59
Vyakarana 16-17
Vyasa 34

Waihand 102
Waqa-i-navis 119
Ward 192
Warren Hastings 142, 184
W.B.Yeats 201
William Cowper 142
William Jones 185-86, 225
World of Fathers 29

Ya Sai 211
Yadava Ramachandra 155
Yama, 7, 9, 19
Yami 45
Yamuna 5, 12, 76
Yajnas (Sacrifices) 9-10
Yajnavalkya 24, 29, 31, 45, 47, 53, 89, 94, 96
Yajurveda 14-16, 18, 23, 33
Yash 230
Yashodabai 207
Yavanas 47, 64
Yeddyurappa 229
Yoga (Patanjali) 54, 160
Yoga (Aurobindo) 204
Yogananda 228
Yogasutras 5, 33, 54
Yoga Vasishtha Ramayana 129
Yolanda King 230
Yue-chis 73

Zain-ul-Abidin 129, 161
Zimmis 114-16, 134-35, 138, 142-43, 187
Zoroaster/Zoroastrianism 47, 86, 113, 137, 209